Cambridge IGCSE
Accounting

Catherine Coucom

CAMBRIDGE
UNIVERSITY PRESS

University Printing House, Cambridge CB2 8BS, United Kingdom

Cambridge University Press is part of the University of Cambridge.

It furthers the University's mission by disseminating knowledge in the pursuit of education, learning and research at the highest international levels of excellence.

Information on this title: education.cambridge.org

© Cambridge University Press 2012

This publication is in copyright. Subject to statutory exception
and to the provisions of relevant collective licensing agreements,
no reproduction of any part may take place without the written
permission of Cambridge University Press.

First Published 2012
9th printing 2016

Printed in Dubai by Oriental Press

A catalogue for this publication is available from the British Library

ISBN 978-1-107-62532-7 Paperback

Cambridge University Press has no responsibility for the persistence or accuracy of URLs for external or third-party internet websites referred to in this publication, and does not guarantee that any content on such websites is, or will remain, accurate or appropriate. Information regarding prices, travel timetables and other factual information given in this work are correct at the time of first printing but Cambridge University Press does not guarantee the accuracy of such information thereafter.

Contents

Introduction	iv
New Terminology	vi
Where to find each section of the syllabus	viii
Acknowledgement	ix
1. Introduction to Accounting	1
2. Double Entry Bookkeeping – Part A	10
3. The Trial Balance	31
4. Double Entry Bookkeeping – Part B	42
5. Petty Cash Books	61
6. Business Documents	72
7. Books of Prime Entry	86
8. Financial Statements – Part A	99
9. Financial Statements – Part B	116
10. Accounting Rules	127
11. Other Payables and Other Receivables	142
12. Depreciation and Disposal of Non-current Assets	166
13. Bad Debts and Provisions for Doubtful Debts	189
14. Bank Reconciliation Statements	207
15. Journal Entries and Correction of Errors	222
16. Control Accounts	243
17. Incomplete Records	260
18. Accounts of Clubs and Societies	285
19. Partnership Accounts	308
20. Accounts of Manufacturing Businesses	328
21. Limited Company Accounts	342
22. Analysis and Interpretation	355
Answers to Review Questions	382
Index	427

Introduction

The aim of this book is to provide an up-to-date text covering the Cambridge International Examinations International General Certificate of Secondary Education Accounting syllabus (0452).

The IGCSE examination consists of two structured papers. Paper 1 tests knowledge and application, with some analysis and evaluation. It may contain some multiple choice questions, some short-answer questions and some structured questions. Paper 2 also tests knowledge and application, but with an emphasis on analysis and evaluation. Questions on Papers 1 and 2 may be set on any topic in the syllabus. It is recommended that students obtain a syllabus for the year in which they intend to sit the examination so that they are aware of what is required. Electronic copies are available at http://www.cie.org.uk

This book covers all the topics included on the latest syllabus for IGCSE Accounting. The topics are not necessarily included in the order in which they appear in the syllabus. They have been presented in what the author's long teaching experience has shown to be a suitable order for an accounting student commencing a course at this level. The table on page viii shows the chapter(s) of the book in which each section of the syllabus may be found.

No prior knowledge of accounting is required as this book provides an introduction to accounting and covers all the topics on the 0452 syllabus. Each chapter is complete in itself and contains appropriate examples. There are also short-answer questions at regular intervals which students can use to test their understanding of each section. The Review Questions at the end of each chapter are taken from past examinations papers wherever possible. Answers to questions marked with an asterisk (*) are given at the end of the book.

The contents of the book have been amended to reflect the move in the IGCSE Accounting syllabus towards applying international accounting terminology. At present this terminology is only used by large-scale companies, but it is probable that it will be used by all businesses in the near future. Only the new terminology will be used in the IGCSE examination papers from 2011, so it is essential that candidates are aware

Introduction

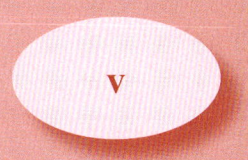

of these terms. The first time an international term is used in this book it will also show the UK equivalent term in brackets. A summary of comparative terms appears on the next page. The terms used in Review Questions which have been taken from past papers have been modified to include the new terminology.

It is always advisable to show all calculations when answering accounting questions. Candidates may respond to the same question in different ways: showing the workings is one way of ensuring that examiners see how the solution was reached. Questions are answered on the actual question paper for both Paper 1 and Paper 2, but space is provided for calculations.

In common with most accounting textbooks, dates used in the examples throughout this book are expressed as 20-0, 20-1, 20-2, and so on. Those Review Questions taken from past papers show the dates as they appeared on the actual examination paper.

New Terminology

International usage	Traditional UK usage
Financial Statements	Final accounts
Income statement	Trading and profit & loss account
Revenue	Sales
Raw materials (ordinary goods purchased)	Purchases
Cost of sales	Cost of goods sold
Inventory (of raw materials and finished goods)	Stock
Work in progress	Work in progress
Gross profit	Gross profit
Other operating expenses	Sundry expenses
Other operating income	Sundry income
Investment revenues	Interest receivable
Finance costs	Interest payable
Profit (before tax) for the year	Net Profit
Balance sheet	Balance sheet
Non-current assets	Fixed assets
Property	Land and buildings
Plant and equipment	Plant and equipment
Investment property	Investments
Intangible assets	Goodwill etc.
Current assets	Current assets
Inventory	Stock
Trade receivables	Debtors
Other receivables	Prepayments

New Terminology

International usage	Traditional UK usage
Cash (and cash equivalents)	Bank and cash
Current liabilities	Current liabilities or Creditors: amounts due within 12 months
Trade payables	Creditors
Other payables	Accruals
Bank overdrafts and loans	Loans repayable within 12 months
Non-current liabilities	Long term liabilities or Creditors: amounts falling due after more than one year
Bank (and other) loans	Loans repayable after 12 months
Capital or Equity	Capital
Share capital	Share capital

IGCSE Accounting

Where to find each section of the syllabus

Chapter	1.1	1.2	1.3	1.4	2.1	2.2	2.3	2.4	3.1	3.2	3.3	3.4	4.1	4.2	4.3	4.4	4.5	5.1	5.2	6.1	6.2	6.3	6.4	6.5	6.6	7.1	7.2	7.3	7.4	7.5	8.1	8.2
One	✓																															
Two	✓		✓	✓																												
Three					✓																											
Four	✓		✓	✓																												
Five			✓	✓																												
Six		✓	✓																													
Seven			✓	✓																												
Eight																		✓														
Nine																			✓	✓												
Ten									✓				✓	✓																		
Eleven																				✓												
Twelve										✓										✓												
Thirteen															✓					✓												
Fourteen											✓																					
Fifteen		✓							✓																							
Sixteen												✓																				
Seventeen																									✓							
Eighteen																							✓									
Nineteen																					✓											
Twenty																									✓							
Twenty one																										✓	✓	✓				
Twenty two																										✓	✓	✓	✓			

Acknowledgement

Cambridge International Examination past papers in relevant parts of the book have been reproduced with permission of University of Cambridge Local Examination Syndicate.

Chapter 1

Introduction to Accounting

In this chapter you will learn to:
- understand the difference between bookkeeping and accounting
- understand why businesses need to keep accounting records
- understand the meaning of the terms assets, liabilities and capital
- understand and apply the accounting equation
- prepare a simple balance sheet.

Introduction

Accounting is regarded as the language of business. Accounting can be divided into two sections:

Bookkeeping

This is a process of **detailed recording of all the financial transactions of a business**. It is necessary for even the smallest business to make a record of every transaction which affects the business. If the records are not maintained, it is likely that something will be forgotten or over-looked. The basis of maintaining these detailed records is **double entry bookkeeping**. The actual records maintained by one business may vary from those maintained by another business because each business is different. However, all businesses apply the same principles while maintaining double entry records.

Accounting

This uses **the bookkeeping records to prepare financial statements at regular intervals**. The owner of a business needs to know whether the business is making a profit or a loss. Periodically (often at yearly intervals), an **income statement** (trading, profit and loss account) is drawn up. This shows the calculation of the profit or loss earned by the business. If the business has earned a profit then the owner is receiving a return on his investment and funds are available for expanding or improving the business. However, if the business has made a loss then it may eventually close down as the owner is not receiving any return on his investment and funds are not available for running or maintaining the business.

The owner of the business also needs to know the financial position at regular intervals so a **balance sheet** is prepared. This shows what the business owns, its **assets**; and what the business owes, its **liabilities**. The term **financial statements** (final accounts) is often used as a collective name for an income statement and a balance sheet.

The progress of the business can be measured by comparing the financial statements of one year with those of previous years, or with those of other similar businesses. The calculation of various accounting ratios is used to measure the relationship between figures within a set of financial statements. These are also useful for comparison purposes.

The information provided by the financial statements shows the owner of the business what has happened during a certain period of time and helps in monitoring the progress of the business. The plans for the future development of the business are also based on these financial statements.

All the accounting terms used above are explained in detail, later in this book.

> **Test your understanding**
> 1. Define the term bookkeeping.
> 2. Define the term accounting.
> 3. State **two** reasons why it is necessary to prepare financial statements at regular intervals.
> 4. State what is included in the term financial statements?

Assets, Liabilities and Capital

It is important to remember that the accounting records of a business relate only to the business. From an accounting viewpoint, the owner of that business is regarded as being completely separate from the business.

Introduction to Accounting

3

When a person decides to start a business he will have to provide the necessary funds (resources). This is often in the form of monetary funds, but may consist of buildings, motors, goods and so on. Any resources provided by the owner of the business are known as **capital**. This represents the amount owed by the business to the owner of that business.

Once the business is formed and capital introduced, the business will own the money or other items provided by the owner. Things owned by the business (or owed to the business) are regarded as the resources of the business or the **assets** of the business.

In addition to the owner, other people may also provide assets to the business. The amount owed by the business to these people is known as **liabilities**.

> **Test your understanding**
> 1. Define **each** of the following terms.
> (a) assets (b) liabilities (c) capital

The Accounting Equation

This is also referred to as the **balance sheet equation**. Like any other mathematical equation, the two sides of the equation will always be equal. The formula for this equation is:

$$\boxed{\text{Assets}} = \boxed{\text{Capital}} + \boxed{\text{Liabilities}}$$

Capital is sometimes referred to as **owner's equity**. So the previous equation can also be written as:

$$\boxed{\text{Assets}} = \boxed{\text{Owner's equity}} + \boxed{\text{Liabilities}}$$

Like any mathematical equation, the accounting equation can be used to find any one of the three elements if the other two are present.

This equation illustrates that the assets of a business (the resources used by a business) are always equal to the liabilities and capital of a business (the resources provided for the business by others). The assets represent how the resources are used by the business and the liabilities and capital represent where these resources come from.

Example 1.1

20-7
January 1 Leena set up a business to trade under the name of The Dress Shop. She opened a business bank account and paid in $20 000 as capital.
2 The business purchased premises, $15 000, and paid by cheque.
3 The business purchased goods, $3000, on credit.
4 The business sold goods, at the cost price of $1000, on credit.

Show the accounting equation after **each** of the above transactions.

Date	Assets	=	Capital	+	Liabilities
January 1	Bank $20 000	=	$20 000	+	Nil
January 2	Premises 15 000 Bank 5 000 $20 000	=	$20 000	+	Nil
January 3	Premises 15 000 Inventory 3 000 Bank 5 000 $23 000	=	$20 000	+	Trade payable $3 000
January 4	Premises 15 000 Inventory 2 000 Trade receivable 1 000 Bank 5 000 $23 000	=	$20 000	+	Trade payable $3 000

- January 1 The assets of the business are equal to the capital of the business.
- January 2 The money in the bank has decreased because a new asset has been bought. The total assets are equal to the capital.
- January 3 Purchasing on credit means that the business does not pay immediately. A new asset **inventory** (stock) has been acquired, but the business has also acquired a liability as

Introduction to Accounting

5

it owes money to the supplier (who is known as a **creditor**). In a balance sheet this is described as a **trade payable**. The total assets are equal to the capital plus the liabilities.

- January 4 Selling on credit means that the business does not immediately receive the money. The inventory has decreased but a new asset has been acquired in the form of money owing to the business by a customer (who is known as a **debtor**). In a balance sheet this is described as a **trade receivable**. The total assets are equal to the capital plus the liabilities. (For the sake of simplicity, the goods were sold to the customer at cost price. In practice, they need to be sold at a price above cost price to enable the business to make a profit.)

Test your understanding
1. Fill in the missing figures in the following table.

	Assets $	Capital $	Liabilities $
(a)	35 000	?	12 500
(b)	?	44 400	19 300
(c)	67 300	55 000	?

The Balance Sheet

The accounting equation may be shown in the form of a balance sheet. This is a **statement of the financial position of a business on a certain date**. It shows the three elements of the accounting equation – the assets, the capital and the liabilities. The balance sheet will be affected every time the business makes changes to the assets, liabilities or capital.

Example 1.2

Prepare the balance sheet of The Dress Shop after **each** of the transactions shown in **Example 1.1** above.

The Dress Shop
Balance Sheet at 1 January 20-7

Assets	$	Liabilities	$
Bank	20 000	Capital	20 000
	20 000		20 000

The Dress Shop
Balance Sheet at 2 January 20-7

Assets	$	Liabilities	$
Premises	15 000	Capital	20 000
Bank	5 000		
	20 000		20 000

The Dress Shop
Balance Sheet at 3 January 20-7

Assets	$	Liabilities	$
Premises	15 000	Capital	20 000
Inventory	3 000	Trade payable	3 000
Bank	5 000		
	23 000		23 000

The Dress Shop
Balance Sheet at 4 January 20-7

Assets	$	Liabilities	$
Premises	15 000	Capital	20 000
Inventory	2 000	Trade payable	3 000
Trade receivable	1 000		
Bank	5 000		
	23 000		23 000

> **Test your understanding**
> 1. Give **two** examples of **each** of the following (excluding those shown in **Example 1.1 and 1.2**):
>   (a) asset (b) liability
> 2. Explain the meaning of **each** of the following terms:
>   (a) creditor (b) debtor

Introduction to Accounting

The balance sheets shown in **Example 1.2** were presented in a horizontal format. There are different ways to present a balance sheet and these are explained in Chapter 9. A balance sheet is also more useful if the assets and liabilities are divided into different types (*see* Chapter 9).

Example 1.1 showed that every single transaction involves a change to the assets and/or the liabilities and/or the capital. This means that it is necessary to prepare a balance sheet after every single transaction, as shown in **Example 1.2**. However, this is not possible in practice as many transactions can take place every hour of each working day. In practice, the day-to-day business transactions are recorded using **double entry bookkeeping** (as explained in Chapters 2 and 4), and a balance sheet is prepared only periodically. This is usually done at the closing of a business on the last day of the financial year as part of the **financial statements**. As the business can be started on any day of the year, its financial year may not necessarily match the calendar year (i.e from 1 January to 31 December). The financial statements are prepared for twelve month periods from the date the business started.

Points to Remember

1. Bookkeeping is the detailed recording of all the financial transactions of a business. Accounting uses these bookkeeping records to prepare financial statements.
2. It is necessary to prepare financial statements to show the profit or loss of the business and the financial position of the business and it will help in decision-making.
3. The accounting equation shows that the assets are always equal to the capital plus the liabilities of the business.
4. A balance sheet is a statement of the financial position of a business on a certain date.

Review Questions

1. Explain why the assets of a business are always equal to the capital plus the liabilities.
2. State whether each of the following is an asset or a liability.
   (a) Land and buildings
   (b) Inventory of goods
   (c) Trade payable
   (d) Trade receivable
   (e) Loan from AB Finance Company
   (f) Cash
*3. Complete the following table to show the effect of each of the following transactions.
   The first one has been completed as an example.
   (a) Bought a motor vehicle and paid by cheque
   (b) Bought goods on credit from a supplier
   (c) Received a cheque from a debtor
   (d) Sold goods on credit
   (e) Paid off a loan in cash

	Effect on assets		Effect on liabilities
		$	$
(a)	Motor vehicles	Increase	No effect
	Bank	Decrease	
(b)			
(c)			
(d)			
(e)			

4. The balance sheet of Bharwani Traders on 31 October 20-4 is shown below.

Bharwani Traders
Balance Sheet at 31 October 20-4

Assets	$	Liabilities	$
Machinery	19 000	Capital	35 000
Motor vehicles	6 000	Trade payables	8 000
Inventory	4 900		
Trade receivables	3 000		
Bank	10 100		
	43 000		43 000

On 1 November 20-4 the following transactions took place.
(a) A cheque for $3000 was paid to a creditor
(b) A debtor paid $500 in cash
(c) A loan for $8000, which was paid into the bank, was received from Lenders Limited
(d) A cheque for $7000 was paid for an additional machine

Prepare the balance sheet of Bharwani Traders on 1 November 20-4 after the above transactions have taken place.

Chapter 2

Double Entry Bookkeeping – Part A

In this chapter you will learn to:
- understand the principles of double entry bookkeeping
- make entries in ledger accounts using double entry principles
- make entries in the ledger for drawings made by the owner of a business
- balance ledger accounts
- prepare ledger accounts using both the "T" format and the running balance format.

Introduction

A business would find it impossible to prepare a balance sheet after every single transaction. The day-to-day transactions are recorded in the books of a business using the **double entry system of bookkeeping**. The term **double entry** is used because the two effects of a transaction (a **giving** and a **receiving**) are both recorded in the ledger.

A business maintains a separate ledger account for each type of asset, expense, liability and income and also for each individual debtor and creditor. Every transaction is recorded in the ledger account relating to that particular item or person.

A **ledger** is traditionally a bound book where each account appears on a separate page. Over the years, the ledger has developed into a loose leaf folder with separate sheets, each containing a ledger account. Recent developments have seen the introduction of a computer file divided into separate ledger accounts.

Double Entry Bookkeeping – Part A

The layout of a ledger account is as follows:

Account name

Debit							Credit
Date	Details	Folio	$	Date	Details	Folio	$

Ledger accounts are divided into two sections by a central vertical line. The left hand side is known as the **debit** side and the right hand side is known as the **credit** side. The term debit is usually abbreviated to "dr" and the term credit is usually abbreviated to "cr". On either side of the account, there are columns to record the date, details and amount of each transaction.

A folio number column is used for reference purposes. The use of folio numbers is not required in the examination syllabus. However, folio numbers have been included in examples present up to Chapter 7 so that the students can appreciate their use and purpose.

In order to record the two aspects of every transaction, every transaction is entered twice – on the debit side of one account and on the credit side of another account. The account which is receiving or gaining the value is debited and the account which is giving the value is credited.

Example 2.1

20-7
January 1 Ajay began business. He opened a business bank account and invested $80 000 as capital **(a)**
         2 Fixtures and equipment costing $30 000 were bought and paid for by cheque **(b)**

Enter the above transactions in Ajay's ledger.

Ajay
Bank account — Page 1

Date	Details	Folio	$	Date	Details	Folio	$
20-7				20-7	Fixtures &		
Jan 1 **(a)**	Capital	2	80 000	Jan 2 **(b)**	equipment	3	30 000

Capital account								Page 2
Date	Details	Folio	$	Date	Details	Folio	$
				20-7 Jan 1 (a)	Bank	1	80 000

Fixtures and equipment account								Page 3
Date	Details	Folio	$	Date	Details	Folio	$
20-7 Jan 1 (b)	Bank	1	30 000				

- The first transaction **(a)** is debited in the bank account, as this is the account which is receiving the money, and credited in the capital account, as this is where the money is coming from.
- The second transaction **(b)** is debited in the fixtures and equipment, to show the value being received, and credited in the bank account, as this is where the money is coming from.
- In each transaction, the details column shows the name of the account in which the other half of the double entry is made.
- The folio number is used for reference purposes and shows the page of the ledger on which the account name in the details column appears.

It is important that a double entry is made for every transaction.

In practice, the information entered in the accounting records is obtained from business documents (see Chapter 6). It is not practical for a set of business documents to be provided in examination so questions usually list the transactions.

In practice, each ledger account has its own page or sheet. As this is not possible in examination questions and exercises, it is usual to find several accounts displayed on one page.

> **Test your understanding**
> 1. Explain why it is necessary to make a double entry in the ledger for each transaction.
> 2. Explain the use of the folio column in a ledger account.

Double Entry Bookkeeping – Part A

Double Entry Records for Assets and Liabilities

A ledger account is opened for each type of asset and liability. Applying the double entry principles, every transaction is entered twice. The account which is receiving the money is debited and the account which is giving the money is credited.

Example 2.2

20-7
January 1 Ajay began business. He opened a business bank account and invested $80 000 as capital
2 Fixtures and equipment costing $30 000 were bought and paid for by cheque
3 A short-term loan of $10 000 was received from AB Loans
5 A motor vehicle costing $9000 was bought and paid for by cheque
6 A long-term loan of $5000 was received from Ajay's sister Mallika

Enter the above transactions in Ajay's ledger.

Ajay

Bank account — Page 1

Date	Details	Folio	$	Date	Details	Folio	$
20-7				20-7			
Jan 1	Capital	2	80 000	Jan 2	Fixtures & equipment	3	30 000
3	AB Loans	4	10 000	5	Motor vehicle	5	9 000
6	Mallika loan	6	5 000				

Capital account — Page 2

Date	Details	Folio	$	Date	Details	Folio	$
				20-7			
				Jan 1	Bank	1	80 000

Fixtures and equipment account   Page 3

Date	Details	Folio	$	Date	Details	Folio	$
20-7 Jan 2	Bank	1	30 000				

AB Loans account   Page 4

Date	Details	Folio	$	Date	Details	Folio	$
				20-7 Jan 3	Bank	1	10 000

Motor vehicles account   Page 5

Date	Details	Folio	$	Date	Details	Folio	$
20-7 Jan 5	Bank	1	9 000				

Mallika loan account   Page 6

Date	Details	Folio	$	Date	Details	Folio	$
				20-7 Jan 6	Bank	1	5 000

Double Entry Records for Expenses and Incomes

A ledger account is opened for each type of expense and income. The same double entry principles applied to assets and liabilities are applied to expenses and incomes. The account which is receiving the money is debited and the account which is giving the money is credited.

Example 2.3

20-7
January   1   Ajay began business with a capital of $80 000 in the business bank account
           1   Paid rent of premises, $400, by cheque
           2   Fixtures and equipment costing $30 000 were bought and paid for by cheque

Double Entry Bookkeeping – Part A

3 Paid insurance, $250, by cheque
3 A short-term loan of $10 000 was received from AB Loans
5 A motor vehicle costing $9000 was bought and paid for by cheque
5 Paid motor expenses, $50, by cheque
6 A long-term loan of $5000 was received from Ajay's sister Mallika
7 Part of the premises were rented out to another business and a cheque for $95 was received

Enter the above transactions in Ajay's ledger.

Ajay

Bank account — Page 1

Date	Details	Folio	$	Date	Details	Folio	$
20-7				20-7			
Jan 1	Capital	2	80 000	Jan 1	Rent	7	400
3	AB Loans	4	10 000	2	Fixtures & equipment	3	30 000
6	Mallika loan	6	5 000	3	Insurance	8	250
7	Rent received	10	95	5	Motor vehicle	5	9 000
				5	Motor expenses	9	50

Capital account — Page 2

Date	Details	Folio	$	Date	Details	Folio	$
				20-7			
				Jan 1	Bank	1	80 000

Fixtures and equipment account — Page 3

Date	Details	Folio	$	Date	Details	Folio	$
20-7							
Jan 2	Bank	1	30 000				

AB Loans account — Page 4

Date	Details	Folio	$	Date	Details	Folio	$
				20-7			
				Jan 3	Bank	1	10 000

Motor vehicles account — Page 5

Date	Details	Folio	$	Date	Details	Folio	$
20-7 Jan 5	Bank	1	9 000				

Mallika loan account — Page 6

Date	Details	Folio	$	Date	Details	Folio	$
				20-7 Jan 6	Bank	1	5 000

Rent account — Page 7

Date	Details	Folio	$	Date	Details	Folio	$
20-7 Jan 1	Bank	1	400				

Insurance account — Page 8

Date	Details	Folio	$	Date	Details	Folio	$
20-7 Jan 3	Bank	1	250				

Motor expenses account — Page 9

Date	Details	Folio	$	Date	Details	Folio	$
20-7 Jan 5	Bank	1	50				

Rent received account — Page 10

Date	Details	Folio	$	Date	Details	Folio	$
				20-7 Jan 7	Bank	1	95

- The motor expenses such as fuel and repairs are shown in an expense account as they do not increase the value of the motor vehicle.

Double Entry Bookkeeping – Part A

- The rent received from a tenant is shown in an income account and is kept separate from the expense of rent payable.
- No lines are left blank in the middle of ledger accounts as each entry is made on the next available line.
- In practice, for ease of reference, accounts of the same type (e.g. assets, expenses and so on) are kept in the same area of the ledger.

> **Test your understanding**
> 1. For **each** of the following transactions, state the name of the account which will be debited and the name of the account which will be credited.
>   (a) Paid property tax by cheque
>   (b) Bought machinery and paid by cheque
>   (c) Received commission by cheque for work done for another business
>   (d) Repaid, by cheque, money borrowed from XYZ Loan Co.

Double Entry Records for Drawings

Whenever the owner of a business takes value from the business for his/her own use this is known as **drawings**. This value may be in the form of money, non-current assets, or goods from the inventory held by the business. It is usual to open a **drawings account** to record these values so that the capital account does not have a large number of entries.

Any drawings are debited in the drawings account to show the value going into that account. The credit entry will be in the account giving the value. When money is withdrawn either the cash or bank account will be credited. When a non-current asset is withdrawn, the appropriate non-current asset account will be credited. When goods are withdrawn, the purchases account will be credited. This is because these goods were originally purchased for resale and the amount of goods available for resale is reduced when goods are taken by the owner.

At the end of the financial year, the total of the drawings account is transferred to the capital account. This reduces the amount owed by the business to the owner of the business.

> **Test your understanding**
> 1. For **each** of the following transactions, state the name of the account which will be debited and the name of the account which will be credited.
>   (a) The owner of a business invested more money in the business.
>   (b) The owner of a business took an unused motor vehicle for personal use.
>   (c) The owner of a business took goods for personal use.

Balancing Ledger Accounts

At the end of each month, it is usual to **balance** any account of assets and liabilities which contain more than one entry. The **balance is the difference between the two sides of the account** and represents the amount which is left in that account.

The steps necessary to balance a ledger account are summarised as follows:
- On a calculator or a separate sheet of paper, add-up each side of the account and find the difference between the two sides.
- Enter this difference on the next available line on the side which is the smallest in money. Enter the date (usually the last day of the month) in the date column and the word "Balance" in the details column. It is usual to insert "c/d" in the folio column. This is the abbreviation for "carried down" and indicates where the double entry for this item will be made.
- Total each side of the account. This is done by drawing total lines and inserting the figure between these lines. It is usual to show a single line above the total and either a single or a double line below the total. The totals of an account must be on the same level and must be the same figure.
- Make the double entry for the balance carried down. On the line below the totals, write the amount of the balance on the opposite side to where the words "Balance c/d" were written. Enter the date (usually the first day of the next month) in the date column and the word "Balance" in the details column. It is usual to insert "b/d" in the folio column. This is the abbreviation for "brought

Double Entry Bookkeeping – Part A

down" and indicates where the double entry for this item was made.

Example 2.4

The bank account prepared in **Example 2.3** shows the entries made by Ajay during the first week of trading. Balance the bank account in Ajay's books on 7 January 20-7.

Ajay

Bank account   Page 1

Date	Details	Folio	$	Date	Details	Folio	$
20-7				20-7			
Jan 1	Capital	2	80 000	Jan 1	Rent	7	400
3	AB Loans	4	10 000	2	Fixtures & equipment	3	30 000
6	Mallika loan	6	5 000	3	Insurance	8	250
7	Rent received	10	95	5	Motor vehicle	5	9 000
					Motor expenses	9	50
				7	Balance	c/d	55 395
			95 095				95 095
20-7							
Jan 8	Balance	b/d	55 395				

Double Entry Records for Sales, Purchases and Returns

It is necessary to open an account to record goods which are purchased for resale and also an account to record goods which are sold by the business. Whilst these are actually the same goods coming into the business and going out of the business, it is necessary to record them in separate accounts as the purchases will be at cost price and the sales at selling price. A **purchases account** and a **sales account** are used rather than a goods account. An **inventory account** is only used to record the goods left at the end of the financial year and not for day-to-day transactions.

The same double entry principles applied to assets and liabilities are applied to purchases, sales and returns.

Purchases

(a) Goods purchased for cash or cheque

Whenever goods are purchased, the purchases account will be debited as the goods are coming into the business and the purchases account is receiving that value. The double entry will be a credit in either the cash account or the bank account depending on whether the amount was paid in cash or by cheque.

(b) Goods purchased on credit

It is common for businesses to buy on credit and pay for the goods at a later date rather than at the time of purchase. The purchases account will be debited in the usual way.

The credit entry will be made in the account of the supplier of the goods to show the value coming from that person. The supplier of goods is known as a **trade creditor**.

When payment is made to the supplier, the bank or cash account will be credited (to show value going out of that account) and the account of the supplier will be debited (to show value going into that account).

Example 2.5

20-7
January   9   Ajay bought goods, $650, on credit from Kolkata & Co.
          10   Ajay bought goods, $150, and paid by cheque.
          13   Ajay paid the amount owing to Kolkata & Co. by cheque

Enter the above transactions in Ajay's ledger.

Ajay
Bank account   Page 1

Date	Details	Folio	$	Date	Details	Folio	$
				20-7			
				Jan 10	Purchases	11	150
				13	Kolkata & Co.	12	650

Double Entry Bookkeeping – Part A

Purchases account   Page 11

Date	Details	Folio	$	Date	Details	Folio	$
20-7							
Jan 9	Kolkata & Co.	12	650				
10	Bank	1	150				

Kolkata & Co account   Page 12

Date	Details	Folio	$	Date	Details	Folio	$
20-7				20-7			
Jan 13	Bank	1	650	Jan 9	Purchases	11	650
			650				650

- The account of Kolkata & Co. is "in balance" as both sides equal $650. The account has been totalled to indicate that the account is now closed.
- It is not necessary to write the month against each transaction, only when it is the first entry for the month.
- If there is more than one entry on the same side of an account on the same date, it is not necessary to write the day of the month each time.

Sales

(a) Goods sold for cash or cheque

Whenever goods are sold, the sales account will be credited as the goods are going out of the business and the sales account is giving out that value. The double entry will be a debit in either the cash account or the bank account depending on whether the amount was received in cash or by cheque.

(b) Goods sold on credit

Just as a business may purchase goods and pay for them at a later date, it may also sell goods on credit. The sales account will be credited in the usual way. The debit entry will be made in the account of the customer to whom the goods were sold to show the value going to that person. The customer who bought the goods on credit is known as a **trade debtor**.

When payment is received from the debtor, the bank or cash account will be debited (to show value coming into that account) and the account of the debtor will be credited (to show value going out of that account).

Example 2.6

20-7
January 16 Ajay sold goods, $175, for cash
         17 Ajay sold goods, $770, on credit to Prerna
         20 Prerna gave Ajay a cheque for $500 on account

Enter the above transactions in Ajay's ledger.

Ajay

Bank account — Page 1

Date	Details	Folio	$	Date	Details	Folio	$
20-7 Jan 20	Prerna	15	500				

Cash account — Page 13

Date	Details	Folio	$	Date	Details	Folio	$
20-7 Jan 16	Sales	14	175				

Sales account — Page 14

Date	Details	Folio	$	Date	Details	Folio	$
				20-7 Jan 16	Cash	13	175
				17	Prerna	15	770

Prerna account — Page 15

Date	Details	Folio	$	Date	Details	Folio	$
20-7 Jan 17	Sales	14	770	20-7 Jan 20	Bank	1	500
				20	Balance	c/d	270
			770				770
20-7 Jan 21	Balance	b/d	270				

Double Entry Bookkeeping – Part A

- The term "on account" indicates that only part of the amount outstanding is being paid. The remainder will be paid at a later date.
- Prerna's account has been balanced following the stages mentioned previously in this Chapter (though this is usually done at the end of the month).
- On 21 January, Prerna is Ajay's debtor as an amount of $270 is owing to Ajay.

Returns

Some times goods which have been purchased have to be returned to the supplier. They may be faulty, damaged or not what was ordered. These goods are known as **purchases returns** or **returns outward**. A special account known as a purchases returns account (or returns outward account) is opened and any returns are credited to this account to show the value going out. The debit entry will be made in the account of the supplier to whom the goods are being returned (to show the value going into that person).

Similarly, a customer may return goods to the business. These goods are known as **sales returns** or **returns inwards**. An account known as the sales returns account (or returns inwards account) is opened and any returns are debited to this account to show the value coming in. The credit entry will be made in the account of the customer who returned the goods (to show the value coming from that person).

Example 2.7

20-7
January 21 Ajay sold goods, $245, on credit to Xavier Traders
22 Xavier Traders returned damaged goods, $55, to Ajay
23 Ajay purchased goods, $820, on credit from Varun
25 Xavier Traders paid their account by cheque
27 Ajay returned faulty goods, $44, to Varun
30 Ajay gave Varun a cheque for $700 on account

Enter the above transactions in Ajay's ledger.

Ajay

Bank account — Page 1

Date	Details	Folio	$	Date	Details	Folio	$
20-7 Jan 25	Xavier Traders	16	190	20-7 Jan 30	Varun	18	700

Purchases account — Page 11

Date	Details	Folio	$	Date	Details	Folio	$
20-7 Jan 23	Varun	18	820				

Sales account — Page 14

Date	Details	Folio	$	Date	Details	Folio	$
				20-7 Jan 21	Xavier Traders	16	245

Xavier Traders account — Page 16

Date	Details	Folio	$	Date	Details	Folio	$
20-7 Jan 21	Sales	14	245 245	20-7 Jan 22 25	Sales returns Bank	17 1	55 190 245

Sales returns account — Page 17

Date	Details	Folio	$	Date	Details	Folio	$
20-7 Jan 22	Xavier Traders	16	55				

Varun account — Page 18

Date	Details	Folio	$	Date	Details	Folio	$
20-7 Jan 27 30 31	Purchases returns Bank Balance	19 1 c/d	44 700 76 820	20-7 Jan 23 20-7 Feb 1	Purchases Balance	11 b/d	820 820 76

Purchases returns account — Page 19

Date	Details	Folio	$	Date	Details	Folio	$
				20-7 Jan 27	Varun	18	44

Double Entry Bookkeeping – Part A

Double Entry Records for Carriage Inwards and Carriage Outwards

The term **Carriage** refers to the **cost of carrying or transporting goods**. **Carriage inwards** is part of the cost of purchasing goods as it occurs when a business has to pay for goods it has purchased to be delivered to its premises. **Carriage outwards** is the selling expense as it occurs when a business pays for goods to be delivered to the customer's premises. It is important that these two expenses are treated separately in the accounts.

Applying the double entry principle to carriage inwards, the carriage inwards account is debited as this is the account receiving the money and the cash account (or the bank account if the money is paid by cheque) is credited as the money is coming from this account. Similarly, if the payment relates to carriage outwards, the cash account or bank account is credited and the carriage outwards account is debited.

If the carriage is not actually paid for at the time, the account of the supplier of the carriage service will be credited instead of the cash account or bank account.

> **Test your understanding**
> 1. Explain how to balance a ledger account.
> 2. Explain the meaning of the term credit purchases.
> 3. State **two** reasons why it may be necessary to return goods to a supplier.
> 4. State an alternative name for sales returns.
> 5. Explain the difference between carriage inwards and carriage outwards.

Three Column Running Balance Accounts

The ledger accounts presented so far have been in the traditional form. This form is also known as the "T" account format.

There is another method of presenting ledger accounts which is commonly used on computer-generated accounts which is known as the three column running balance format. This form of presentation uses only one column each for the date, details and folio and has three money columns side-by-side – one for debit, one for credit and one for balance after each transaction. The layout of a ledger account using this format is as follows:

Date	Details	Folio	Debit $	Credit $	Balance $

The advantage of this method is that it shows the balance of the account after every transaction. When the accounts are prepared manually, it involves extra calculations which may lead to errors.

Example 2.8

20-7
January
1 Ajay began business. He opened a business bank account and invested $80 000 as capital
1 Paid rent of premises, $400, by cheque
2 Fixtures and equipment costing $30 000 were bought and paid for by cheque
3 Paid insurance, $250, by cheque
3 A short-term loan of $10 000 was received from AB Loans
5 A motor vehicle costing $9000 was bought and paid for by cheque
5 Paid motor expenses, $50, by cheque
6 A long-term loan of $5000 was received from Ajay's sister Mallika
7 Part of the premises were rented out to another business and a cheque for $95 was received

Enter the above transactions in the bank account in Ajay's ledger using the three column running balance format.

Double Entry Bookkeeping – Part A

Ajay
Bank account   Page 1

Date	Details	Folio	Debit	Credit	Balance
20-7			$	$	$
Jan 1	Capital		80 000		80 000 dr
	Rent			400	79 600 dr
2	Fixtures and equipment			30 000	49 600 dr
3	Insurance			250	49 350 dr
	AB Loans		10 000		59 350 dr
5	Motor vehicle			9 000	50 350 dr
	Motor expenses			50	50 300 dr
6	Mallika loan		5 000		55 300 dr
7	Rent received		95		55 395 dr

- It is common for the abbreviation "dr" or "cr" to appear after the figure in the balance column to indicate the nature of the balance.

As students often find the traditional form of ledger accounts easier to understand, the "T" format is used in all ledger accounts throughout this book. Where ledger accounts are required in examinations, either form of presentation is acceptable.

Examination questions frequently ask candidates to show the entries in one ledger account only, rather than asking for a complete set of double entry records. This is simply an examination technique to enable greater syllabus coverage within the limited time of the examination paper.

IGCSE Accounting

POINTS TO REMEMBER

1. Every transaction must be entered twice – on the debit side of one account and on the credit side of another account.
2. The debit entry is made in the account which is receiving the value and the credit entry is made in the account which is giving the value.
3. Each type of asset, liability, expense and income has its own ledger account.
4. Any value taken from the business by the owner of the business is known as drawings.
5. At the end of the period, the accounts of assets and liabilities which contain more than one entry should be balanced.
6. The entries for purchases and sales, and purchases returns and sales returns are recorded in separate accounts.
7. Carriage is the cost of transporting goods.

REVIEW QUESTIONS

1. A trader provides the following information.

20-7		$
February 1	Balance of cash	250
2	Paid property tax in cash	52
3	Cash sales	94
4	Bought stationery and paid in cash	13
5	Received cash from M Ghosh, a debtor	120
6	The owner withdrew cash for personal use	50
7	Bought goods and paid in cash	200

   Enter the above transactions in the trader's cash account. Balance the account on 7 February and bring down the balance on 8 February 20-7.

Double Entry Bookkeeping – Part A

2. Copy out the following table and insert the name of the account to be debited and the name of the account to be credited for **each** transaction.

Transaction	Account to be debited	Account to be credited
(a) Sold goods for cash		
(b) Bought goods on credit from M Arora		
(c) The owner took cash for her own use		
(d) Returned goods to M Arora		
(e) Sold goods on credit to B Jindal		
(f) Paid for carriage on goods sold to B Jindal		
(g) Paid wages of employees in cash		
(h) Bought motor vehicle and paid by cheque		

*3. On 1 July 20-6 Mumtaz started a business. The following are her transactions for the first two weeks of trading.

July 1 Mumtaz paid capital, $50 000, into the business bank account
      2 Bought premises, $25 000, and paid by cheque
      4 Bought equipment, $4000, and paid by cheque
      6 Bought goods, $1500, on credit from Mayur Vihar Traders
      7 Paid advertising expenses, $60, by cheque
      9 Sold goods, $200, and received a cheque
     12 Sold goods, $310, on credit, to Ridhima
     13 Ridhima returned damaged goods, $20
     14 Paid $1000 by cheque on account to Mayur Vihar Traders

Enter the above transactions in the ledger of Mumtaz. Balance the bank account and the accounts of Mayur Vihar Traders and Ridhima on 14 July and bring down the balances on 15 July 20-6.

*4. From the following information, write up the account of Manish in the books of Rahman for the month of May 20-1. Prepare the account in three column running balance format.

May 1 Manish owes Rahman $920
14 Rahman sold goods, $440, on credit to Manish
16 Manish returned goods, $175, to Rahman
19 Manish paid Rahman $100 in cash
21 Rahman sold goods, $93, on credit to Manish
26 Manish paid Rahman $900 by cheque

5. On 1 September 20-3 Adarsh started a business. The following are his transactions for the first month of trading.

September 1 Adarsh paid capital, $90 000, into the business bank account
2 Paid rent, $400, by cheque
4 Bought goods, $2100, on credit from Vinod
8 Cash sales $170
11 Paid sundry expenses, $32, in cash
14 Bought goods, $900, on credit from Vinod
19 Sold goods, $380, on credit to Kaveri
21 Returned faulty goods, $110, to Vinod
25 Paid shop assistant's wages in cash, $120
27 Paid the amount owing to Vinod by cheque
29 Adarsh took goods costing $130 for his own use

Enter the above transactions in the ledger of Adarsh. Balance the bank account and the cash account on 30 September and bring down the balances on 1 October 20-3.

6. The following account appears in the ledger of Marine Drive Stores.

Central Wholesalers account

Date	Details	Folio	$	Date	Details	Folio	$
20-4				20-4			
May 17	Returns		120	May 1	Balance	b/d	180
20	Bank		300	10	Purchases		410
31	Balance	c/d	170				
			590				590
				20-4			
				June 1	Balance	b/d	170

Explain **each** entry in the above account and also state where the double entry for **each** entry will be found.

Chapter 3 The Trial Balance

In this chapter you will learn to:
- understand the purpose of a trial balance
- prepare a trial balance
- understand the errors which affect a trial balance
- understand the errors which do not affect a trial balance.

Introduction

A trial balance is **a list of the balances on the accounts in the ledger at a certain date**. A trial balance is prepared to check the arithmetical accuracy of the double entry bookkeeping. The name of each account is listed in the trial balance. The balance on each account is shown according to whether it is a debit balance or a credit balance. The trial balance will show if the total of the debit balances is equal to the total credit balances.

It is important to remember that the trial balance is **not** a part of the double entry system of bookkeeping as it is simply a list of balances. If the ledger accounts are balanced monthly then a trial balance may also be drawn up at the end of each month.

The trial balance should be headed with the term "trial balance" along with the date on which it was prepared.

The layout of a trial balance is as follows:

Trial Balance at ………. *

Details	Folio	Debit $	Credit $

*The date on which it is prepared.

The Purpose of a Trial Balance

1. The trial balance can help in locating arithmetical errors. However, the balancing of the trial balance is not proof that the entries in the ledger accounts are completely free from errors.

2. A trial balance is useful in preparing financial statements (see Chapters 8 and 9).

The Preparation of a Trial Balance

All the ledger accounts which are "open" (those which still have an amount of money showing in the account) are listed together with the balance on each account. If the debit side of the account is larger in money than the credit side then that account has a debit balance and the amount of the balance (or difference) is entered in the debit column of the trial balance. If the credit side of the account has more money than the debit side then that account has a credit balance and the amount of the balance (or difference) is entered in the credit column of the trial balance.

The debit column and the credit column are totalled. If the totals agree, it indicates that the double entry bookkeeping is arithmetically correct.

Example 3.1

Ajay started his business on 1 January 20-7. His transactions for his first week of trading were shown in the solution to **Exercise 2.3** in Chapter 2.

Prepare a trial balance for Ajay on 7 January 20-7.

The Trial Balance

Ajay
Trial Balance at 7 January 20-7

	Folio	Debit $	Credit $
Bank	1	55 395	
Capital	2		80 000
Fixtures & equipment	3	30 000	
AB Loans	4		10 000
Motor vehicles	5	9 000	
Mallika loan	6		5 000
Rent	7	400	
Insurance	8	250	
Motor expenses	9	50	
Rent received	10		95
		95 095	95 095

- Folio numbers do not always appear in a trial balance.
- It is common to find the words "debit" and "credit" abbreviated to "dr" and "cr".
- In this particular example, the totals of the trial balance are same as the totals of the bank account. This will not always be the case. It occurred in this example as all the transactions passed through the bank account.

> **Test your understanding**
> 1. Explain what a trial balance is.
> 2. State **two** purposes of preparing a trial balance.
> 3. Explain what determines whether the balance of an account is entered in the debit column or the credit column of a trial balance.
> 4. Explain what is indicated if the totals of a trial balance agree.

In practice, a trial balance is drawn-up using the actual ledger accounts. However, in examination questions this does not always occur. Sometimes students are presented with a list of balances and asked to prepare a trial balance; sometimes a trial balance containing errors is presented and students are asked to prepare a corrected trial balance. In these situations students cannot look at the ledger account in order to determine whether the account has a debit or a credit balance. It is necessary to know the type of accounts which have a debit balance and those which have a credit balance. These are shown in the table below.

Debit balances	Credit balances
Assets	Liabilities
Expenses	Incomes
Drawings	Capital
Purchases	Sales
Sales returns	Purchases returns

Example 3.2

The following trial balance was prepared by an inexperienced bookkeeper and contains errors.

Prepare a corrected trial balance at 31 December 20-9.

Jasmine
Trial Balance for the year ended 31 December 20-9

	Debit $	Credit $
Cash		300
Bank overdraft	3 000	
Capital		42 500
Drawings		750
Land and buildings	30 000	
Office equipment		1 050
Loan	2 200	
Inventory	7 500	
Purchases		9 850
Sales	10 650	
Sales returns		940
Purchases returns	1 030	
Carriage inwards		400
Wages	1 500	
Rent received	830	
Sundry expenses	1 290	
Trade receivables		12 300
Trade payables	5 670	
	63 670	68 090

The Trial Balance

35

Jasmine
Corrected Trial Balance at 31 December 20-9

	Debit $	Credit $
Cash	300	
Bank overdraft		3 000
Capital		42 500
Drawings	750	
Land and buildings	30 000	
Office equipment	1 050	
Loan		2 200
Inventory	7 500	
Purchases	9 850	
Sales		10 650
Sales returns	940	
Purchases returns		1 030
Carriage inwards	400	
Wages	1 500	
Rent received		830
Sundry expenses	1 290	
Trade receivables	12 300	
Trade payables		5 670
	65 880	65 880

- The heading of the trial balance was incorrect and required amending.
- Each item had to be considered to decide whether it was in the correct column or it required amending.

Test your understanding

1. State the column of a trial balance in which the balance of **each** of the following accounts would appear. Give a reason for your answer in each case.
   (a) loan from WQ loans
   (b) motor expenses
   (c) motor vehicles
   (d) bank overdraft
   (e) carriage outwards
   (f) commission received

The Trial Balance and Errors

If the trial balance fails to balance

It is obvious that an error has been made somewhere. This may be:
1. An error of addition within the trial balance
2. An error of addition within one of the ledger accounts
3. Entering a different figure on the credit to that entered on the debit when making a double entry in the ledger
4. Making a single entry for a transaction rather than a double entry
5. Entering a transaction twice on the same side of the ledger

> **Check list for locating errors**
> - Check the addition of the trial balance
> - Check the addition of the balance of each ledger account
> - Check that each ledger account balance has been entered in the correct column of the trial balance
> - Check that every ledger account balance has been entered in the trial balance
> - Look for a transaction equal to the difference in the trial balance and check that a double entry has been made for that transaction
> - Look for a transaction equal to half the difference in the trial balance and check if it has been entered twice on the same side of the ledger rather than once on each side
> - Check the double entry for every transaction entered in the books since the date of the last trial balance

If the trial balance balances

When a trial balance balances, it simply means that the total of the debit balances is equal to the total of the credit balances. It does not imply that the double entry is error-free. The trial balance will still balance if any of the following errors are made.

The Trial Balance

Name of error	Description of error	Example
Error of commission	This occurs when a transaction is entered using the correct amount and on the correct side, but in the wrong account of the same class.	Cash received from Malini credited to Mallika's account.
Error of complete reversal	This occurs when the correct amount is entered in the correct accounts, but the entry has been made on the wrong side of each account.	Cash drawings debited to the cash account and credited to the drawings account.
Error of omission	This occurs when a transaction has been completely omitted from the accounting records. Neither a debit entry nor a credit entry has been made.	Payment of wages not entered in the books.
Error of original entry	This occurs when an incorrect figure is used when a transaction is first entered in the accounting records. The double entry will therefore use the incorrect figure.	Goods, $100, bought on credit but recorded as $1000.
Error of principle	This occurs when a transaction is entered using the correct amount and on the correct side, but in the wrong class of account.	Motor expenses debited to the motor vehicles account.
Compensating errors	These occur when two or more errors cancel each other out.	Purchases account under-added by $100 and sales returns account over-added by $100.

Test your understanding
1. For **each** of the following state the type of error which has been made.
    (a) Rent of premises debited to the premises account
    (b) Sales to R Singh debited to H Singh's account
    (c) Balance on cash account over-stated by $10 and balance on sales account over-stated by $10
    (d) Cash sales debited to the sales account and credited to the cash account

Points to Remember

1. A trial balance is a list of the balances on the accounts in the ledger at a certain date.
2. A trial balance is prepared to check the arithmetical accuracy of the double entry bookkeeping.
3. If a trial balance fails to balance, it indicates that an error has been made.
4. There are six types of error which are not revealed by a trial balance.

Review Questions

1. Danbi Wyske runs her business from rented premises. The following balances were extracted from her books on 30 April 2003.

	$
Inventory 1 May 2002	4 000
Sales	80 000
Purchases	62 000
Trade receivables	10 000
Trade payables	9 000
Electricity paid	3 000
General expenses	7 000
Cash at bank	5 000
Drawings	8 000
Rent and insurance paid	6 000
Equipment	29 000
Capital	?

Prepare Danbi's trial balance at 30 April 2003, showing her capital account balance. **[Based on IGCSE 2003]**

2. A trial balance drawn up at the end of Jim's financial year balanced. The following errors were then discovered.

The Trial Balance

1. Goods returned to K Weston had been debited to K Wilton.
2. Repairs to office equipment had been debited in the office equipment account.
3. An invoice, $1000, for goods sold on credit to Jacob & Co had been recorded in the accounts as $100.
4. Goods purchased on credit from Brixton Ltd had been debited in Brixton's account and credited in the purchases account.

Required

(a) State the type of error made in **each** of the errors 1-4 above.
(b) Name **two** further errors not revealed by a trial balance.

*3. Hilota has a business supplying spare parts for cars. His financial year ends on 31 March. At 31 March 2006 his account showed the following balances.

	$
Non-current assets	12 700
Inventory at 1 April 2005	3 200
Bank balance (Dr)	4 550
Sales	56 000
Purchases	34 200
Carriage outwards	950
Rent	4 000
Wages	7 200
General expenses	2 600
Trade receivables	2 100
Trade payables	3 000
Capital	20 000
Drawings	7 500

Required

(a) Prepare Hilota's trial balance at 31 March 2006.
(b) State **one** limitation of a trial balance.
(c) State **two** uses of a trial balance.

[Based on IGCSE 2006]

4. (a) Define a trial balance.
   (b) Explain the purpose of a trial balance.
   (c) Explain how a trial balance is different from a balance sheet.

(d) A trader's trial balance fails to balance. Explain how **each** of the following checks would be useful to help in discovering the error(s)
   (i) Looking for a transaction equal to the difference in the trial balance
   (ii) Looking for a transaction equal to half the difference in the trial balance.
(e) (i) List **four** types of error which would not be revealed by a trial balance
   (ii) Give an example of **each** of these four types of error
   (iii) Explain **why each** of these errors would not be revealed by a trial balance.

5. At the end of April 2000, an inexperienced bookkeeper prepared the following trial balance for Khalid Hassan.

	Dr. $	Cr. $
Sales	95 300	
Purchases		51 600
Inventory 1 May 1999	5 000	
Wages	18 200	
General expenses	7 300	
Repairs and maintenance		2 700
Machinery and equipment	58 550	
Motors	15 900	
Trade receivables		15 800
Trade payables	7 300	
Cash		350
Bank overdraft	3 800	
Drawings		12 000
Capital (balancing figure)		128 900
	211 350	211 350

In addition to the obvious errors in the trial balance, the accountant was also able to discover the following errors, which the trial balance failed to disclose.
1. $150 for the cost of repairing a motor had been debited to the motors account.
2. $50 cash paid for general expenses had not been recorded.

The Trial Balance

41

3. Errors of addition had been made resulting in the sales being overcast by $100 and the wages being overcast by the same amount.
4. When an invoice for goods purchased on credit was recorded the amount was entered as $1000 instead of $100.
5. A cheque received from a debtor for $200 had been debited to the debtor's account and credited to the bank account.

(a) For **each** of the above items (1–5) state the type of error that was made.
(b) Prepare an amended trial balance for Khalid Hassan at 30 April showing the correct capital balance.
(c) Khalid's brother Yousef also has a business. When Yousef prepared his trial balance on 31 March 2000, he found that the credit side exceeded the debit side by $250. Describe **four** procedures that Yousef could carry out to find the errors that caused the difference on the trial balance.

[IGCSE 2000]

Chapter 4

Double Entry Bookkeeping – Part B

In this chapter you will learn to:
- understand how the ledger is divided into specialist areas
- prepare a two column cash book
- make contra entries in a cash book
- understand cash discounts – allowed and received
- prepare a three column cash book.

Introduction

Chapter 2 introduced the basic principles of double entry bookkeeping. It was explained how a ledger account is opened for each type of asset, expense, liability and income, and for every individual debtor and creditor. As the business grows, so does the number of ledger accounts, so it becomes necessary to divide the ledger into different sections.

Division of the Ledger into Specialist Areas

Dividing the ledger into sections makes it more convenient to use as the same type of accounts can be kept together and the task of maintaining the ledger can be divided between several people. The ledger is usually divided into the following specialised areas:

Sales Ledger	This is also referred to as the **debtors ledger**. All the **personal** accounts of debtors (credit customers) are kept in the sales ledger.
Purchases Ledger	This is also referred to as the **creditors ledger**. All the **personal** accounts of creditors (credit suppliers) are kept in the purchases ledger.

Double Entry Bookkeeping – Part B

Nominal Ledger	This is also referred to as the **general ledger**. Apart from the cash account, the bank account and the accounts of debtors and creditors, all the remaining accounts are kept in the nominal ledger. This ledger will contain accounts of assets, liabilities, expenses, incomes, sales, purchases and returns. Asset accounts are known as **real** accounts. Accounts for expenses, income and capital are known as **nominal** accounts.
Cash books	These contain the main cash book (see later) and the petty cash book (see Chapter 5)

> **Test your understanding**
> 1. State **one** advantage of dividing the ledger into specialist areas.
> 2. State in which ledger **each** of the following accounts would appear.
>   (a) rent account
>   (b) AB Finance Co. loan account
>   (c) XY Stores account (a supplier)
>   (d) capital account
>   (e) sales returns account
>   (f) Gee Tee Traders account (a customer)

The Two Column Cash Book

Chapter 2 explained how two separate accounts – a cash account and a bank account – are maintained to record the movements of money. In practice, it is common for these accounts to be moved from the ledger and shown in a separate book known as the cash book. The cash account and the bank account appear side-by-side in the cash book.

The rules of double entry bookkeeping are still applied. Any money received is debited in the cash book. If the money is placed in the cash till, it will be entered in the cash column and if it is paid into the bank, it will be entered in the bank column. Any money paid out is credited in the cash book. If the money is paid in cash, it will be entered in the cash column and if it is paid out of the bank, it will be entered in the bank column.

Whilst the cash account and the bank account appear side-by-side, they still keep their own identity and must be balanced separately as described in Chapter 2.

Since the cash a book is part of the double entry system, it represents ledger accounts for both cash and bank. It is, however, also a **book of prime entry** (see Chapter 7).

Contra entries

Sometimes surplus cash is paid into the bank, or money may be withdrawn from the bank to place in the cash. Such transactions are known as **contra entries** because they appear on both sides of the cash book: debited to one account and credited to the other. These transactions are recorded by applying the usual rules of double entry by debiting the account receiving the money and crediting the account giving the money. The name of the account where the double entry is made is written in the details column. The entries are summarised as follows:

To record surplus cash paid into the bank
Debit the bank account and write "cash" in the details column
Credit the cash account and write "bank" in the details column

To record cash withdrawn from the bank for office use
Debit the cash account and write "bank" in the details column
Credit the bank account and write "cash" in the details column

In each case, the letter "c" is usually entered in the folio column to indicate that the double entry is on the opposite side of the same book.

Example 4.1

20-6
December   1   Mamata started business with a capital of $20 000 which she paid into a business bank account
           2   Paid rent of premises, $650, by cheque
           5   Purchased goods, $9500, on credit from Lodi Road Traders

Double Entry Bookkeeping – Part B

9 Withdrew $150 from the bank account for office use
14 Paid advertising expenses, $90, in cash
18 Sold goods, $4120, on credit to Central Dealers
23 Paid Lodi Road Traders' account by cheque
26 Bought motor vehicle, $5760, and paid by cheque
28 Mamata took $3000 from the business bank account for personal use

Enter the above transactions in the books of Mamata. The cash account and the bank account should be shown in a two column cash book. The ledger should be divided into sales ledger, purchases ledger and nominal ledger. Balance the cash book on 31 December.

Mamata

Sales Ledger
Central Dealers account   Page 1

Date	Details	Folio	$	Date	Details	Folio	$
20-6 Dec 18	Sales	nl 5	4 120				

Purchases Ledger
Lodi Road Traders account   Page 1

Date	Details	Folio	$	Date	Details	Folio	$
20-6 Dec 23	Bank	cb 1	9 500 9 500	20-6 Dec 5	Purchases	nl 3	9 500 9 500

Nominal Ledger
Capital account   Page 1

Date	Details	Folio	$	Date	Details	Folio	$
				20-7 Dec 1	Bank	cb 1	20 000

Rent account   Page 2

Date	Details	Folio	$	Date	Details	Folio	$
20-6 Dec 2	Bank	cb 1	650				

Purchases account — Page 3

Date	Details	Folio	$	Date	Details	Folio	$
20-6 Dec 5	Lodi Road Traders	pl 1	9 500				

Advertising account — Page 4

Date	Details	Folio	$	Date	Details	Folio	$
20-6 Dec 14	Cash	cb 1	90				

Sales account — Page 5

Date	Details	Folio	$	Date	Details	Folio	$
				20-6 Dec 18	Central Dealers	sl 1	4 120

Motor vehicle account — Page 6

Date	Details	Folio	$	Date	Details	Folio	$
20-6 Dec 26	Bank	cb 1	5 760				

Drawings account — Page 7

Date	Details	Folio	$	Date	Details	Folio	$
20-6 Dec 28	Bank	cb 1	3 000				

Test your understanding
1. Explain what is meant by a contra entry in a cash book.
2. Give two examples of contra entries in a cash book.

Double Entry Bookkeeping – Part B

Mamata
Cash Book

Page 1

Date	Details	Folio	Cash $	Bank $	Date	Details	Folio	Cash $	Bank $
20-6					20-6				
Dec 1	Capital	nl 1		20 000	Dec 2	Rent	nl 2		650
9	Bank	c	150		9	Cash	c		150
					14	Advertising	nl 4	90	
					23	Lodi Road Traders	nl 1		9 500
					26	Motor Vehicle	nl 6		5 760
					28	Drawings	nl 7		3 000
					31	Balance	c/d	60	940
			150	20 000				150	20 000
20-7									
Jan 1	Balance	b/d	60	840					

Bank overdraft

As explained earlier, the cash column and the bank column of a cash book are balanced separately as they represent two separate accounts.

The balance on the cash column will always be brought down as a debit balance at the start of the next trading period. The only exception to this is when there is no cash left in the cash account in which case the balance will be nil. **It is not possible to have a credit balance on a cash account.**

It is, however, possible to have a credit balance on a bank account. The bank may allow the business to have a **bank overdraft**. This means that the bank allows the business to pay out more from the bank than is put into the bank (interest will be charged by the bank on the amount overdrawn). In the cash book, the bank account is balanced in the usual way and the balance will be brought down on the credit side. This represents the amount the business owes the bank and is a liability.

Example 4.2

Mamata started business on 1 December 2006. Her transactions for the first month of trading were the same as those shown in **Example 4.1** except that her drawings on 28 December amounted to $5000 rather than $3000.

Enter Mamata's transactions for December 20-6 in her two column cash book. Balance the book on 31 December and bring down the balances on 1 January 20-7. The solution is shown on page 49.

The Three Column Cash Book

Many businesses maintain a three column cash book rather than a two column cash book. The difference is that a three column cash book has an extra money column on each side to record **cash discount**.

Cash discount

This is an allowance given to a customer when an account is settled within a time limit set by the supplier. An account does not have to be paid in cash to qualify for cash discount. The *time* of payment is the deciding factor rather than *how* the account is paid. Cash discount is a means of encouraging customers to pay their accounts promptly. The supplier will receive an amount slightly less than the due amount. However, the money is paid earlier and so it is available for use within the business.

Double Entry Bookkeeping – Part B

Mamata
Cash Book

Page 1

Date	Details	Folio	Cash $	Bank $	Date	Details	Folio	Cash $	Bank $
20-6					20-6				
Dec 1	Capital	nl 1		20 000	Dec 2	Rent	nl 2		650
9	Bank	c	150		9	Cash	c		150
31	Balance	c/d		1 060	14	Advertising	nl 4	90	
					23	Lodi Road Traders	nl 1		9 500
					26	Motor Vehicle	nl 6		5 760
					28	Drawings	nl 7		5 000
					31	Balance	c/d	60	
			150	21 060				150	21 060
20-7					20-6				
Jan 1	Balance	b/d	60	840	Jan 1	Balance	b/d		1 060

Discount allowed is the discount a business allows its credit customers (debtors) when they pay their accounts within a set time. This is an expense of the business as it is the cost of having debts settled promptly. **Discount received** is the discount a business receives from its credit suppliers (creditors) when it pays their accounts within a set time. This is an income of the business as it is the benefit received from settling debts promptly. It is important to realise that discount received does not involve the receipt of money: the supplier simply accepts less money in settlement of the account.

In addition to recording the cash or cheque in settlement of debt, it is also necessary to record cash discount. The entries are summarised as follows:

1. **When an account is paid by a debtor and a discount is allowed**
   Credit the discount in the debtor's account to show that this amount is no longer owing.
   Enter the amount of the discount in the discount allowed column of the cash book.
2. **When an account of a creditor is paid and a discount is received**
   Debit the discount in the creditor's account to show that this amount is no longer owing.
   Enter the amount of the discount in the discount received column of the cash book.

The discount columns in the cash book are **not** a part of the double entry system. They are used for convenience to make a note of discount at the time an account is paid or received. At the end of the trading period the totals must be transferred to the double entry system. The steps for this are as follows:

1. Total each discount column.
2. Debit the discount allowed account in the nominal ledger with the total of the discount allowed column. This now represents the double entry for all the individual credits in the accounts of debtors.
3. Credit the discount received account in the nominal ledger with the total of the discount received column. This now represents the double entry for all the individual debits in the accounts of creditors.

Double Entry Bookkeeping – Part B

Dishonoured cheque

A dishonoured cheque is a cheque received, which the debtor's bank refuses to pay. This may occur because the debtor does not have enough money in his/her bank account, or it may be because of an error on the cheque e.g. no signature, no date, the amount in words and the amount in figures do not agree.

If a cheque is dishonoured, it is returned to the business that paid the cheque into the bank. The business must record the return of this cheque by crediting the bank account and debiting the debtor's account (the reverse of the entries made when the cheque was received). The business will also inform the debtor that this amount is unpaid.

> **Test your understanding**
> 1. Explain why it is **not** possible to have a credit balance brought down in the cash column of a cash book.
> 2. Explain the meaning of the term bank overdraft.
> 3. Explain why a business may allow its credit customers cash discount.
> 4. Explain the meaning of the term "dishonoured cheque".

Example 4.3

Enter the following transactions in the books of Mamata. She maintains a three column cash book and divides the ledger into three sections – sales ledger, purchases ledger and nominal ledger.

Balance the cash book on 31 January 20-7 and transfer the totals of the discount columns to the relevant accounts in the nominal ledger. Balance the accounts in the sales and purchases ledgers where necessary.

20-7
January   1   Mamata had a cash balance of $60 and a bank overdraft of $1060
           4   Bought goods, $5200, on credit from Lodi Road Traders
           8   Returned goods, $200, to Lodi Road Traders
          12   Sold goods, $770, on credit to A & J Singh
          14   Cash sales $680

17 Paid $650 cash into the business bank account
21 Received a cheque from A & J Singh in settlement of their account
24 Sold goods, $1200, on credit to North East Stores
26 A & H Singh's cheque was dishonoured and returned by the bank
28 Paid Lodi Road Traders the amount due, by cheque, after deducting a discount of 2½%
31 North East Stores paid the amount due by cheque less a cash discount of 3%

Mamata

Sales Ledger
A & J Singh account   Page 2

Date	Details	Folio	$	Date	Details	Folio	$
20-7				20-7			
Jan 12	Sales	nl 5	770	Jan 21	Bank	cb 2	770
26	Bank (dis-honoured cheque)	cb 2	770	31	Balance	c/d	770
			1 540				1 540
20-7							
Feb 1	Balance	b/d	770				

North East Stores account   Page 3

Date	Details	Folio	$	Date	Details	Folio	$
20-7				20-7			
Jan 24	Sales	nl 5	1 200	Jan 31	Bank	cb 2	1 164
					Discount	cb 2	36
			1 200				1 200

Double Entry Bookkeeping – Part B

Purchases Ledger
Lodi Road Traders account — Page 1

Date	Details	Folio	$	Date	Details	Folio	$
20-7 Jan 8	Purchases Returns	nl 8	200	20-7 Jan 4	Purchases	nl 3	5 200
28	Bank	cb 2	4 875				
	Discount	cb 2	125				
			5 200				5 200

Nominal Ledger
Purchases account — Page 3

Date	Details	Folio	$	Date	Details	Folio	$
20-7 Jan 4	Lodi Road Traders	pl 1	5 200				

Sales account — Page 5

Date	Details	Folio	$	Date	Details	Folio	$
				20-7 Jan 12	A & J Singh	sl 2	770
				14	Cash	cb 2	680
				24	North East Stores	sl 3	1 200

Purchases returns account — Page 8

Date	Details	Folio	$	Date	Details	Folio	$
				20-7 Jan 8	Lodi Road Traders	pl 1	200

Discount allowed account — Page 9

Date	Details	Folio	$	Date	Details	Folio	$
20-7 Jan 31	Total for month	cb 2	36				

Discount received account — Page 10

Date	Details	Folio	$	Date	Details	Folio	$
				20-7 Jan 31	Total for month	cb 2	125

Mamata
Cash Book
Page 2

Date	Details	Folio	Discount Allowed $	Cash $	Bank $	Date	Details	Folio	Discount Received $	Cash $	Bank $
20-7						20-7					
Dec 1	Balance	b/d		60		Jan 1	Balance	b/d			1 060
14	Sales	nl 5		680		17	Bank	c		650	
17	Cash	c			650	26	A & J Singh (dishonoured cheque)	sl 2			770
21	A & J Singh	sl 2			770	28	Lodi Road Traders	pl 1	125		4 875
31	North East Stores	sl 3	36		1 164	31	Balance	c/d		90	
	Balance	c/d			4 121						
			36	740	6 705				125	740	6 705
			nl 9						nl 10		
20-7						20-7					
Jan 1	Balance	b/d		90		Jan 1	Balance	b/d			4 121

Double Entry Bookkeeping – Part B

> ### POINTS TO REMEMBER
>
> 1. The ledger is usually divided into three specialist areas – sales ledger, purchases ledger and nominal ledger.
> 2. The cash account and the bank account are usually kept side-by-side in a cash book.
> 3. A contra entry appears on both sides of a cash book.
> 4. A credit balance brought down in the bank column of a cash book indicates a bank overdraft.
> 5. Cash discount is given to encourage customers to pay their accounts within a set time limit.
> 6. The totals of the discount columns in the cash book are transferred to the discount accounts in the ledger.

> ### REVIEW QUESTIONS
>
> 1. The balances on Ella's cash and bank accounts at 1 March 1999 were:
>
> | | $ |
> |------------------|-------|
> | Bank overdraft | 2 300 |
> | Cash in hand | 200 |
>
>   Transactions for the month of March 1999 were:
>
>   March 1 Received and banked cheque for $195 from Josiah Buko
>   5 Paid cheques to C Brown, $240, and A Greenly, $288
>   11 Cash sales $400
>   16 Banked spare cash $300
>   25 Ella paid further capital into the bank, $3000
>   30 Received and banked cheque for $1170 from PQ Ltd.
>
>   Record the transactions for March 1999 in the bank and cash

accounts in Ella's cash book and bring down the cash and bank balances on 1 April 1999.

[IGCSE 1999]

2. (a) State **two** advantages of dividing the ledger into specialist areas.
   (b) Indicate by means of a tick (✓) the ledger in which **each** of the following accounts would appear.

Account	Sales ledger	Purchases ledger	Nominal ledger
(a) Tom (a creditor)			
(b) Jim (a debtor)			
(c) Sales			
(d) Purchases returns			
(e) Drawings			

*3. Jonah is a sole trader who keeps full double entry accounting records including a three column cash book. All cheques received are banked on the same day.

On 30 June 2004, balances in his books included the following:

		$
Debtors	H Syde	500
	B Sharp	800
	M Yaveli	630
Creditors	J Teime	400
	P Mulder	1000
Cash		600
Bank (dr)		2500

Jonah's transactions for the month of July 2004 included the following:

$

July 3 H Syde paid the amount he owed by cheque after deducting cash discount of $10
     7 Cash was withdrawn from bank for office use   200

Double Entry Bookkeeping – Part B

    10 Paid J Teime by cheque after deducting $15 cash discount
    12 Paid wages in cash   400
    14 B Sharp paid the amount he owed by cheque after deducting cash discount of $20
    17 Paid P Mulder by cheque after deducting cash discount of $25
    20 Cash sales paid directly into the bank   350
    21 M Yaveli paid the amount he owed by cheque
    24 Paid wages in cash   250
          Paid electricity bill by cheque   600
    29 Jonah's bank returned M Yaveli's cheque for $630 as dishonoured

(a) Enter the above transactions in Jonah's cash book. Balance the cash book at 31 July and bring down the balances on 1 August 2004.

(b) Make the entries required in the discount accounts in Jonah's ledger on 31 July 2004.

[IGCSE 2004]

4. Benjamin Ngaara started business on 1 August 2001 with a capital of $9500 which was paid into a business bank account.

Transactions for the month of August 2001 were:

August 2 Purchased furniture and equipment and paid by cheque, $2750
             4 Withdrew $200 cash from bank for business use
             6 Paid rent of premises in cash, $150
           13 Received a cheque from Tanko Ltd. for $75 which was paid into the bank
           18 Paid a cheque to Mary Jones in settlement of her account of $350 less 2% cash discount
           20 The cheque paid into the bank on 13 August was returned by the bank dishonoured
           31 Banked a cheque received from Jacob Smythe for $194 in full settlement of his account of $200

(a) Write up Benjamin's three column cash book for August 2001. Balance the cash and bank columns and bring down the balances on 1 September 2001.

(b) Benjamin is unsure how to transfer the totals of the discount columns to the ledger.
   (i) State to which ledger account, and to which side of that account, the total of the discount allowed column is posted.
   (ii) State to which ledger account, and to which side of that account, the total of the discount received column is posted.

[IGCSE 2001]

*5. A trader's cash book includes the following entries:

Cash Book

	Discount Allowed	Cash	Bank		Discount Received	Cash	Bank
20-6	$	$	$	20-6	$	$	$
June 1 Balance b/d		240		June 1 Balance b/d			3130
2 Cash	c		200	2 Bank	c		200
3 Rohit			500	7 ADT Ltd.		10	390
				10 Rohit (dishonoured cheque)			500

(a) Explain **each** entry in the above cash book and also state where the double entry for **each** entry will be found.
(b) Explain the purpose of the discount columns in a three column cash book.

6. Abdul Anwar is a sole trader who keeps a full set of double entry records including a three column cash book.
The balances on his books on 1 May 2009 included the following:

	$
Cash	100
Bank	490 credit
Debtor – Sameen Atif	150
Creditor – Mohsen Ali	320

Abdul's transactions for the month of May 2009 included the following:

Double Entry Bookkeeping – Part B

May 6 Cash sales, $280, of which $200 was paid into the bank on that date
    13 Received a cheque from Sameen Atif in settlement of her account
    18 Paid a cheque to Mohsin Ali in settlement of his account after deducting cash discount of 2 ½%
    24 Sameen Atif's cheque was dishonoured and was returned by the bank
    30 Paid all the remaining cash into the bank except $50

Required

(a) Enter the above transactions in Abdul's cash book. Balance the cash book at 31 May and bring down the balances on 1 June 2009.

Abdul Anwar's financial year ends on 31 October.

Apart from those mentioned above, Abdul Anwar had no other transactions with Sameen Atif during the six months ended 31 October 2009.

Required

(b) Write up Sameen Atif's account as it would appear in Abdul's ledger for the six months ended 31 October 2009.

[IGCSE 2009]

7. Kalpana is a trader. On 1 February 20-8 she had the following balances on her books.

	$
Cash book – Cash	100
Bank overdraft	480
Sales ledger – Srivastava	200
Purchases ledger – Ahmed	320
Nominal ledger – Premises	60 000
Fixtures and fittings	5 500
Capital	65 000

Enter the above balances in the appropriate accounts on 1 February 20-8.

The following transactions took place during the month of February 20-8.

February 3 Sold goods, $300, on credit to Srivastava
          7 Srivastava returned faulty goods, $50
         11 Purchased goods, $390, paying by cheque
             Paid $10 by cheque for carriage on goods purchased
         15 Cash sales, $610, of which $600 was paid into the bank
         19 Srivastava paid the amount owing on 1 February by cheque, after deducting 3% cash discount
         21 Paid general expenses, $75, in cash
         23 Paid Ahmed a cheque for the amount due, less a cash discount of 2½%
         25 Sublet part of the premises and received $400 rent in cash
         27 Paid $15 by cheque for repairs to fixtures
         28 Paid all the cash into the bank except $100

Enter the above transactions in the books of Kalpana.

Balance the cash book and the personal accounts on 28 February.

Transfer the totals of the discount columns to the nominal ledger on 28 February.

Draw up a trial balance at 28 February 20-8.

Chapter 5   Petty Cash Books

In this chapter you will learn to:
- understand the purpose of a petty cash book
- understand the imprest system of petty cash
- prepare a petty cash book
- post transactions to and from a petty cash book.

Introduction

A **petty cash book** is used to record low-value (petty) cash payments. These may include postages and stationery, cleaning, travelling expenses, and even small cash payments to creditors.

The petty cash book serves two purposes: (a) it lists the transactions for transferring to ledger accounts; (b) it also acts as a ledger account for petty cash transactions. Like the cash book, the petty cash book is a book of prime entry and since it is part of the double entry system, it is also a ledger account.

Maintaining a petty cash book means that it is not necessary to record small cash payments individually in either the cash book or the ledger. This reduces the number of entries in these books.

The task of maintaining a petty cash book is often given to a junior member of staff who is given an amount of cash to act as a **float** from which to make small cash payments. Whilst this allows the chief cashier to concentrate on more important tasks, it also provides valuable training for a junior member of staff. The chief cashier must check the work of the petty cashier at regular intervals.

When a member of staff wishes to obtain some petty cash he/she should present the petty cashier with a completed **petty cash voucher**.

This should show the purpose for which the money is required, the date and the signature of the person receiving the cash. At regular intervals the petty cashier should check these vouchers against the total cash spent.

> **Test your understanding**
> 1. State **two** advantages of maintaining a petty cash book.
> 2. Explain the purpose of a petty cash voucher.

The Imprest System

Most petty cash books are maintained using the imprest system. Under this system the petty cashier starts each period (week, fortnight, month etc.) with a fixed amount of money. This is known as the **imprest amount** or the **float**. During the period, payments are made out of this cash and are recorded in the petty cash book. At the end of the period, after the petty cash book is balanced, the chief cashier will provide the petty cashier with enough cash to restore the balance to the amount of the imprest (float). The petty cashier therefore starts each period with the same amount of cash.

Under this system the chief cashier is aware of exactly how much petty cash has been spent in each period. The amount of the imprest can be adjusted as necessary if it is too much or not enough.

> **Test your understanding**
> 1. Explain the meaning of the imprest system of petty cash.
> 2. Explain what the petty cashier should do if he/she thinks that the imprest amount is inadequate.

The Layout of a Petty Cash Book

A petty cash book resembles a ledger account with several money columns on the credit side. These are known as **analysis columns** and are used to divide the payments into different categories. A column is used for each of the main types of expenses paid out of petty cash. Instead of a folio column on the credit side there is a column for recording the number of the voucher to which the payment relates.

Petty Cash Books

The number of columns and the main types of expenses will be determined by each individual business. In examinations, guidance is given regarding the columns required.

A layout of a petty cash book is shown as follows:

Petty Cash Book

Dr											Cr
Date	Details	Folio	Total Received $	Date	Details	Vo. No.	Total Paid $	Analysis Columns			
								$	$	$	

"Vo. No." is the abbreviation for "voucher number"

Preparation of a Petty Cash Book

The entries in a petty cash book are summarised as follows:

During the period

1. **Money received**
   (a) Debit the total received column with any money received from the chief cashier.
   Insert the word "cash" or "bank" in the details column.
   (b) Debit the total received column with any money received from any other source.
   Insert the name of the account to be credited in the details column e.g. the name of a debtor (where a debtor pays an account in cash), travel expenses (where an employee reimburses the petty cash for private travel expenses), telephone expenses (where an employee reimburses the petty cash for private telephone calls), and so on.

2. **Money paid**
   Credit the total paid column with any money paid out and also enter the amount in the analysis column for that particular expense.

A brief description of the reason for the payment should be entered in the details column.

At the end of the period

1. Add the total paid column. Insert the total.
2. Add each of the analysis columns and insert the totals. If these totals are then added horizontally they should agree with the total paid column. The analysis columns are now complete.
3. Balance the total received column and the total paid column in the same way as balancing any other ledger account. Carry down the balance from the credit side to the debit side to start the new period.
4. When the imprest is restored enter as described earlier.
5. Complete the double entry for the totals of the analysis columns.
   (a) The totals of the analysis columns for expenses should be debited to the appropriate expense account in the nominal ledger. To indicate that the double entry has been completed the folio number of the relevant account is often written below the total of the appropriate analysis column in the petty cash book.
   (b) Any entries in the analysis column headed ledger accounts should be debited individually to the purchase ledger account of the creditor who made the payment.

Example 5.1

Maitreyi keeps an analysed petty cash book using the imprest system. The amount of the imprest is $150. She provided the following information.

20-1		$	Voucher Number
November	1 Balance	150	
	5 Paid window cleaner	10	1
	8 Bought pens and pencils	4	2
	14 Paid H Singh, a creditor	20	3
	17 Paid taxi fare	9	4
	21 Bought computer paper	7	5
	25 Paid bus fares	3	6

Petty Cash Books

(a) & (b)

Maitreyi
Petty Cash Book

Page 1

Date	Details	Fo	Total Received $	Date	Details	Vo	Total Paid $	Cleaning $	Stationery $	Travel expenses $	Ledger accounts $
20-1 Nov 1	Balance	b/d	150	20-1 Nov 5	Window cleaner	1	10	10			
				8	Pens & pencils	2	4		4		
				14	H Singh	3	20				20
				17	Taxi fare	4	9			9	
				21	Computer paper	5	7		7		
				25	Bus fares	6	3			3	
				27	A Sharma	7	32				32
				29	Office cleaner	8	30	30			
							115	40	11	12	52
				30	Balance	c/d	35	nl 11	nl 17	nl 24	
			150				150				
20-1 Dec 1	Balance Cash	b/d	35 115								

27	Paid A Sharma, a creditor	32	7
29	Paid office cleaner	30	8

(a) Write up Maitreyi's petty cash book for the month of November 20-1. The petty cash book should have four analysis columns - cleaning, stationery, travel expenses, and ledger accounts.
(b) Balance the petty cash book on 30 November and carry down the balance. Show the restoration of the imprest on 1 December 20-1.
(c) Make the necessary entries in Maitreyi's nominal ledger and purchases ledger on 30 November 20-1.

(c)

Maitreyi

Nominal Ledger

Cleaning account — Page 11

Date	Details	Folio	$	Date	Details	Folio	$
20-1 Nov 30	Petty cash	pcb1	40				

Stationery account — Page 17

Date	Details	Folio	$	Date	Details	Folio	$
20-1 Nov 30	Petty cash	pcb1	11				

Travel expenses account — Page 24

Date	Details	Folio	$	Date	Details	Folio	$
20-1 Nov 30	Petty cash	pcb1	12				

Purchases Ledger

H Singh account — Page 73

Date	Details	Folio	$	Date	Details	Folio	$
20-1 Nov 14	Petty cash	pcb1	20				

Petty Cash Books

A Sharma account   Page 69

Date	Details	Folio	$	Date	Details	Folio	$
20-1 Nov 27	Petty cash	pcb1	32				

Note: Each of the accounts in the purchases ledger would have shown a credit balance representing the amount due. The payment from petty cash will cancel this amount.

Test your understanding

1. Explain the use of analysis columns in a petty cash book.
2. State where the double entry will be made for **each** of the following items appearing in a petty cash book:
   (a) amount received to restore the imprest
   (b) payment from petty cash to a trade creditor.

POINTS TO REMEMBER

1. A petty cash book is used to record small cash payments (and occasionally small cash receipts).
2. The imprest system of petty cash means that the petty cashier starts each period with the same amount.
3. A petty cash book is a book of prime entry and also a ledger account.
4. The totals of the analysis columns are posted to the appropriate nominal ledger accounts at the end of each period.
5. Any payments to trade creditors are posted individually to purchase ledger account of the creditor to whom the payment was made.

Review Questions

*1. Mel Rose is a sole trader who keeps a petty cash book on the imprest system. The book has four analysis columns - stationery, postage, travel, and cleaning. The imprest amount is $100. Mel's transactions for the month of March 2002 were as follows.

		$
March 1	Balance of cash	100
3	Travelling expenses	10
6	Office expenses	12
10	Postages	5
14	Cleaner's wages	20
17	Envelopes	3
22	Bus fares	6
25	Postages	4
28	Cleaner's wages	20

(a) Write up Mel's petty cash book to record her transactions for the month of March 2002.
(b) Balance the petty cash book on 31 March 2002 and bring down the balance.
(c) Make the entry on 1 April 2002 to restore the petty cash imprest amount. **[IGCSE 2002]**

2. John Paihia, a trader, maintains a petty cash book using the imprest system.

Required
(a) Explain what is meant by the imprest system in relation to petty cash books.

John Paihia's imprest amount is $300. His transactions for the month of September 2007 were as follows:

		$
Sept 1	Balance brought down	48
	Petty cash restored to imprest amount	?
6	Bought postage stamps	15
11	Paid to Paul Ahipara, a creditor	95

Petty Cash Books

	19	Paid cleaner	24
	23	Paid travelling expenses	9
	25	Bought office stationery	72
	29	Received cash refund from stationery supplier for overcharge	6

Required

(b) Enter the above transactions in John Paihia's petty cash book. The book should have four analysis columns – postages and stationery, travelling expenses, cleaning and ledger accounts.

Balance the book on 30 September 2007 and carry down the balance.

Make the entry on 1 October 2007 to restore the petty cash to the imprest amount.

(c) Explain to John Paihia how the double entry is completed for the items recorded in the analysis columns of the petty cash book.

[IGCSE 2007]

3. Raminder is a sole trader. He operates a petty cash book using the imprest system with a float of $100 at the beginning of each month. The imprest was restored on 30 April so there is an opening balance of $100 on 1 May.

Details of petty cash vouchers presented during May were as follows.

		Voucher number	Total amount $
May	1 Milk, tea and sugar	9	5.20
	6 Postage stamps	10	10.50
	14 Cleaner's wages	11	30.00
	17 Envelopes	12	7.40
	21 Parcel postage	13	2.90
	24 Milk and tea	14	3.10
	28 Cleaner's wages	15	30.00
	30 Computer paper	16	4.70

(a) Write up Raminder's petty cash book for May. Use analysis columns for postages, cleaning, stationery, and refreshments. Total and balance the book on 31 May.

(b) (i) State **one** reason why a business may operate a petty cash book.
   (ii) State **one** advantage of operating the imprest system of petty cash.

4. Philo is in business and keeps his petty cash on the imprest system with a balance of $200.

   On 31 March 2009 there was $129 in the petty cash box and on 1 April 2009 Philo's cashier made a transfer from the business bank account to restore the imprest balance. All the petty cash vouchers for March related to expenses incurred in that month.

   Required
   (a) What were the total expenses paid from petty cash in the month of March 2009?

   When the cash was counted on 30 April 2009, there was $117.50 in the petty cash box and the following petty cash vouchers were found.

		$
April	5 Postage stamps	20.00
	10 Refreshments	17.00
	13 Menon – loan	100.00
	17 Flowers for office	21.00
	24 Stationery	14.40

   Menon had repaid his loan in cash on 29 April.

   Required
   (b) What were the total expenses paid from petty cash in the month of April 2009?
   (c) Calculate the amount of cash which **should** be in the petty cash box on 30 April.
   (d) Suggest **two** reasons for the difference in the actual amount of cash in the petty cash box and the amount which should be there.

   The petty cashier remembered a further petty cash payment of $10 was made on 28 April for cleaning the office windows.

   Required
   (e) Advise Philo's petty cashier about the importance of keeping a record of business expenditure.

Petty Cash Books

(f) Make the necessary entries for the month of April in the petty cash book. The book should have five analysis columns – postages and stationery, refreshments, flowers, cleaning, and other payments. Balance the book and carry down the balance. Show the entry on 1 May to restore the imprest balance to the correct amount.

[IGCSE 2009]

*5. Shilpa is a sole trader. She pays all receipts into the bank at the end of each day's trading and all payments are made by cheque, except for those less than $20 which are regarded as petty cash items.

She provides the following information.

Date	Detail	Amount	
20-9		$	
Feb 21	Balance at bank	3120	
	Petty cash imprest	50	
22	Paid South West Traders	721	to settle an account of $750
24	Received cheques:		
	Janpath Stores	410	to settle an account of $425
	AB Trading	220	
26	Paid:		
	Window cleaner	7	
	Speedy Motors	85	
	Petrol	11	
27	Paid:		
	Refreshments	5	
	Ghandi Stores	12	

(a) Write up the petty cash book for the week ending 28 February 20-9. Use analysis columns for refreshments, cleaning, motor expenses, and ledger accounts.
Balance the book on 27 February 20-9 and restore the imprest on 28 February 20-9.

(b) Write up the cash book for the week ending 28 February 20-9. Balance the book at 28 February 20-9 (after the restoration of the petty cash imprest).

Chapter 6 Business Documents

In this chapter you will learn to:
- recognise and understand the use of business documents
- understand trade discounts.

Introduction

As explained in Chapter 2, the entries in the accounting records of a business are made using business documents. Both documents received and issued by a business are used.

The main business documents and their uses are described later in this chapter.

Invoice

When a business sells goods on credit it will issue an invoice to the purchaser. Each business has its own style of invoice, but they all contain the following information:

- the name and address of the supplier
- the name and address of the customer
- the date
- full details, quantities and prices of the goods supplied

Sometimes the supplier allows the customer **trade discount**. This is a reduction in the price of the goods and the rate of this discount often increases according to the quantity purchased (so encouraging customers to buy in bulk). It is also given to businesses in the same trade. Such businesses will not be prepared to pay the full rate as they need to make a profit when they sell the goods.

Business Documents

It is important to distinguish between **cash discount** and **trade discount**. Cash discount was explained in Chapter 4. **Trade discount** is shown as a deduction on the invoice. Cash discount is not shown as a deduction from an invoice as it is only allowed if the invoice is paid within a set time limit.

> **Test your understanding**
> 1. State **two** reasons why a supplier may allow a customer trade discount.
> 2. Explain the difference between trade discount and cash discount.

Example 6.1

Sew and Sew is a curtain-making business. On 3 April 20-9 goods were purchased on credit from The Weaving Shed and the following invoice was received.

Invoice No. I 3624

INVOICE

The Weaving Shed
14 Industrial Street
Hightown
Telephone 111 01357

Sew and Sew
92 The Avenue
Lowtown

3 April 20-9

Quantity	Description	Unit Price $	Amount $
30 metres	Brocade fabric Design: B320 Colour: Crimson	15	450 00
10 metres	Polycotton fabric Design:P21 Colour: Lemon	6	60 00
			510 00
	Less 20% Trade discount		102 00
			408 00
	Terms: 2½% cash discount if account paid by 31 May 20-9		

- The customer receives the original invoice and uses it to record the purchase of goods on credit.
- The supplier keeps a copy of the invoice and uses it to record the sale of goods on credit.

> **Test your understanding**
> 1. List **four** items of information shown on an invoice.
> 2. Karnail sells goods on credit to Harbhajan and issues an invoice.
>   (a) Name the account to be debited and the account to be credited in Karnail's books.
>   (b) Name the account to be debited and the account to be credited in Harbhajan's books.

Debit Note

The customer should check that goods received are in a satisfactory condition and that they are exactly what was ordered (in respect of price, quantity and quality).

The supplier must be informed of any shortages, overcharges and faults. This is done by issuing a **debit note** to the supplier. Each business has its own style of debit note, but they all contain the following information:

- the name and address of the supplier
- the name and address of the customer
- the date
- full details and quantities (and sometimes the prices) of the goods returned or overcharged

When a price is included on a debit note it is the price which the customer was actually charged for those goods (the price after the deduction of trade discount).

Example 6.2

On 6 April 20-9 Sew and Sew returned goods to The Weaving Shed and issued the following debit note.

Business Documents

	DEBIT NOTE	**Debit Note Number 29**

Sew and Sew
92 The Avenue
Lowtown

The Weaving Shed
14 Industrial Street
Hightown   6 April 20-9

The following goods have been returned:

	Price $	Amount $
10 Metres Polycotton Fabric Design P21 Colour Lemon	6	60 00
Less 20% Trade Discount		12 00
		48 00
Reason for return – Wrong colour supplied		
Please issue a Credit Note		

- Neither the supplier nor the customer makes any entries in their accounting records in respect of a debit note.
- A debit note is merely a request to the supplier to reduce the total of the original invoice.

Test your understanding
1. State two reasons why a customer may send a debit note to a supplier of goods on credit.

Where there has been an overcharge on an invoice most businesses will issue an additional invoice. However, some businesses may issue a debit note instead. This will be entered in the books of both the supplier and the customer in the same way as the original invoice.

Credit Note

When goods are returned, reported faulty, or where there has been an overcharge on an invoice, the supplier may issue a **credit note**. As with all documents, each business has its own style of credit note, but they all contain the following information:

- the name and address of the supplier
- the name and address of the customer
- the date
- full details, quantities and prices of the goods returned or overcharged

To distinguish them from invoices, credit notes are sometimes printed in red.

Example 6.3

On 6 April 20-9 Sew and Sew returned goods to The Weaving Shed and issued a debit note. The Weaving Shed issued the following credit note to Sew and Sew on 9 April 20-9.

Credit Note
C 529

CREDIT NOTE

The Weaving Shed
14 Industrial Street
Hightown
Telephone 111 01357

Sew and Sew
92 The Avenue
Lowtown

9 April 20-9

Quantity	Description	Unit Price $	Amount $
10 metres	Polycotton fabric Design: P21 Colour: Lemon	6	60 00
	Less 20% Trade discount		12 00
			48 00
	Reason for issue of credit note: Wrong colour supplied		

Business Documents

- The customer receives the original credit note and uses it to record the purchases returns.
- The supplier keeps a copy of the credit note and uses it to record the sales returns.

> **Test your understanding**
> 1. State **two** reasons why a supplier may send a credit note to a customer.
> 2. Harbhajan issues a credit note to Karnail.
>   (a) Name the account to be debited and the account to be credited in Karnail's books.
>   (b) Name the account to be debited and the account to be credited in Harbhajan's books.

Statement of Account

At the end of each month, a supplier will usually issue each customer with a **statement of account**. This is a summary of the transactions for the month. The style of a statement of an account may vary, but they all contain the following information:

- the name and address of the supplier
- the name and address of the customer
- the date
- the balance owing at the start of the period
- invoices and credit notes issued
- payments received
- any cash discounts allowed
- the balance owing at the end of the period

Example 6.4

The Weaving Shed issued the following statement of account to Sew and Sew on
30 April 20-9.

STATEMENT OF ACCOUNT				
The Weaving Shed *14 Industrial Street* *Hightown* *Telephone 111 01357*				
Sew and Sew 92 The Avenue Lowtown 30 April 20-9				
Date	Reference	Debit $	Credit $	Balance $
20-9 April 3 9	Invoice Number I 3624 Credit Note Number C529	408 00	 48 00	408 00 360 00
The last amount shown in the balance column is the amount due. Terms: 2½% cash discount if account is paid by 31 May 20-9.				

- Neither the supplier nor the customer makes any entries in their accounting records in respect of a statement of account.
- A statement of account is a reminder to the customer of the amount outstanding. This can be checked against the customer's own records to ensure that no errors have been made by either the supplier or the customer.

Test your understanding
1. State **one** purpose of a statement of account.

Business Documents

Cheque

Many accounts are paid by means of a cheque. Other methods of payment through the banking system are credit transfers and standing orders. A **cheque** is a written order to a bank to pay a stated sum of money to the person or business named on the order. A book of pre-printed cheques is issued by the bank, and the customer is only required to complete the necessary details of date, amount and payee (the person or business to whom the money is to be paid).

Example 6.5

On 28 May 20-9 Sew and Sew sent a cheque to The Weaving Shed for the amount due on that date less cash discount. The cheque and its counterfoil are shown as follows.

	The ABC Bank Limited South District Branch Delhi	
Date 28th May 20-9		Date 28th May 20-9
Payee The Weaving Shed	**Pay** The Weaving Shed Three hundred & Fifty one dollars only	$ 351--00
		S. Dhoni **Trading as Sew and Sew**
$351-00		
Cheque No 00039	**Cheque No** 00039	**Branch Sort Code** **Account No** 05 22 30 3996829

Cheque counterfoil   Actual cheque

- The supplier receives the cheque. A paying-in slip is completed when the cheque is paid into the bank. The counterfoil of this paying-in slip is used to make the entry in the cash book to show the money paid into the bank and to make a note of the discount in the discount allowed column.
- The customer keeps the cheque counterfoil and uses it to make the entry in the cash book to show the money paid out of the bank and to make a note of the discount in the discount received column.

Receipt

A **receipt** is a written acknowledgement of money received and acts as proof of payment. Since a cheque passes through the banking system it can act as a receipt, so many businesses do not issue receipts if accounts have been paid by cheque. Where goods are sold for cash the customer is usually provided with a receipt.

Example 6.6

The Weaving Shed issued the following receipt to Sew and Sew on 30 May 20-9.

RECEIPT	Receipt No. 44
The Weaving Shed 14 Industrial Street Hightown	
Received from Sew and Sew the sum of $351 (three hundred and fifty one dollars) by cheque	
30 May 20-9 K Singh	Chief cashier

Business Documents

POINTS TO REMEMBER

1. A supplier of goods on credit issues an invoice to the customer.
2. A supplier may allow a customer trade discount if the businesses are in the same trade and also for buying in bulk.
3. If goods are returned or there is an overcharge, a customer may issue a debit note to the supplier asking for a reduction in the invoice.
4. A supplier issues a credit note to notify the customer of any reduction in the total of an invoice.
5. A supplier issues a statement of account at the end of each month to notify the customer of the amount owing and provide a summary of the account.
6. Many accounts are paid by cheque, in which case it is not necessary to issue a receipt as proof of payment.

REVIEW QUESTIONS

1. Give a description of the purpose of **each** of the following business documents.
   (a) invoice (b) statement of account
   (c) credit note (d) receipt
*2. (a) Zak is a trader.
   Arrange the following business documents in the order they would be issued by Zak to a credit customer.
   Statement of account: Credit note   Receipt   Invoice
   (b) Explain why a credit customer may send a debit note to Zak.
   (c) Give **four** items of information you would expect to find on a statement of account.

(d) On 1 August 2007 Zak made a sale on credit to Sasha of 170 pencils at $0.85 each.
Complete the following invoice for the sale to Sasha using the information given above.

```
                        Zak Trading

   [            ]

                                        Date [          ]

     Quantity            Price $              Amount $
   [          ]        [          ]         [          ]

   Terms: 2.5% for settlement within 14 days
```

(e) Zak received payment by cheque from Sasha on 12 August. Show the entries to be made in Zak's cash book to record the payment of the invoice.
(f) Zak allows trade discount of 5% for orders of more than 200 pencils. Sasha orders 250 pencils.
   (i) State the amount of the trade discount given by Zak on this order.
   (ii) State the net amount of the invoice for this order.
   (iii) Sasha pays this invoice within 14 days. Calculate the amount of cash discount to be allowed.

[Based on IGCSE 2007]

3. Agrotech sells farming equipment and supplies on credit. A new customer, Chalk Farm, has recently been supplied with goods shown on the invoice as follows:

Business Documents

83

```
                         AGROTECH
                          INVOICE
Unit 2
Downyer Way                              Invoice No: 0/5721
Midtown                                  Date: 6 April 2002
─────────────────────────────────────────────────────────────
DESCRIPTION          QUANTITY        PRICE              TOTAL
                                      $                   $
Sacks of Groquick fertiliser  50 sacks  $20 per sack (i)  ☐
Tractor tyres (type B/6)       4        $125 each         500

                     Total goods              (ii)        ☐
                     20% trade discount       (iii)       ☐
             INVOICE TOTAL (NET GOODS)        (iv)        ☐
Chalk Farm
Springfield
OXTON
Terms: 3% for settlement within one month
```

(a) Calculate the missing amounts at **(i)**, **(ii)**, **(iii)** and **(iv)** on the invoice.

(b) When the goods were delivered, one tractor tyre was found to be faulty. Agrotech could not replace the tyre and issued a credit note to Chalk Farm on 17 April 2002.
Calculate the net amount shown on the credit note issued by Agrotech to Chalk Farm. Show your workings.

(c) Chalk Farm paid the amount due to Agrotech from these transactions by cheque on 24 April, deducting cash discount of 3%.
Write up the ledger account of Agrotech in Chalk Farms books from the above information.

[IGCSE 2002]

4. On 2 May 2000 Marianne Jones received the document shown below from her supplier, Zen Wholesale.

ZEN WHOLESALE

Riverside Warehouse
New Street
South Town

Tel. 0796 151023

Date	Details		Dr $	Cr $	Balance $
2000					
April 1	Balance	b/f	1 000	1 000 Dr	
12	Sales		300		1 300 Dr
19	Sales returns			50	1 250 Dr
30	Bank			975	
	Discount			25	

Ms M Jones
High Street
South Town

A/c No: J/2657
Date: 30 April 2000

(a) Name the above document.
(b) Calculate the balance due from Marianne to Zen Wholesale on 30 April 2000. Show your workings.
(c) (i) For the transactions on 12 and 19 April, insert the names of the documents sent by Zen Wholesale to Marianne in the following sentences.
   1 12 April Zen Wholesale sent .... to Marianne.
   2 19 April Zen Wholesale sent .... to Marianne.
   (ii) Complete the boxes below to show the ledger account entries recording the transactions on 12 and 19 April in the books of Zen Wholesale.

Date of transaction	Ledger account to be debited (dr)		Ledger account to be credited (cr)	
2000	Account name	Amount $	Account name	Amount $
12 April	....	....	....	....
19 April	....	....	....	....

   (iii) Calculate the percentage rate of the discount allowed to Marianne on 24 April. Show your workings.

[IGCSE 2000]

Business Documents

85

*5. Pieter Burg is in business and buys goods from the General Supply Company. He received the following invoice from them.

	GENERAL SUPPLY COMPANY		
	SALES INVOICE		
Pieter Burg			25 September 2005
Quantity	Description	Unit Price	$
(i)	Bolt fastenings	$0.40	1200 00
1000	Grommets	$0.10	(ii)
	Total		(iii)
Terms: 3%	(iv)	for payment within 14 days of invoice	

(a) Write down the missing words or figures from the invoice.

(i) .... (ii) ....
(iii) .... (iv) ....

Pieter had previously bought goods for $2500 from the General Supply Company on 28 August, and this amount was unpaid at 31 August.

Pieter paid this amount on 5 September. He did not pay the September invoice until 30 October.

An extract from the payments side of Pieter's cash book is shown below.

Date	Details	Discount received $	Bank $
5 Sept	General Supply Co.	(i)	(ii)
30 Oct	General Supply Co.	(i)	(ii)

(b) Write down the amounts missing from the cash book.

(i) .... (ii) ....
(iii) .... (iv) ....

(c) From the information in (a) and (b) show the entries in the General Supply Company's account in Pieter Burg's purchases ledger for the months of September and October 2005.

[IGCSE 2005]

Chapter 7   Books of Prime Entry

> **In this chapter you will learn to:**
> - enter sales, purchases and returns of goods in the books of prime entry
> - post entries relating to sales, purchases and returns of goods from the books of prime entry to ledger accounts.

Introduction

In Chapter 4 it was explained how the ledger is divided into specialist areas and how the cash and the bank account are usually maintained in a cash book rather than in the ledger. Businesses use **books of prime entry** to record goods sold on credit, goods purchased on credit, sales returns and purchases returns. These books are basically listing devices, which mean that a lot of detail is removed from the ledger. It also means that bookkeeping can be divided between several people.

Books of prime entry are also known as **books of original entry** or **subsidiary books**. The name of these books has arisen because all transactions should be recorded in one of these books *before* they are entered in the ledger.

The books of prime entry are:

    Cash book
    Petty cash book
    Sales journal
    Purchases journal
    Sales returns journal
    Purchases returns journal
    General journal.

Books of Prime Entry

The cash book and the petty cash book have already been explained in Chapters 4 and 5. The uses of the journal will be explained in Chapter 15. This Chapter concentrates on the sales, purchases and returns journals.

Sales Journal

This is a list of the names of businesses to which credit sales were made, the value of the sales, and the dates on which the sales were made. The sales journal is sometimes referred to as the **sales book** or the **sales day book**.

This journal is written up using the copies of the invoices sent to the customers. The entries are summarised as follows:

1. When goods are sold on credit

- Enter the date, name of the customer and the total of the invoice in the sales journal.
- Debit the customer's account in the sales ledger with the total of the invoice.

2. At the end of the month

- Credit the sales account in the nominal ledger with the total of the sales journal.
- This will now form the double entry for all the individual debit entries in the sales ledger.

Sales Returns Journal

This is a list of the names of businesses, the value of goods returned and the dates on which the returns were made. The sales returns journal is also known as the **sales returns book** or the **returns inwards book** (or **returns inwards journal**).

This journal is written up using the copies of the credit notes sent to the customers. The entries are summarised as follows:

1. When goods are returned by a credit customer

- Enter the date, name of the customer and total of the credit note in the sales returns journal.

- Credit the customer's account in the sales ledger with the total of the credit note.

2. At the end of the month

- Debit the sales returns account in the nominal ledger with the total of the sales returns journal.
- This will now form the double entry for all the individual credit entries in the sales ledger.

> **Test your understanding**
> 1. List **seven** books of prime entry.
> 2. When a trader sells goods on credit, he lists them in the sales journal and debits the accounts of customers. Explain where and when the double entry for these debit entries is made.

Example 7.1

20-9
April   3   The Weaving Shed issued an invoice to Sew and Sew for goods, $510, subject to a trade discount of 20%
        9   The Weaving Shed issued a credit note to Sew and Sew for goods returned, list price $60
       13   The Weaving Shed sold goods on credit to Fine Furnishings, $1000, subject to a trade discount of 25%, and issued an invoice on the same day
       20   The Weaving Shed sent Jaffar & Company an invoice for $220 for goods supplied on credit
       28   The Weaving Shed issued a credit note to Jaffar & Company for $10 because of an overcharge

Make the necessary entries in the books of The Weaving Shed for April 20-9

Books of Prime Entry

The Weaving Shed

Sales Journal   Page 1

Date	Name	Invoice Number	Folio	Amount $
20-9				
April 3	Sew and Sew	I 3624	sl 22	408
13	Fine Furnishings	I 3625	sl 14	750
20	Jaffar & Company	I 3626	sl 16	220
30	Transfer to sales account		nl 35	1 378

Sales Returns Journal   Page 1

Date	Name	Credit Note Number	Folio	Amount $
20-9				
April 9	Sew and Sew	C 529	sl 22	48
28	Jaffar & Company	C 530	sl 16	10
30	Transfer to sales returns account		nl 36	58

Sales Ledger

Sew and Sew account   Page 22

Date	Details	Folio	$	Date	Details	Folio	$
20-9				20-9			
Apl 3	Sales	sj 1	408	Apl 9	Sales returns	srj 1	48

Fine Furnishings account   Page 14

Date	Details	Folio	$	Date	Details	Folio	$
20-9							
Apl 13	Sales	sj 1	750				

Jaffar & Company account   Page 16

Date	Details	Folio	$	Date	Details	Folio	$
20-9				20-9			
Apl 20	Sales	sj 1	220	Apl 28	Sales returns	srj 1	10

Nominal Ledger

Sales account   Page 35

Date	Details	Folio	$	Date	Details	Folio	$
				20-9 Apl 30	Credit sales for month	sj 1	1 378

Sales returns account   Page 36

Date	Details	Folio	$	Date	Details	Folio	$
20-9 Apl 30	Returns for month	srj 1	58				

- Trade discount does **not** appear in the ledger accounts. Trade discount **may** be shown in the books of prime entry for information purposes only.
- The entry in the sales account on 30 April is the double entry for the three individual debits in the customers' accounts in the sales ledger.
- The entry in the sales returns account on 30 April is the double entry for the two individual credits in the customers' accounts in the sales ledger.

Purchases Journal

This is a list of the names of businesses from which credit purchases were made, the value of the purchases, and the dates on which the purchases were made. The purchases journal is also called the **purchases book** or the **purchases day book**.

This journal is written up using the invoices received from suppliers. The entries are summarised as follows:

1. When goods are purchased on credit

- Enter the date, name of the supplier and the total of the invoice in the purchases journal.

Books of Prime Entry

- Credit the supplier's account in the purchases ledger with the total of the invoice.

2. At the end of the month

- Debit the purchases account in the nominal ledger with the total of the purchases journal.
- This will now form the double entry for all the individual credit entries in the purchases ledger.

Purchases Returns Journal

This is a list of the names of businesses, the value of goods returned and the dates on which the returns were made. The purchases returns journal is also known as the **purchases returns book** or the **returns outward book** (or **returns outward journal**).

This journal is written up using the credit notes received from suppliers. The entries are summarised as follows:

1. When goods are returned to a credit supplier

- Enter the date, name of the supplier and the total of the credit note in the purchases returns journal.
- Debit the supplier's account in the purchases ledger with the total of the credit note.

2. At the end of the month

- Credit the purchases returns account in the nominal ledger with the total of the purchases returns journal.
- This will now form the double entry for all the individual debit entries in the purchases ledger.

> **Test your understanding**
> 1. State **two** advantages of maintaining sales, purchases and returns journals.
> 2. Complete the following sentence. The total of the purchases journal is .... to the .... account in the .... ledger.

Example 7.2

20-9
April   3   Sew and Sew received an invoice for goods purchased from The Weaving Shed for $510, less a trade discount of 20%
         9   Sew and Sew received a credit note from The Weaving Shed for goods returned, list price $60
        24   Sew and Sew received an invoice for goods purchased on credit from The Curtain Company for $280, less 15% trade discount
        29   Sew and Sew discovered that half of the goods purchased on 24 April were faulty and these goods were returned to The Curtain Company who issued a credit note

Make the necessary entries in the books of Sew and Sew for April 20-9

Sew and Sew

Purchases Journal   Page 1

Date	Name	Invoice Number	Folio	Amount $
20-9				
April 3	The Weaving Shed	I 3624	pl 8	408
24	The Curtain Company	I 117	pl 5	238
30	Transfer to purchases account		nl 4	646

Purchases Returns Journal   Page 1

Date	Name	Credit Note Number	Folio	Amount $
20-9				
April 9	The Weaving Shed	C 529	pl 8	48
29	The Curtain Company	C 43	pl 5	119
30	Transfer to purchases returns account		nl 5	167

Purchases Ledger

The Weaving Shed account   Page 8

Date	Details	Folio	$	Date	Details	Folio	$
20-9				20-9			
Apl 9	Purchases returns	prj 1	48	Apl 3	Purchases	pj 1	408

Books of Prime Entry

The Curtain Company account — Page 5

Date	Details	Folio	$	Date	Details	Folio	$
20-9 Apl 29	Purchases returns	prj 1	119	20-9 Apl 24	Purchases	pj 1	238

Nominal Ledger

Purchases account — Page 4

Date	Details	Folio	$	Date	Details	Folio	$
20-9 Apl 30	Credit purchases for month	pj 1	646				

Purchases returns account — Page 5

Date	Details	Folio	$	Date	Details	Folio	$
				20-9 Apl 30	Returns for month	prj 1	167

- Trade discount does **not** appear in the ledger accounts. Trade discount **may** be shown in the books of prime entry for information purposes only.
- The entry in the purchases account on 30 April is the double entry for the two individual credits in the suppliers' accounts in the purchases ledger.
- The entry in the purchases returns account on 30 April is the double entry for the two individual debits in the suppliers' accounts in the purchases ledger.
- The Weaving Shed and Sew and Sew each record the transactions between the two businesses from their own viewpoint – The Weaving Shed is selling the goods and Sew and Sew are purchasing the goods.

Points to Remember

1. All transactions should be entered in a book of prime entry before they are entered in the ledger.
2. The sales journal is written up from copies of invoices sent to customers and the sales returns journal is written up from copies of credit notes sent to customers.
3. The purchases journal is written up from invoices received from suppliers and the purchases returns journal is written up from credit notes received from suppliers.
4. At the end of each month the totals of the sales, purchases and returns journals are transferred to the sales, purchases and returns accounts, respectively.

Review Questions

1. Ombeya sells musical instruments. In September he had the following transactions.

Date	Details	Reference	Amount ($)
September 4	Sale to Hales Orchestra	INV23	1200
15	Sale to Sing Song Band	INV24	450
17	Returns from Hales Orchestra	RT7	300
28	Sale to Town School	INV25	700

   Required

   (a) Show the entries to be made for September in Ombeya's sales journal and sales returns journal.

Books of Prime Entry

(b) Using the information in Ombeya's sales journal and sales returns journal, write up the following accounts in his ledger for September.
  (i) Sales account
  (ii) Sales returns account
  (iii) Hales Orchestra account
  (iv) Sing Song Band account
  (v) Town School account

[IGCSE 2008]

*2. Redd keeps full accounting records and makes up his final accounts to 31 March each year.
The following are extracts from his accounting records for March 2005.

Purchases Journal

		$
5 March	Block	320
17 March	Quayle	500
29 March	Block	270

Purchases Returns Journal

		$
8 March	Block	100

Cash Book (Cr)

		Discount Received $	Bank $
30 March	Block		220
30 March	Quayle	15	485

Required

Write up the accounts of Block and Quayle in Redd's purchases ledger for the month of March 2005, showing any balances carried and brought down.

[IGCSE 2005]

3. Ahmed is a sole trader who keeps full accounting records for all his purchases and sales on credit. Entries are posted monthly from prime (original) entry books to ledger accounts, but the entries for April 2004 have not yet been made.

   (a) The following information is provided.

	Total for April 2004 $
Purchases journal	50 000
Sales journal	85 000
Purchases returns journal	6 000
Sales returns journal	8 000

   Make the entries required on 30 April 2004 in the following ledger accounts:

   Purchases account
   Purchases returns account
   Sales account
   Sales returns account

   (b) In which of Ahmed's ledgers are the above accounts kept?

   [IGCSE 2004]

*4. On 1 September 2001 Joseph sold goods on credit to Billy Jones, a new customer, for $1000.

   On 10 September 2001, Billy Jones returned $200 worth of the goods as they were badly damaged. Joseph could not replace the goods so he made an allowance to Billy for their cost.

   (a) Complete the boxes below to show **in Billy's books**:
   (i) the names of the business documents
   (ii) the books of prime entry

   used to record the above transactions.

		(i)	(ii)
Date	Transaction	Business document used by Billy	Billy's prime entry book
2001 1 September	Goods bought	....	....
10 September	Goods returned	....	....

Books of Prime Entry

97

(b) On 25 September 2001 Billy paid Joseph the amount he owed for the above transactions, claiming cash discount of 2½%.
How much did Billy pay? Show your workings.

(c) Joseph's records for the month of September 2001 include the following

	$
Total of sales journal	15 000
Total of sales returns journal	1 800

Complete the following sentences to show how these totals are recorded in Joseph's ledger accounts.

1. The total of the sales journal is posted to the .... side of the .... account.
2. The total of the sales returns journal is posted to the .... side of the .... account.

(d) Using the information in (a) and (b), write up the ledger account of Billy Jones as it would appear **in Joseph's ledger**.

[IGCSE 2001]

5. Shilpa Bassra is a trader who keeps a full set of accounting records. She divides her ledger into three specialist areas – nominal ledger, purchases ledger and sales ledger.

Required

(a) State **one** advantage of dividing the ledger into these three areas.

Shilpa Bassra's books of prime entry show the following transactions for March 2007.

Purchases Journal

2007		$	$
March 8	Omar El Gamal		
	Goods		440
21	Mohammed El Wakil		
	Goods	380	
	Trade discount	76	304
31	Total for month		744

Purchases Returns Journal

2007			$	$
March 24	Mohammed El Wakil			
		Goods	160	
		Trade discount	32	128
31	Total for month			128

Cash Book (credit side)

			Discount Received	Cash	Bank
2007			$	$	$
March 19	Omar El Gamal		11		429
26	Mohammed El Wakil			110	
31	Cash purchases for month				990

Required

(b) Write up the accounts of Omar El Gamal and Mohammed El Wakil as they would appear in Shilpa Bassra's purchases ledger for the month of March 2007. There were no balances on these accounts on 1 March 2007.

(c) Write up the purchases account and the purchases returns account as they would appear in Shilpa Bassra's nominal ledger for the month of March 2007.

[IGCSE 2007]

Chapter 8 Financial Statements – Part A

In this chapter you will learn to:
- prepare the trading account section of an income statement and understand its purpose
- prepare the profit and loss account section of an income statement of a trading business and understand its purpose
- close ledger accounts by transfer to the income statement
- make transfers to, and balance the capital account at the end of the financial year
- prepare an income statement of a service business and understand its purpose

Introduction

When a person starts a business his/her aim is to make a profit. The profit (or loss) is calculated in the financial statements which are usually prepared at the end of each financial year. Financial statements basically consist of two parts:
1. An **income statement** which consists of two sections:
    A **trading account** in which the **gross profit** of the business is calculated
    A **profit and loss account** in which the **profit for the year**, the **net profit**, of the business is calculated.
   The trading account and the profit and loss account are both part of the double entry system.
2. A **balance sheet** which shows the **financial position** of the business at a certain date. The balance sheet is not part of the double entry system.

Financial statements are usually prepared from a trial balance. **Every item in a trial balance appears *once* in a set of financial statements.** As each item is used, it is useful to place a tick (✓) against the item. This ensures that no items are overlooked.

It is common to find notes accompanying a trial balance about various adjustments which are to be made (these are explained in the following chapters). **Any notes to a trial balance are used *twice* in a set of financial statements.** To ensure that this is done, it is useful to place a tick (✓) against the notes each time they are used.

Example 8.1

The following trial balance was extracted from the books of Samir at 31 May 20-8.

This trial balance will be used in **Example 8.2** to **Example 8.7**.

Samir
Trial Balance at 31 May 20-8

	Dr $	Cr $
Revenue (Sales)		95 700
Sales returns	1 000	
Purchases	65 000	
Purchases returns		500
Carriage inwards	1 500	
Inventory 1 June 20-8	7 100	
Discount received		400
Discount allowed	900	
Wages	11 200	
General expenses	2 800	
Property tax	600	
Loan interest	500	
Premises	80 000	
Fixtures and equipment	13 900	
Trade receivables	7 500	
Trade payables		7 800
Bank	3 300	
Cash	100	
Long-term loan		10 000
Capital		90 000
Drawings	9 000	
	204 400	204 400

Financial Statements – Part A

Notes
1. The inventory at 31 May 20-8 was valued at $7600.
2. During the year ended 31 May 20-8, Samir took goods costing $300 for his own use. No entries have been made in the accounting records.

Trading Account Section of the Income Statement

The **trading account** is concerned with buying and selling, and its purpose is to calculate the profit earned on the goods sold. This is known as the **gross profit**. The formula for calculating gross profit is:

| Gross profit | = | Selling price of goods | – | Cost of sales |

The selling price represents the total sales less any sales returns.
The cost of sales represents the total cost of the goods actually sold. This is not necessarily the cost of goods purchased during the year: some goods may have been in stock at the start of the year, and some of the goods purchased during the year may remain unsold at the end of the year. The formula for calculating cost of sales is:

| Cost of sales | = | Opening inventory | + | Purchases | – | Closing inventory |

The purchases figure represents the total cost of purchases less any purchases returns. If carriage inwards has been paid on goods purchased this must be added to the purchases as it increases the cost of the goods. If the owner of the business has withdrawn goods for personal use the cost of these is credited to the purchases account, so reducing the cost of goods available for sale. If goods taken by the owner have not already been recorded they must be deducted from the purchases. The formula for calculating the net purchases figure is:

| Net purchase | = | Purchases | – | Purchases returns | + | Carriage inwards | – | Goods for own use |

The calculation of gross profit is shown in the trading account section of the income statement. This must have a heading which includes the period of time covered by the statement. It is also usual to include the name under which the business trades.

> **Test your understanding**
> 1. State what is calculated in
>   (a) a trading account
>   (b) a profit and loss account
> 2. State the formula for calculating gross profit.
> 3. State the formula for calculating cost of sales.

There are two ways in which a trading account can be prepared – **horizontal** and **vertical**.

The **horizontal format** is similar to a traditional ledger account. Using this method, the sales revenue is shown on the credit side and the cost of sales on the debit side. The difference (or balance) between the two sides equals the gross profit.

Example 8.2

Using the trial balance and accompanying notes shown in **Example 8.1**, prepare the trading account section of the income statement of Samir for the year ended 31 May 20-8. Use the horizontal format.

Samir
Income Statement (Trading Account Section) for the year ended 31 May 20-8

	$	$		$	$
Opening inventory		7 100	Revenue (Sales)	95 700	
Purchases	65 000		Less Sales returns	1 000	94 700
Less Purchases returns	500				
	64 500				
Less Goods for own use	300				
	64 200				
Carriage inwards	1 500	65 700			
		72 800			
Less Closing inventory		7 600			
Cost of sales		65 200			
Gross profit c/d		29 500			
		94 700			94 700

- As the above items are entered in the trading account, they should be ticked-off in the trial balance and accompanying notes.

Financial Statements – Part A

- The gross profit is carried down to the profit and loss account (see later in this Chapter).
- The term **revenue** is often used instead of **sales** in a trial balance and in an income statement.

A trading account can also be prepared using the **vertical format**. This is the format used by most businesses. A trading account prepared using this method contains the same information as a horizontal account, but looks like an arithmetic calculation.

Example 8.3

Using the trial balance and accompanying notes shown in **Example 8.1**, prepare the trading account section of the income statement of Samir for the year ended 31 May 20-8. Use the vertical format.

Samir
Income Statement (Trading Account Section) for the year ended 31 May 20-8

	$	$	$
Revenue (Sales)		95 700	
Less Sales returns		1 000	94 700
Less Cost of sales			
Opening inventory		7 100	
Purchases	65 000		
Less Purchases returns	500		
	64 500		
Less Goods for own use	300		
	64 200		
Carriage inwards	1 500	65 700	
		72 800	
Less Closing inventory		7 600	65 200
Gross profit			29 500

Profit and Loss Account Section of the Income Statement

The **profit and loss account** is concerned with profits and losses, gains and expenses. Its purpose is to calculate the final profit after all running expenses and other items of income. This is known as the **profit for the year or the net profit**. The formula for calculating net profit is:

| Net profit | = | Gross profit | + | Other income | – | Expenses |

The profit and loss account section of an income statement must have a heading which includes the period of time covered by the statement. It is also usual to include the name under which the business trades.

As with a trading account, a profit and loss account can be prepared using either the **horizontal** or the **vertical** method. Using the horizontal format, the gross profit and any other income are shown on the credit side and the expenses are shown on the debit side. The difference (or balance) between the two sides equal the **profit for the year (net profit)** (if the credit side is the largest) or the **loss for the year (net loss)** (if the debit side is the largest).

Example 8.4

Using the trial balance and accompanying notes shown in **Example 8.1**, prepare the profit and loss account section of the income statement of Samir for the year ended 31 May 20-8. Use the horizontal format.

Samir
Income Statement (Profit and Loss Account Section)
for the year ended 31 May 20-8

	$	$		$	$
Discount allowed		900	Gross profit b/d		29 500
Wages		11 200	Discount received		400
General expenses		2 800			
Property tax		600			
Loan interest		500			
Profit for the year (net profit)		13 900			
		29 900			29 900

- As the above items are entered in the profit and loss account they should be ticked-off in the trial balance and accompanying notes.
- The gross profit is brought down from the trading account where it was calculated.

A profit and loss account can also be prepared using the vertical format. This format is used by most businesses. As with a vertical trading account, the vertical profit and loss account looks like an arithmetic calculation.

Financial Statements – Part A

Example 8.4

Using the trial balance and accompanying notes shown in **Example 8.1**, prepare the profit and loss account section of the income statement of Samir for the year ended 31 May 20-8. Use the vertical format.

Samir
Income Statement (Profit and Loss Account Section)
for the year ended 31 May 20-8

	$	$	$
Gross profit			29 500
Add Discount received			400
			29 900
Less Discount allowed		900	
Wages		11 200	
General expenses		2 800	
Property tax		600	
Loan interest		500	16 000
Profit for the year (net profit)			13 900

> **Test your understanding**
> 1. List **six** business expenses (excluding those shown in the above examples).
> 2. State the formula for calculating net profit.

The two sections of the income statement are usually presented in the form of one combined statement, which is normally presented in vertical format. The profit and loss account section follows on immediately after the trading account section, with the words "gross profit" being written only once. The heading of the income statement includes the period of time covered by the statement and the name under which the business trades.

As most businesses prepare their income statements using the vertical format this method will be followed in the remainder of this book.

Example 8.5

Using either the trial balance and accompanying notes shown in **Example 8.1** or the separate sections of the income statement prepared in

Examples 8.3 and 8.4, prepare the income statement of Samir for the year ended 31 May 20-8.

Samir
Income Statement for the year ended 31 May 20-8

	$	$	$
Revenue (sales)		95 700	
Less Sales returns		1 000	94 700
Less Cost of sales			
Opening inventory		7 100	
Purchases	65 000		
Less Purchases returns	500		
	64 500		
Less Goods for own use	300		
	64 200		
Carriage inwards	1 500	65 700	
		72 800	
Less Closing inventory		7 600	65 200
Gross profit			29 500
Add Discount received			400
			29 900
Less Discount allowed		900	
Wages		11 200	
General expenses		2 800	
Property tax		600	
Loan interest		500	16 000
Profit for the year			13 900

- "Profit for the year" is often used in place of "Net profit".

Transferring Ledger Account Totals to the Income Statement

Anything appearing in the income statement must have a double entry in another account. Anything credited to the income statement must be debited in the appropriate ledger account: anything debited to the income statement must be credited in the appropriate ledger account.

When something is deducted from a debit item in the income statement this is equal to a credit entry, so a debit entry is required in the ledger. In the same way, when something is deducted from a credit item in the income statement this is equal to a debit entry, so a credit entry is required in the ledger.

Financial Statements – Part A

Example 8.6

Using the income statement prepared for Samir in the previous example, prepare the following ledger accounts to show how **each** is closed by transfer to the income statement:
- (a) purchases account
- (b) purchases returns account
- (c) discount received account
- (d) wages account

Samir
Nominal Ledger

(a) **Purchases account**

Date	Details	Folio	$	Date	Details	Folio	$
20-8 May 31	Total to date		65 000	20-8 May 31	Income statement		65 000
			65 000				65 000

(b) **Purchases returns account**

Date	Details	Folio	$	Date	Details	Folio	$
20-8 May 31	Income statement		500	20-8 May 31	Total to date		500
			500				500

(c) **Discount received account**

Date	Details	Folio	$	Date	Details	Folio	$
20-8 May 31	Income statement		400	20-8 May 31	Total to date		400
			400				400

(d) **Wages account**

Date	Details	Folio	$	Date	Details	Folio	$
20-8 May 31	Total to date		11 200	20-8 May 31	Income statement		11 200
			11 200				11 200

- The entries shown as "totals to date" represent the total of the individual entries made in the account for the year ended 31 May 20-8.
- All the other items in the income statement (excluding inventory, gross profit and profit for the year) have similar transfers from the appropriate ledger accounts.
- The gross profit technically has a double entry within the income statement as it is transferred from the trading account section to the profit and loss account section (refer to **Examples 8.2 and 8.4**).
- The entries for inventory and profit for the year are explained below.

There are two entries for inventory in the income statement – the inventory at the start of the year and the inventory at the end of the year. The inventory account will have a debit balance representing the inventory at the start of the year – this is credited to the inventory account and transferred to the debit of the income statement. The inventory at the end of the year is shown as a deduction from the debit entries in the income statement (which is equal to a credit entry), so this must be debited in the inventory account.

Example 8.7

Using the income statement prepared for Samir in a previous example, prepare the inventory account in Samir's ledger on 31 May 20-8.

Samir
Nominal Ledger
Inventory account

Date	Details	Folio	$	Date	Details	Folio	$
20-7 June 1	Balance	b/d	7 100	20-8 May 31	Income statement		7 100
			7 100				7 100
20-8 May 31	Income statement		7 600				

Financial Statements – Part A

- The entry of $7600 on the debit side representing the inventory at the end of the financial year on 31 May 20-8 becomes the opening inventory for the year beginning 1 June 20-8.

A profit for the year (net profit) represents the return on the owner's investment. This will appear as a debit entry in the income statement and should be transferred to the credit of the capital account as it increases the amount the business owes the owner. A loss for the year (net loss) will appear as a credit entry in the income statement and should be transferred to the debit of the capital account as it reduces the amount the business owes the owner.

As explained in Chapter 2, the total of the drawings account is transferred to the capital account at the end of the year.

Example 8.8

On 1 June 20-7 the credit balance on Samir's capital account was $90 000. For the year ended 31 May 20-8 his drawings were $9000 and his profit for the year was $13 900.

Prepare the capital account and the drawings account in Samir's ledger on 31 May 20-8.

Samir
Nominal Ledger
Capital account

Date	Details	Folio	$	Date	Details	Folio	$
20-8				20-7			
May 31	Drawings		9 000	June 1	Balance	b/d	90 000
	Balance	c/d	94 900	20-8			
				May 31	Profit		13 900
			103 900				103 900
				20-8			
				June 1	Balance	b/d	94 900

Drawings account

Date	Details	Folio	$	Date	Details	Folio	$
20-8				20-8			
May 31	Total to date		9 000	May 31	Capital		9 000
			9 000				9 000

Test your understanding
1. Explain why it is necessary to make two transfers from the income statement to the inventory account at the end of the financial year.
2. Explain why a loss for the year is debited to the owner's capital account.

Income Statement of a Service Business

A **service business** is one which does not buy and sell goods such as an accountant, an insurance company, a travel agent, a hairdresser and so on. At the end of the financial year, these businesses still need to prepare financial statements. However, the trading account section of the income statement is not prepared as no goods are bought and sold. Only the profit and loss section of the income statement and a balance sheet are prepared.

In the income statement all the items of revenue received such as fees from clients, commission and other income are credited and expenses are debited. The balance sheet is exactly the same as the balance sheet of a trading business.

Example 8.9

Anita is a business consultant. She provided the following information at the end of her financial year on 30 September 20-5.

	$
Property tax	6 400
General expenses	8 950
Insurance	2 670
Printing and stationery	4 560
Loan interest	1 500
Wages	43 500
Rent received	7 300
Commissions received	92 150

(a) Prepare the income statement for Anita for the year ended 30 September 20-5. Use the horizontal format.

Financial Statements – Part A

Anita
Income Statement for the year ended 30 September 20-5

	$	$		$	$
Property tax		6 400	Commissions received		92 150
General expenses		8 950	Rent received		7 300
Insurance		2 670			
Printing and stationery		4 560			
Loan interest		1 500			
Wages		43 500			
Profit for the year		31 870			
		99 450			99 450

(b) Prepare the income statement for Anita for the year ended 30 September 20-5. Use the vertical format.

Anita
Income Statement for the year ended 30 September 20-5

	$	$	$
Commissions received			92 150
Add Rent received			7 300
			99 450
Less Property tax		6 400	
General expenses		8 950	
Insurance		2 670	
Printing and stationery		4 560	
Loan interest		1 500	
Wages		43 500	67 580
Profit for the year			31 870

POINTS TO REMEMBER

1. The difference between the selling price and the cost price is known as the gross profit. This is calculated in the trading account section of the income statement.
2. The difference between the gross profit plus other income less expenses is known as the net profit. This is calculated in the profit and loss account section of the income statement.
3. All the items appearing in the income statement are transferred from the ledger accounts to complete the double entry.

4. A profit for the year is transferred to the credit of the capital account and a loss for the year is transferred to the debit of the capital account.
5. A business which provides a service only prepares the profit and loss account section of the income statement.

Review Questions

1. Martha Adebuyo owns a retail shop. Her financial year ends on 31 August. Her income statement for the year ended 31 August 2004 is shown below. Some words and figures are missing.
   In **each** of the boxes **(i)** to **(vii)** enter the missing word(s) or figure.

   Income statement for the year ended 31 August 2004

	$	$	$
Revenue (sales)		106 000	
Less Sales returns	(i)		100 000
Less Cost of goods sold			
Opening **(ii)**		12 000	
Purchases **(iii)**			
Less Purchases returns	4 000		
	67 000		
Plus Carriage **(iv)**	5 000	72 000	
		84 000	
Less Closing inventory	(v)		70 000
Gross profit			30 000
Add Rent **(vi)**			6 000
Less Wages		14 000	36 000
Insurance		3 000	
General expenses	(vii)		
			24 000
Profit for the year			12 000

   [IGCSE 2004]

Financial Statements – Part A

*2. Piyush is a financial adviser. He provided the following information on 31 October 20-6.

	$
Commissions earned	72 100
Interest received	2 900
Staff salaries	28 500
Rent	9 400
Postages and telephone expenses	5 700
Light and heat	1 100
Insurance	800
General expenses	3 500

Prepare Piyush's income statement for the year ended 31 October 20-6.

*3. Rani owns a retail store. For the year ended 31 December 20-9 she made a gross profit of $35 000. She provided the following information for that year.

	$
Drawings	17 000
Wages and salaries	23 000
Rent received from subletting	6 000
General expenses	13 500
Loan interest	1 000
Discount allowed	500
Discount received	870
Advertising	680
Property tax	1 240
Motor expenses	2 550

(a) Starting with the gross profit, prepare the profit and loss section of the income statement for the year ended 31 December 20-9.
(b) Prepare Rani's capital account as it would appear in her ledger for the year ended 31 December 20-9. On 1 January 20-9 her capital was $46 000.

4. (a) Explain the difference between:
   (i) carriage inwards and carriage outwards
   (ii) discount allowed and discount received

The following accounts were drawn up for Jasper Cato, who has a furniture shop, by his bookkeeper who only had a limited knowledge of preparing final accounts.

Financial statements as at 30 September 2000

	$		$
Purchases	25 200	Reveneue (sales)	37 600
Inventory 1 October 1999	4 500	Returns outward	900
Inventory 30 September 2000	6 000	Discount received	280
Profit on goods c/d	3 080		
	38 780		38 780
Carriage inwards	1 200	Profit on goods b/d	3 080
Returns inward	1 600	Discount allowed	160
Administration expenses	7 230	Carriage outwards	1 480
Sundry expenses	170	Loss for year c/d	5 480
	10 200		10 200
Loss for year b/d	5 480	Capital 1 October 1999	27 000
Capital left	21 520		
	27 000		27 000

(b) Redraft the income statement under the correct heading to show the correct gross profit (or loss) and the profit (or loss) for the year.

[IGCSE 2000]

5. Khalid earns fees and commissions from his insurance business. His capital account at 1 November 2008 showed $3000 credit.
A summary of the bank columns in his cash book for the year ended 31 October 2009 showed:

Details	Bank $	Details	Bank $
Clients – fees received	12 000	Rent	9 600
Clients – commissions received	32 000	Staff wages	8 800
		Office expenses	6 400
		Motor expenses	3 600
		Drawings - Khalid	25 000

Financial Statements – Part A

Fees are invoiced when work is completed. Trade receivables for fees were:

	$
1 November 2008	2600
31 October 2009	4100

Required
(a) Calculate the fees earned by Khalid for the year ended 31 October 2009.
(b) From the information above and your answer to (a), prepare Khalid's income statement for the year ended 31 October 2009.
(c) Prepare Khalid's capital account for the year ended 31 October 2009 and bring down the balance at 1 November 2009.
(d) Suggest **two** ways in which Khalid might reduce or eliminate the deficit on his capital account.

[IGCSE 2009]

Chapter 9

Financial Statements – Part B

In this chapter you will learn to:
- understand the purpose of a balance sheet
- recognise and understand the different types of assets
- recognise and understand the different types of liabilities
- prepare a balance sheet.

Introduction

As explained in Chapter 8, the financial statements are prepared at the end of each financial year. These consist of an **income statement** and a **balance sheet**.

A **balance sheet** is a **statement of the financial position of a business on a certain date**. It shows the assets of a business (what the business owns and what is owing to the business) and the liabilities of a business (what the business owes). The assets show how the resources are being used and the liabilities show where they come from.

> **Test your understanding**
> 1. Define a balance sheet.
> 2. Explain the meaning of **each** of the following terms:
> (a) asset
> (b) liability

Some very elementary balance sheets were prepared in Chapter 1. However, it is usual to arrange the assets and liabilities into different groups according to their type.

Financial Statements – Part B

Assets

Assets are divided into two types. These are:

1. Non-current assets

These are long-term assets which are obtained for use rather than for resale. These assets help the business earn revenue.

Examples of non-current assets include land and buildings, machinery, fixtures and motors.

In a balance sheet, it is usual for the **non-current** to be **arranged in increasing order of liquidity**. This means that the most permanent assets are shown first.

A typical order for showing non-current assets in a balance sheet is as follows:
- Land and buildings
- Machinery
- Fixtures and equipment
- Motor vehicles

2. Current assets

These are short-term assets. Because they arise from the normal trading activities of the business their values are constantly changing. These are assets which are either in the form of cash or which can be turned into cash relatively easily.

Examples of current assets include inventory, trade receivables, bank and cash.

In a balance sheet, it is usual for **current assets** to be **arranged in increasing order of liquidity**. This means that the assets furthest away from cash are shown first.

A typical order for showing current assets in a balance sheet is:
- Inventory
- Trade receivables
- Bank
- Cash

Liabilities

Liabilities are divided into three types. These are:

1. Capital

This represents the owner's investment in the business and is the amount owed by the business to the owner.

2. Non-current liabilities

These are amounts owed by the business which are not due for repayment within the next 12 months.
  Examples of non-current liabilities include long-term loan and mortgage.

3. Current liabilities

These are short-term liabilities. Since current liabilities, like current assets, arise from the normal trading activities of the business, their values are constantly changing. They are amounts owed by the business which are due for repayment within the next 12 months.
  Examples of current liabilities include trade payables and bank overdraft.

Test your understanding
1. Define the term non-current assets. Illustrate your answer by giving **two** examples.
2. State the order in which current assets are arranged in a balance sheet.
3. Explain how to distinguish between a non-curent liability and a current liability.

A balance sheet must have a heading which includes the date to which it relates. It is also usual to include the name under which the business trades.

There are two ways in which a balance sheet can be prepared – **horizontal** and **vertical**. A **horizontal** balance sheet is prepared in a two-sided format. It is usual for the assets to be listed on the left and the

Financial Statements – Part B

liabilities to be listed on the right (but it is equally correct to show the assets on the right and the liabilities on the left).

Example 9.1

The following trial balance was extracted from the books of Samir at 31 May 20-8.

This trial balance was used in Chapter 8 to prepare an income statement for the year ended 31 May 20-8.

The profit for the year of $13 900 was calculated in the income statement.

Samir
Trial Balance at 31 May 20-8

	Dr $	Cr $
✓ Revenue (sales)		95 700
✓ Sales returns	1 000	
✓ Purchases	65 000	
✓ Purchases returns		500
✓ Carriage inwards	1 500	
✓ Inventory 1 June 20-8	7 100	
✓ Discount received		400
✓ Discount allowed	900	
✓ Wages	11 200	
✓ General expenses	2 800	
✓ Property tax	600	
✓ Loan interest	500	
Premises	80 000	
Fixtures and equipment	13 900	
Trade receivables	7 500	
Trade payables		7 800
Bank	3 300	
Cash	100	
Long-term loan		10 000
Capital		90 000
Drawings	9 000	
	204 400	204 400

Notes
✓ 1 The inventory at 31 May 20-8 was valued at $7600.
✓ 2 During the year ended 31 May 20-8 Samir took goods costing $300 for his own use. No entries have been made in the accounting records.

As explained in Chapter 8, every item within a trial balance is used once in the preparation of a set of financial statements, and any notes to a trial balance are used twice. The items already used in the preparation of the income statement in Chapter 8 have been ticked.

Example 9.2

Using the trial balance and accompanying notes shown in **Example 9.1**, prepare a balance sheet for Samir at 31 May 20-9. Use the horizontal format.

Samir
Balance Sheet at 31 May 20-9

	$	$		$	$
Non-current assets			**Capital**		
Premises		80 000	Opening balance		90 000
Fixtures & equipment		13 900	Plus Profit for the year		13 900
		93 900			103 900
Current assets			Less drawings		
			(9000 + 300)		9 300
Inventory	7 600				94 600
Trade receivables	7 500		**Non-current liabilities**		
Bank	3 300		Loan		10 000
Cash	100	18 500	**Current liabilities**		
			Trade payables		7 800
		112 400			112 400

- As the above items are entered in the balance sheet they should be ticked-off in the trial balance and accompanying notes.
- Once the balance sheet is completed all the items in the trial balance should have a tick and the notes to the trial balance should have two ticks.
- The assets and liabilities have been arranged in their different categories.
- The balance on the capital account has increased because the business made a profit (which the business owes to the owner of the business), but has decreased because the owner made drawings (money and goods).

If a balance sheet is prepared using the **vertical** format, the assets are listed (showing how the resources are used) and underneath them the

Financial Statements – Part B

liabilities are listed (showing where the resources have come from). It is also acceptable to list the liabilities first followed by the assets.

Example 9.3

Using the trial balance and accompanying notes shown in **Example 9.1**, prepare a balance sheet for Samir at 31 May 20-9. Use the vertical format.

Samir
Balance Sheet at 31 May 20-9

	$	$	$
Non-current assets			
Premises			80 000
Fixtures and equipment			13 900
			93 900
Current assets			
Inventory		7 600	
Trade receivables		7 500	
Bank		3 300	
Cash		100	
		18 500	
Current liabilities			
Trade payables		7 800	
Net current assets			10 700
			104 600
Non-current liabilities			
Loan			10 000
			94 600
Financed by			
Capital			
Opening balance			90 000
Plus Profit for the year			13 900
			103 900
Less Drawings (9000 + 300)			9 300
			94 600

- There is only one current liability so this has been shown in the centre column. If there had been more than one they would have been listed in the first column and the total shown in the centre column.
- The main advantage a vertical balance sheet has over a horizontal balance sheet is that it shows the figure for net current assets. This may also be called working capital. This is very important to a business. It will be explained in Chapter 24.

- The non-current liability has been deducted in the first section of the balance sheet. Alternatively, it could have been added to the final balance of the capital account in the second section of the balance sheet.

As most businesses prepare their balance sheets using the vertical format, this method will be followed in the remainder of this book.

Test your understanding
1. Explain the two ways in which a non-current liability may be shown in a vertical balance sheet.
2. State **one** advantage of preparing a balance sheet in vertical format.

POINTS TO REMEMBER

1. A balance sheet is a statement of the financial position of a business on a certain date.
2. Non-current assets are long-term assets. In a balance sheet the most permanent are shown first.
3. Current assets are short-term assets and their values are constantly changing. In a balance sheet the furthest away from cash are shown first.
4. Non-current liabilities are amounts which are not due for repayment within the next 12 months.
5. Current liabilities are amounts which are due for repayment within the next 12 months.

REVIEW QUESTIONS

1. Bonnie Clyde makes parts for cars and her financial year ends on 31 March. After preparing her income statement for the year ended 31 March 2005, her trial balance shows the following items.

Financial Statements – Part B

	$	
Bank	500	Dr
Bank loan repayable 2008	2 800	
Trade payables	700	
Machinery	8 000	
Inventory	3 000	
Drawings	4 500	
Capital account at 1 April 2004	6 000	
Profit for the year	7 500	
Trade receivables	1 000	

Prepare Bonnie's balance sheet at 31 March 2005.

[Based on IGCSE 2005]

2. The balance sheet of Amy Dootes is given below with some words and figures missing.

   Enter the missing words and figures in the boxes **(i)** to **(vi)** on the balance sheet.

Balance Sheet at 31 March 2004

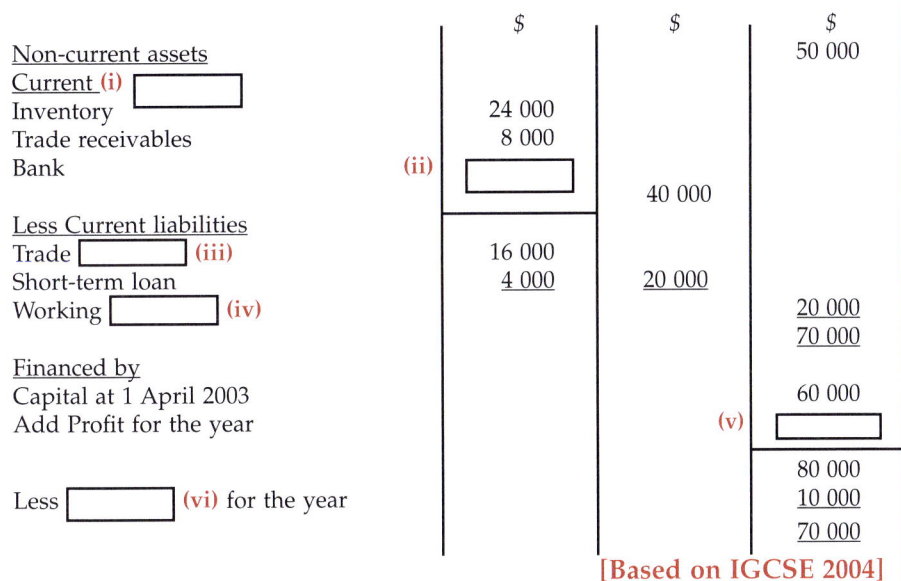

	$	$	$
Non-current assets			50 000
Current **(i)** [ ]			
Inventory	24 000		
Trade receivables	8 000		
Bank **(ii)** [ ]		40 000	
Less Current liabilities			
Trade [ ] **(iii)**	16 000		
Short-term loan	4 000	20 000	
Working [ ] **(iv)**			20 000
			70 000
Financed by			
Capital at 1 April 2003			60 000
Add Profit for the year		**(v)** [ ]	
			80 000
Less [ ] **(vi)** for the year			10 000
			70 000

[Based on IGCSE 2004]

3. Morgan is in business as a printer. He has prepared the following trial balance (after calculating his profit for the year) from his accounting records for the year ended 31 August 2006.

Morgan
Trial Balance at 31 August 2006

	$	$
Machinery	5 600	
Office equipment	1 500	
Bank		2 200
Cash	200	
Trade payables		2 100
Trade receivables	4 100	
Loan from Nicola repayable 2011		5 000
Inventory 31 August 2006	3 900	
Capital		9 000
Drawings	21 000	
Profit for the year		18 000
	36 300	36 300

(a) Prepare Morgan's balance sheet at 31 August 2006.

(b) Morgan's business has a bank overdraft at 31 August 2006. Suggest **one** way in which he could reduce or eliminate the overdraft.

(c) Nicola has given Morgan an additional long term loan of $2000 paid into the bank on 1 September 2006.
In the table below, place a tick (P) under the correct heading to indicate the effect of the additional loan on the following items in Morgan's balance sheet:

Effect of additional loan

	Increase	Decrease	No effect
(i) Bank overdraft			
(ii) Loan account			
(iii) Net current assets			
(iv) Profit for the year			
(v) Capital			

[Based on IGCSE 2006]

*4. Prepare an income statement for the month ended 30 November 20-7 and a balance sheet at 30 November 20-7 from the following trial balance of Y Singh.

Financial Statements – Part B

	Dr $		Cr $
Inventory 1 December 20-7	1 184	Revenue (sales)	9 300
Purchases	5 937	Purchases returns	161
Sales returns	103	Trade payables	866
Carriage inwards	100	Capital	7 320
Carriage outwards	160		
Wages	1 933		
Rent and insurance	235		
Motor vehicle expenses	440		
General expenses	240		
Equipment	3 500		
Motor vehicle	2 975		
Bank	240		
Drawings	600		
	17 647		17 647

The inventory at 31 December 20-7 was valued at $980

*5. The following trial balance of Pathan Stores was drawn up after the preparation of the trading account section of the income statement for the year ended 31 December 20-1.

	Dr $	Cr $
Gross profit		58 500
Wages	19 150	
Office expenses	1 300	
Rent and property tax	5 170	
Insurance	910	
Carriage outwards	4 270	
Motor expenses	7 770	
Sundry expenses	410	
Commission received		3 000
Inventory at 31 December 20-1	25 000	
Trade receivables	13 350	
Bank	9 400	
Cash	1 000	
Trade payables		8 430
Long-term loan from AB Finance		20 000
Machinery	20 000	
Motor vehicles	11 000	
Capital		38 800
Drawings	10 000	
	128 730	128 730

(a) Prepare the profit and loss account section of the income statement of Pathan Stores for the year ended 31 December 20-1.
(b) Prepare the balance sheet of Pathan Stores at 31 December 20-1.

6. Abhinav is a trader.
Using the following information taken from Abhinav's books on 30 June 20-8, you are required to:
(a) Prepare a trial balance at 30 June 20-8
(b) Prepare an income statement for the year ended 30 June 20-8
(c) Prepare a balance sheet at 30 June 20-8

	$
Capital	54 400
Drawings	1 300
Premises	30 000
Fixtures	4 000
Sales	82 000
Purchases	70 100
Inventory 1 July 20-7	18 600
Carriage inwards	400
Carriage outwards	1 500
Trade receivables	14 000
Trade payables	8 000
Discount received	210
Insurance	390
Sundry expenses	340
Wages	10 300
Property tax	1 200
Loan interest	500
Long-term loan from ABC Loans Ltd.	10 000
Bank	1 980

Inventory at 30 June 20-8 was valued at $20 100.

Chapter 10 Accounting Rules

> **In this chapter you will learn to:**
> - understand the accounting rules which are applied in the preparation of accounting statements
> - understand the ways in which the quality of information in accounting statements can be measured
> - understand the difference between capital and revenue expenditure, and capital and revenue receipts
> - understand the basis of inventory valuation and prepare simple inventory valuation statements.

Introduction

Accounting has developed a number of rules which must be applied by everyone who is involved with the recording of financial information. If every accountant or bookkeeper followed their own rules it would be impossible for others to fully understand the financial position of a business. In the same way, it would be impossible to make a comparison between the financial results of two or more businesses if they had each applied their own rules in the preparation of their accounting statements. The accounting principles which must be applied by every business are explained in this chapter.

It also describes how capital and revenue expenditure and capital and revenue receipts should be recorded. It is important that all businesses follow the same procedures for these items. Similarly, all businesses should apply the same principles of inventory valuation. This is also explained later in this chapter.

> **Test your understanding**
> 1. State **one** reason why accounting rules are necessary.

Accounting Principles

Accounting principles are sometimes referred to as **concepts** and **conventions**. A **concept** is a rule which sets down how the financial activities of a business are recorded. A **convention** is an acceptable method by which the rule is applied to a given situation. Some of the main accounting principles have already been applied to the practical accounting examples in the previous chapters.

The main accounting principles are explained below.

Business Entity

This is also known as the **accounting entity** principle. This means that the **business is treated as being completely separate from the owner of the business**. The personal assets of the owner, the personal spending of the owner etc. do not appear in the accounting records of the business. The accounting records relate only to the business and record the assets of the business, the liabilities of the business, the money spent by the business and so on. Everything is recorded from the viewpoint of the business.

If there is a transaction concerning both the business and its owner then it is recorded in the accounting records of the business. When the owner introduces capital into the business, it is credited to the capital account (to show the funds coming from the owner). The capital account shows a credit balance representing the amount owed by the business to the owner. When the owner makes drawings from the business a debit entry will be made in the drawings account (to show the value going to the owner) which reduces the amount owed by the business to the owner.

The practical application of the principle of accounting entity has already been explained in the chapters on double entry bookkeeping and financial statements.

Duality

This is also referred to as the **dual aspect** principle. It has been explained in previous chapters how **every transaction has two aspects – a giving and a receiving**. The term **double entry** is used to describe how these two aspects of a transaction are recorded in the accounting records.

Money measurement

This accounting principle means that **only information which can be expressed in terms of money can be recorded in the accounting records**.

Accounting Rules

Money is a recognised unit of measure and is a traditional way of valuing transactions. It does not rely on personal opinions and it is factual.

There are many aspects of a business which cannot be measured in terms of money and, therefore, do not appear in the accounting records. The morale of the workforce, the effectiveness of a good manager, the benefits of a staff training course all play an important part in the success of the business, but they will not appear in the accounting records as their value cannot be expressed in monetary terms. In a similar way, the launch of a rival product or increased competition cannot be recorded in the accounting records as their effects cannot be measured in monetary terms.

> **Test your understanding**
> 1. Explain the meaning of the term business entity.
> 2. Explain how the principle of duality is carried out in recording the day-to-day transactions of a business.
> 3. No entry is made in the accounting records of Park Street Stores when a competitor reduces his prices by 15%. Explain why.

Realisation

This principle emphasises the importance of not recording a profit until it has actually been earned. This means that **profit is only regarded as being earned when the legal title to goods or services passes from the seller to the buyer**, who has then an obligation (liability) to pay for those goods.

When an order is placed by a customer no goods change hands, and no profit is earned. Profit is regarded as being realised when the goods actually change hands. This is the same even if the goods are sold on credit and the customer does not pay for them immediately.

Consistency

There are some areas of accounting where a choice of method is available. For example, there are several different ways to calculate the depreciation of a non-current asset (see Chapter 12). Where a choice of method is available, the one with the most realistic outcome should be selected. Once a method has been selected, **the method must be used consistently from one accounting period to the next**. If this is not done, a comparison of the financial results from year to year is impossible, and the profit of a particular year can be distorted.

There may be a good reason why it is necessary to change a method or valuation. In such a situation, the charge may be made, but the effects of this should be noted in the financial statements.

Accruals

This is also referred to as the **matching principle**. This is an extension of the realisation principle. As explained earlier, profit is earned when the ownership of goods passes to the customer, not when the goods are actually paid for. The accruals principle extends this beyond the purchase and sale of goods to include other income and expenses. **The revenue of the accounting period is matched against the costs of the same period** (the timing of the actual receipts and payments is ignored).

The figures shown in an income statement must relate to the period of time covered by that statement, whether or not any money has changed hands. This means that a more meaningful comparison can be made of the profits, sales, expenses and so on from year to year. Chapter 11 will explain why it is sometimes necessary to adjust the items of income and expense in an income statement for amounts **prepaid** or **accrued**.

The accruals principle is also applied to capital and revenue expenditure. This is explained later in this chapter.

> **Test your understanding**
> 1. A customer orders goods on 2 February. The goods are delivered to the customer on 16 February. A cheque in full settlement is received from the customer on 28 February. State the date on which the profit is regarded as realised. Give a reason for your answer.
> 2. State why a business should apply the principle of consistency.
> 3. Explain what is meant by the principle of accruals.

Prudence

This is also known as the principle of **conservatism**. This principle ensures that the accounting records present a realistic picture of the position of the business. **Accountants should ensure that profits and assets are not overstated and that liabilities are not understated**. The phrase "never anticipate a profit, but provide for all possible losses" is often used to describe the principle of **prudence**. Profit should only be recognised when

Accounting Rules

it is reasonably certain that such a profit has been realised and all possible losses should be provided for.

Later chapters will explain how it is necessary to provide for the loss in value of non-current assets and to recognise that it may be necessary to make allowance for those customers who do not pay their accounts. If this is not done, the value of such assets will be overstated in the balance sheet.

Prudence is a very important principle. If a situation arises where applying another accounting principle would be contrary to the principle of prudence, then the principle of prudence is applied (this principle overrules all the other principles). For example, under the realisation principle, profit is earned when goods actually change hands; but if the customer fails to pay after a reasonable time, the principle of prudence may be applied and the debt is written off.

Going concern

The accounting records of a business are always maintained on the basis of assumed continuity. This means that **it is assumed that the business will continue to operate for an indefinite period of time and that there is no intention to close down the business or reduce the size of the business by any significant amount**.

This continuity means that the non-current assets shown in a balance sheet will appear at their book value, which is the original cost less depreciation (see Chapter 12), and inventory will appear at the lower of cost or net realisable value (see later in this chapter).

If it is expected that the business will cease to operate in the near future the asset values in the balance sheet will be adjusted. Assets will be shown at their expected sale values which are more meaningful than their book value in this situation.

Materiality

This principle applies to items of very low value (items which are not "material") which are not worth recording as separate items. Other principles can be ignored if the time and cost involved in recording such low value items far outweigh any benefits to be gained from the strict application of these principles. For example, a pocket calculator purchased for office use is strictly a non-current asset, part of its value being "lost" each year through normal usage. The cost of calculating and recording this each year would amount to more than the cost of the asset. Instead of the calculator being recorded as a non-current asset, it would be regarded as an office expense in the year of purchase. What is material for one business may not be so for another business. A lap top computer may be regarded as immaterial for a large multi-national business, but would be material for a small sole trader. A large business may decide that non-current assets costing less than $1000 will be regarded as immaterial and be charged as expenses. A small business may have a much lower figure.

This principle is also applied by entering small expenses in one account known as "general expenses" or "sundry expenses" rather than having individual ledger accounts for office expenses like light bulbs, flower displays etc. Materiality is also applied in relation to inventories of office supplies like envelopes when the total cost of envelopes purchased during the year is treated as an expense even though there are some left at the end of the year.

Historical cost

This principle requires that **all assets and expenses are recorded in the ledger accounts at their actual cost**. It is closely linked to the money measurement principle. Cost is a known fact and can be verified.

Applying this principle makes it difficult to make comparisons about transactions occurring at different times because of the effect of inflation.

Sometimes it is necessary to adopt a more prudent approach to ensure that the non-current assets are shown at a more realistic value, so the cost price is reduced by depreciation (see Chapter 12).

Accounting period

The principle of going concern assumes that a business will continue to operate for an indefinite period of time. It is clearly not sensible or practical to wait until a business ceases trading before a report on its progress is made. **Because reports are required at regular intervals, the life of the business is divided into accounting periods – usually years**. This allows meaningful comparisons to be made between different periods for the same business and between one business and another business.

Financial statements are prepared for each time period and transactions are regarded as occurring in either one period or another. The practical application of this has been shown in earlier chapters when the balance of a ledger account at the end of one trading period was carried down to become the opening balance of the next accounting period. It was also shown when the expenses for the period were totalled and transferred to the income statement for the period.

Accounting Rules

> **Test your understanding**
> 1. "If in doubt, understate profits and overstate losses". State which accounting principle is being described.
> 2. State **one** situation when the principle of going concern is **not** applied.
> 3. Explain why the principle of materiality may be applied to the purchase of an office stapler.
> 4. State **two** reasons why it is useful for the life of a business to be divided into accounting periods of one year.

Objectives in Selecting Accounting Policies

The quality of information contained in financial statements determine the usefulness of these statements. This quality of information can be measured in terms of four factors – relevance, reliability, comparability and understandability.

Relevance

Financial statements provide information about a business's financial performance and position. These can be used as the basis for financial decisions. It is important that the information is provided in time for these decisions to be made: information not available when required is of little use.

It is also important that the information is relevant to users of the financial statements. This means that it can be used to confirm, or correct, prior expectations about past events and also to help forming, revising or confirming expectations about the future.

Reliability

The information provided in financial statements can be reliable if it is
- Capable of being depended upon by users as being a true representation of the underlying transactions and events which it is representing
- Capable of being independently verified
- Free from bias
- Free from significant errors
- Prepared with suitable caution being applied to any judgements and estimates which are necessary.

Comparability

The information contained in financial statements can be useful if it can be compared with similar information about the same business for another accounting period or at another point in time. It is also useful to be able to compare the information with similar information about other business.

In order to make comparisons, it is necessary to be aware of any different policies used in the preparation of the financial statements, any changes in these policies and the effects of such changes. It is important to be able to identify similarities and differences between the information in the financial statement and the information relating to other accounting periods or other businesses.

Understandability

It is important that financial statements can be understood by the users of those statements. This depends partly on the clarity of the information provided.

It also depends on the abilities of the users of the financial statements. It is normally assumed that users of financial statements have a reasonable knowledge of business and economic activities and accounting and that they will be reasonably diligent when studying the financial statements. However, information should not be omitted from financial statements because it is decided that it is too difficult for users to understand.

> **Test your understanding**
> 1. State **two** ways in which information can be regarded as being relevant.
> 2. State **three** ways in which information can be regarded as being reliable.
> 3. Explain why it is necessary to know any changes in accounting policy when comparing financial statements with those of a previous year.
> 4. Explain the meaning of the term "understandability".

Capital and Revenue Expenditure and Receipts

Capital expenditure

This is money spent by a business on purchasing non-current assets and improving or extending non-current assets. This includes all the legal

Accounting Rules

costs incurred in the purchase of non-current assets, costs of carriage for the delivery of non-current assets and costs of installing non-current assets.

These costs will appear as non-current assets in the balance sheet of a business. They should **not** be charged as expenses in the year of purchase as they benefit the business for several years. The value of non-current assets often decreases because of depreciation (see Chapter 12). This cost will be matched against the annual revenue which the non-current asset has helped the business to earn.

Revenue Expenditure

This is money spent on running a business on a day-to-day basis. This includes the administration expenses, the selling expenses, the financial expenses, and the cost of maintaining and running non-current assets. It also includes the cost of goods purchases for the purpose of resale.

These costs will appear in the income statement. They are matched against the revenue of the period.

If these two types of expenditure are treated incorrectly the profit for the year will be inaccurate and the balance sheet (whilst still balancing) will also be incorrect. For example, if repairs to a machine were treated as an improvement to that machine the expenses in the income statement would be understated, so the profit for the year would be overstated. In the balance sheet, the non-current assets would be overstated and the capital would also be overstated because of the incorrect profit for the year.

Capital Receipt

A capital receipt occurs when a capital item such as a non-current asset is sold. A capital receipt should **not** be entered in the income statement. If, however, a profit or loss is made on the sale of a non-current asset then this will be included in the income statement for the year in which the asset was sold (this is explained in the section on disposal of non-current assets in Chapter 12).

Revenue Receipt

Revenue receipts are sales or other income such as rent received, commission received, discount received and so on. These arise from the normal trading activities and are entered in the income statement.

> **Test your understanding**
> 1. Explain why it is important to distinguish between capital expenditure and revenue expenditure.
> 2. Give **one** example of **each** of the following (a) capital receipt (b) revenue receipt

Inventory Valuation

It is necessary for a business to value its inventory at the end of each financial year. As explained earlier, the inventory at the end of one year becomes the inventory at the start of the next year. If an incorrect value is placed on the inventory it will affect the gross profit and the net profit (profit for the year) for both the current financial year and the following financial year. Incorrect values will also be shown for both current assets and capital in the balance sheet.

Inventory is always valued at the **lower of cost or net realisable value**. This is an application of the principle of **prudence** as over-valuing the inventory causes both the profit and the assets to be over-valued.

The cost of the inventory is the actual purchase price plus any additional costs (such as carriage inwards) incurred in bringing the inventory to its present position and condition. The net realisable value is the estimated receipts from the sale of the inventory, less any costs of completing the goods or costs of selling the goods.

Usually the cost of the inventory will be lower than the net realisable value. It may happen that the goods are damaged or there is no demand for such type of goods because of change in taste or fashion. In this situation, the net realisable value will be lower than cost.

> **Test your understanding**
> 1. State the basis on which inventory should be valued.
> 2. Explain the meaning of the term "net realisable value".

Example 10.1

Devnani Traders sell two different types of goods (Type A and B). They provide the following information at 31 December 20-6.

Accounting Rules

Type	Units	Cost price per unit	Net realisable value per unit
A	94	$20	$18
B	38	$15	$19

Calculate the value of the closing inventory of Devnani Traders at 31 December 20-6.

Devnani Traders
Valuation of inventory at 31 December 20-6

	$
Type A – 94 units at $18 per unit	1692
Type B – 38 units at $15 per unit	<u>570</u>
	2262

- Type A has been valued at net realisable value as this is below the cost price.
- Type B has been valued at cost price as this is below the net realisable value.

Points to Remember

1. Accounting has developed a set of principles which are applied in the preparation of accounting statements.
2. The main accounting principles are – business entity, duality, money measurement, realisation, consistency, matching, prudence, going concern, materiality, historical cost and accounting period.
3. The quality of information contained in financial statements can be measured in terms of four factors – relevance, reliability, comparability and understandability.
4. It is important to distinguish between capital and revenue expenditure and also between capital and revenue receipts. If these items are treated incorrectly the financial statements will also be inaccurate.
5. At the end of every financial year inventory must be valued. It is always valued at the lower of cost or net realisable value.

Review Questions

1. State what is meant by going concern.
   [IGCSE 2005]
2. Name the accounting principle which is described in the following sentence. "The same accounting treatment should be applied to similar items at all times".
   [IGCSE 2003]
3. Name the accounting principle which states that only the financial transactions of the business should be recorded in the business's books.
   [IGCSE 2002]
4. "Profit should not be overstated by ignoring foreseeable losses and revenue should not be recorded before it is earned." Name the accounting principle described in this statement.
   [IGCSE 2002]
5. The quality of the information in a set of financial statements determines how useful those statements are.
   There are **four** ways in which the quality of information in a trader's financial statements can be measured. One of them is reliability. State the other **three**.
   [IGCSE 2005]
*6. The quality of information in financial statements can be measured in terms of comparability and reliability.

Required

   (a) Jane Joda, a trader, could compare her results for the year ended 30 April 2005 with those for the previous year.
       State **one** other comparison Jane could make.
   (b) Suggest **one** way in which Jane might use the results of any comparisons she makes.
   (c) Jane Joda must be able to rely on the information provided in the financial statements prepared for her business.

Accounting Rules

One condition which must be present for information to be regarded as reliable is that:

"The information must be capable of being depended on as being a true statement of the transactions and events which are being recorded."

State **two** other conditions. [IGCSE 2005]

7. Peter Mpho knows that he will soon have to make decisions about the accounting policies he needs to apply.

Required

(a) List four objectives which Peter Mpho must consider when selecting accounting policies.

The first has been completed as an example.

  (i) *Relevance*
  (ii) ....
  (iii) ....
  (iv) ....

(b) Explain to Peter Mpho what is meant by the term "relevance". [IGCSE 2007]

8. (a) Explain the difference between capital expenditure and revenue expenditure.

(b) Tina decides to start a business driving a taxi. She buys a suitable motor car on 1 April 2008 but has to spend more money installing a meter. Each year she has to pay for a taxi licence and for taxi insurance.

In the table below, place a tick (✓) under the correct heading for each item of expenditure incurred by Tina.

	Capital expenditure	*Revenue expenditure*
(i) Purchase of taxi		
(ii) Installing meter		
(iii) Taxi licence		
(iv) Taxi insurance		
(v) Filling taxi with fuel		
(vi) Servicing engine		

[Based on IGCSE 2008]

*9. Michael Ong started a business on 1 July 2007. He had very little knowledge of bookkeeping but attempted to prepare a set of financial statements at the end of his first year of trading.

The financial statements Michael prepared, containing errors, are shown below.

Income statement

	$	$
Sales of goods	80 000	
Sales of motor vehicle (AB 246) at book value)	2 000	82 000
Purchases of goods	60 000	
Purchase of new motor vehicle (CD 357)	8 000	
	68 000	
Closing inventory of goods	12 000	56 000
Gross profit		26 000
General expenses	10 800	
Bad debts	200	11 000
Profit for the year		15 000

Balance Sheet

	$
Equipment	2 000
Bank	1 000
Trade receivables	7 000
Closing inventory of goods	12 000
Purchases of stationery	200
Commission received	500
	22 700
Trade payables	17 000
Capital (balancing figure)	5 700
	22 700

Required

(a) (i) Explain the difference between capital expenditure and revenue expenditure.

(ii) Explain the difference between capital receipts and revenue receipts.

(b) Calculate Michael Ong's correct profit for the year ended 30 June 2008.

[N.B. Bad debts are the amounts that will not be received from debtors and are regarded as an expense to the business.]

[IGCSE 2008]

Accounting Rules

*10. A trader provides the following information about his stock at 30 November 20-8.

Inventory code number	Number of units in inventory	Cost per unit $	Selling price per unit $
BD 20	300	1.50	2.30
BD 23	119	0.95	0.80
BD 29	410	1.78	1.85

The trader had to pay carriage inwards on inventory Code Number BD 20 at the rate of $5 per 100 units (not included in the cost per unit shown above).

Calculate the total value of inventory which should appear in the trader's balance sheet on 30 November 20-8. Show your calculations.

11. Ah Sung has a business buying and selling parts for machines. You are given the following information about Part Q.
At 1 April there were 200 units in the warehouse which cost $3.20 each. In the month of April purchases were:

April	Units	Cost per unit
5	100	$3.20
10	150	$3.00
27	100	$3.00

At 30 April there were 300 units in the warehouse and the net realisable value of each unit was $3.00.

Required

Calculate the following for Part Q. Show all workings.
(a) The value of inventory at 1 April.
(b) The total cost of purchases for April.
(c) The value of inventory at 30 April.
(d) The number of units sold in April.
(e) The cost of goods sold for the month of April.

[IGCSE 2008]

Chapter 11 — Other Payables and Other Receivables

> **In this chapter you will learn to:**
> - recognise and understand prepaid and accrued expenses
> - recognise and understand prepaid and accrued income
> - make ledger entries to record prepaid and accrued expenses and income
> - make entries to record prepaid and accrued expenses and income in the financial statements.

Introduction

It is often necessary to make adjustments to the accounting records in order to present a more accurate view of the profit or loss of the business and the financial position of the business. Such adjustments are referred to as **year-end adjustments**. These adjustments are considered in this chapter and also in Chapters 12 and 13.

The examples used in previous chapters assumed that all the expenses in the profit and loss account section of the income statement were paid until the end of the financial year, with nothing paid beyond that date and nothing unpaid. A similar approach was used in relation to revenue items within the profit and loss account section of the income statement when it was assumed that all the items were received up to the end of the financial year with nothing relating to a period beyond that date and nothing outstanding. In practice, this is rarely the case: it is common to find expenses or income unpaid, or to find expenses or income paid in one financial year but which relate to other financial years.

It was explained in Chapter 8 how an income statement is prepared for a definite period of time (the period of time covered by the statement being

Other Payables and other Receivables

included as part of the statement heading). **Only items relating to that particular time period should be included in the statement: the timing of the actual receipts and payments is not relevant**. This is a practical application of the **accruals principle** (see Chapter 10). It is, therefore, necessary to adjust the items within an income statement for amounts **prepaid** or **accrued**. This means that the profit or loss will be shown at a more accurate figure, and it allows for more meaningful comparisons of the financial statements from year to year.

The use of a simple diagram is often helpful when calculating the expense or income relating to a particular financial year. This is illustrated in the examples used in this chapter.

Accrued and Prepaid Expenses

Accrued expenses

An accrual is an amount due in an accounting period which remains unpaid at the end of that accounting period. **Where an expense is accrued it means that some benefit or service has been received during the accounting period but this benefit or service has not been paid for by the end of the period.**

It was explained in Chapter 8 how the totals of expense accounts in the nominal ledger are transferred to the income statement at the end of the financial year. To apply the **accruals principle**, the amount transferred to the income statement should represent the expense for the accounting period covered by that account. This means that **any amount due but unpaid at the end of the financial year must be added to the amount paid** and the total expense relating to the accounting period transferred to the income statement.

The expense account will now show a balance equal to the amount unpaid. To complete the double entry, this **balance is brought down on the credit side of the ledger account**. As the balance represents an amount owing, due for payment in the near future, it will be included as a **current liability** in the **balance sheet**.

The entries are summarised as follows:

During the year – debit the expense account and credit the cash book with the amount paid

At the year end – debit the expense account with any amount due but unpaid and carry down as a credit balance

credit the expense account and debit the income statement with the difference on the expense account (this represents the expense for the year)

include the balance on the expense account as a current liability in the balance sheet.

> **Test your understanding**
> 1. State what is meant by an accrued expense.
> 2. State where an accrued expense is shown in a balance sheet.
> 3. Explain why accrued expenses should be included when calculating the profit.

Example 11.1

Salman started a business on 1 April 20-7.

He receives an invoice for telephone expenses quarterly in arrears. During the year ended 31 March 20-8 his payments for expenses included the following:

20-7	30 June	Telephone expenses paid in cash $44
	4 October	Telephone expenses paid by cheque $56
20-8	3 January	Telephone expenses paid by cheque $62

An invoice for telephone expenses for $59 was received on 31 March 20-8. This was for telephone expenses up to the end of March, but was not paid until 5 April 20-8.

(a) Write up the telephone expenses account in Salman's nominal ledger for the year ended 31 March 20-8.
(b) Prepare a relevant extract from Salman's income statement for the year ended 31 March 20-8.
(c) Prepare a relevant extract from Salman's balance sheet at 31 March 20-8.

Other Payables and other Receivables

> Before attempting to answer the question it may be helpful to consider the problem by the use of a diagram.
>
> ```
> <------Financial Year 1 April 20-7 to 31 March 20-8------------>
>   A   M   J   J   A   S   O   N   D   J   F   M
> |---|---|---|---|---|---|---|---|---|---|---|---|
>
> |---|---|---|---|---|---|---|---|
>   <   $162 paid to 31 December 20-7   ><$59 owing>
> ```
>
> The diagram shows that the expenses paid do not match the period covered by the financial year, so it is necessary to add the amount owing at the end of the year.

(a)

Salman
Nominal Ledger
Telephone expenses account

Date	Details	Folio	$	Date	Details	Folio	$
20-7				20-8			
June 30	Cash		44	Mar 31	Income		
Oct 4	Bank		56		Statement		221
20-8							
Jan 3	Bank		62				
Mar 31	Balance	c/d	59				
			221				221
				20-8			
				Apl 1	Balance	b/d	59

(b)

Salman
Extract from Income Statement for the year ended 31 March 20-8

	$
Expenses – Telephone expenses	221

(c)

Salman
Extract from Balance Sheet at 31 March 20-8

	$
Current liabilities	
Other payables	59

- The telephone expenses relating to the financial year ended on 31 March 20-8 amount to $221, which is the total paid plus the amount unpaid.
- The telephone expenses would be listed with the other expenses in the income statement and deducted from the gross profit.
- Where there are several accrued expenses it is usual to show one combined figure in the balance sheet under other payables rather than showing the amount of each separate accrual.

Prepaid expenses

A prepayment is an amount that is paid in advance. **Where an expense is prepaid it means that a payment has been made during the financial year for some benefit or service to be received in a future accounting period.**

As with accrued expenses, the **accruals principle** must be applied so that the amount transferred to the income statement represents the expense for the accounting period covered by that statement. Any amount paid during the financial year relating to a future accounting period must be deducted from the amount paid so that only the expense relating to the accounting period is transferred to the income statement.

The expense account will now show a balance equal to the amount paid in advance. To complete the double entry, this **balance is brought down on the debit side of the ledger account**. As the balance represents a short term benefit, which the business has paid for but which is not used up, it will be included as a **current asset** in the **balance sheet**.

The entries are summarised as follows:

During the year – debit the expense account and credit the cash book with the amount paid

At the year end – credit the expense account with any amount paid in advance and carry down as a debit balance

credit the expense account and debit the income statement with the difference on the expense account (this represents the expense for the year)

include the balance on the expense account as a current asset in the balance sheet.

Other Payables and other Receivables

147

> **Test your understanding**
> 1. State what is meant by a prepaid expense.
> 2. State where a prepaid expense is shown in a balance sheet.
> 3. Explain how the accruals principle is applied to expenses shown in the income statement.

Example 11.2

Salman started a business on 1 April 20-7.

Salman rented premises until 1 July 20-7 when he purchased premises. He paid a cheque for $600 for one year's insurance on his premises on 1 July 20-7.

(a) Write up the insurance account in Salman's nominal ledger for the year ended 31 March 20-8.
(b) Prepare a relevant extract from Salman's income statement for the year ended 31 March 20-8.
(c) Prepare a relevant extract from Salman's balance sheet at 31 March 20-8.

> Before attempting to answer the question it may be helpful to consider the problem by the use of a diagram.
>
> ```
> <-----Financial Year 1 April 20-7 to 31 March 20-8------->
>  A   M   J   J   A   S   O   N   D   J   F   M
> |---|---|---|---|---|---|---|---|---|---|---|---|
>                                             A   M   J
>                 |---|---|---|---|---|---|---|---|---|---|---|---|
>          <        $600 paid to 30 June 20-8           >
> ```
>
> The diagram shows that the expenses paid do not match the period covered by the financial year, so it is necessary to deduct that portion of the $600 which falls outside the financial year (3 months/12 months or ¼ of $600 relates to the following financial year).

(a)

Salman
Nominal Ledger
Insurance account

Date	Details	Folio	$	Date	Details	Folio	$
20-7 July 1	Bank		600	20-8 Mar 31	Income statement		450
					Balance	c/d	150
			600				600
20-8 Apl 1	Balance	b/d	150				

(b)

Salman
Extract from Income Statement for the year ended 31 March 20-8

	$
Expenses – Insurance	450

(c)

Salman
Extract from Balance Sheet at 31 March 20-8

	$
Current assets	
Other receivables	150

- The insurance relating to the financial year ended on 31 March 20-8 amounts to $450, which is the insurance from 1 July 20-7 to 31 March 20-8.
- The insurance expense would be listed with the other expenses in the income statement and deducted from the gross profit.
- Where there are several prepaid expenses it is usual to show one combined figure in the balance sheet under other receivables rather than showing the amount of each separate prepayment.

If a business has an inventory of stationery, postage stamps, wrapping paper etc. at the end of a financial year, this can be regarded as a prepaid expense. Money has been spent, but the benefit will not be received until the following accounting period, when the stationery, wrapping paper etc. is actually used. The entries are similar to those for a prepaid expense.

Other Payables and other Receivables

Example 11.3

Salman started a business on 1 April 20-7.
During the year ended 31 March 20-8 he purchased stationery costing $113.
On 31 March 20-8 the inventory of stationery was valued at $36.
Write up the stationery account in Salman's nominal ledger for the year ended 31 March 20-8.

Salman
Nominal Ledger
Stationery account

Date	Details	Folio	$	Date	Details	Folio	$
20-8 Mar 31	Bank		113	20-8 Mar 31	Income statement Balance	c/d	77 36
			113				113
20-8 Apl 1	Balance	b/d	36				

- The date of 31 March 20-8 has been used for the total paid as no individual dates and amounts were shown in the question.
- The expense of $77 would be listed with the other expenses in the income statement and deducted from the gross profit.
- The balance representing the inventory at 31 March 20-8 would appear as a current asset in the balance sheet.
- The inventory must not be included in the inventory of goods for resale.

Opening balances on expense accounts

The trader mentioned in **Examples 11.1** to **11.3** was in his first year of business, so none of the expense accounts prepared in these examples had an opening balance. There was, however, a closing balance on each account which became the opening balance for the second year of trading. This must be considered when calculating the expense relating to the next financial year.

Example 11.4

Salman's financial year ends on 31 March.

He receives an invoice for telephone expenses quarterly in arrears.

On 1 April 20-8 the telephone expenses account in Salman's nominal ledger showed a credit balance of $59.

During the year ended 31 March 20-9 his payments for expenses included the following:

20-8	5 April	Telephone expenses paid in cash $59
20-8	30 June	Telephone expenses paid by cheque $60
	2 October	Telephone expenses paid by cheque $48
	31 December	Telephone expenses paid by cheque $56

An invoice for telephone expenses for $63 was received on 31 March 20-9. This was for telephone expenses up to the end of March, but was not paid until 2 April 20-9.

Write up the telephone expenses account in Salman's nominal ledger for the year ended 31 March 20-9.

Before attempting to answer the question it may be helpful to consider the problem by the use of a diagram.

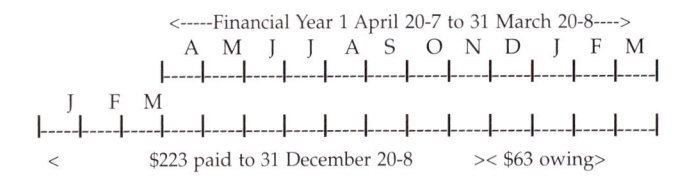

```
                    <-----Financial Year 1 April 20-7 to 31 March 20-8---->
                     A   M   J   J   A   S   O   N   D   J   F   M
                     |---|---|---|---|---|---|---|---|---|---|---|---|
         J   F   M
         |---|---|---|---|---|---|---|---|---|---|---|---|---|---|---|
         <          $223 paid to 31 December 20-8      >< $63 owing>
```

The diagram shows that the expenses paid do not match the period covered by the financial year, so it is necessary to:

1. deduct that portion of the $223 which falls outside the financial year ($59 was paid during this financial year but related to the previous accounting period)

2. add the $63 owing at the end of present financial year.

Other Payables and other Receivables

Salman
Nominal Ledger
Telephone expenses account

Date	Details	Folio	$	Date	Details	Folio	$
20-8				20-8			
Apl 5	Cash		59	Apl 1	Balance	b/d	59
June 30	Bank		60	20-9			
Oct 2	Bank		48	Mar 31	Income		
Dec 31	Bank		56		statement		227
20-9							
Mar 31	Balance	c/d	63				286
			286				
				20-9			
				Apl 1	Balance	b/d	63

Example 11.5

Salman's financial year ends on 31 March.

On 1 April 20-8 the insurance account in Salman's nominal ledger showed a debit balance of $150.

He paid a cheque for $636 for one year's insurance on his premises on 1 July 20-8.

Write up the insurance account in Salman's nominal ledger for the year ended 31 March 20-9.

Before attempting to answer the question it may be helpful to consider the problem by the use of a diagram.

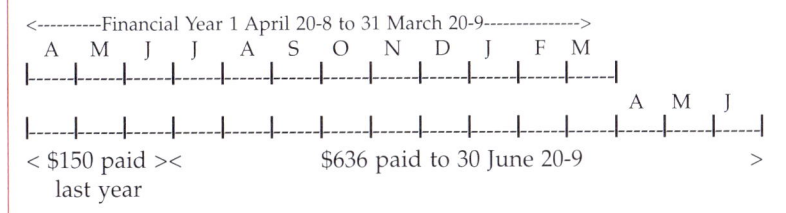

```
<---------Financial Year 1 April 20-8 to 31 March 20-9--------------->
  A    M    J    J    A    S    O    N    D    J    F    M
  |----|----|----|----|----|----|----|----|----|----|----|----|
                                                              A    M    J
                                                              |----|----|----|
  < $150 paid ><         $636 paid to 30 June 20-9                        >
     last year
```

The diagram shows that the expenses paid do not match the period covered by the financial year, so it is necessary to:
1. deduct that portion of the $636 which falls outside the financial year (3 months/12 months or ¼ of $636 relates to the following financial year).
2. add the $150 paid in the previous financial year as it falls within the present financial year.

Salman
Nominal Ledger
Insurance account

Date	Details	Folio	$	Date	Details	Folio	$
20-8				20-8			
Apl 1	Balance	b/d	150	Mar 31	Income statement		627
July 1	Bank		636		Balance	c/d	159
			786				786
20-9							
Apl 1	Balance	b/d	159				

> **Test your understanding**
> 1. Anisha started business on 1 April 20-1. Property tax amounted to $800 for the year ended 31 March 20-2 and $880 for the year ended 31 March 20-3. Property tax of $600 was paid during the year ended 31 March 20-2 and $860 was paid during the year ended 31 March 20-3.
> For **each** of the years ended 31 March 20-2 and 31 March 20-3 state:
> (a) the amount charged for property tax in the income statement.
> (b) the amount shown for property tax in the balance sheet, indicating whether it is a current asset or a current liability.

Accrued and Prepaid Income

Accrued income

Where an item of income is accrued it means that another person receiving a benefit or service from the business during the accounting period has not paid for that benefit or service by the end of the period.

Chapter 8 explained how the totals of income accounts in the nominal ledger are transferred to the income statement at the end of the financial year. The **accruals principle** is applied to income in the same way as it is to expenses so that the amount transferred to the income statement represents the income for the accounting period covered by that statement.

Other Payables and other Receivables

153

This means that **any amount due but not received at the end of the financial year must be added to the amount received** and the total income relating to the accounting period transferred to the income statement.

The income account will now show a balance equal to the amount not yet received. To complete the double entry, this **balance is brought down on the debit side of the ledger account**. As the balance represents an amount owing to the business, due to be received in the near future, it will be included as a **current asset** in the **balance sheet**.

The entries are summarised as follows:

During the year – credit the income account and debit the cash book with the amount received.

At the year end – credit the income account with any amount due but not received and carry down as a debit balance

debit the income account and credit the income statement with the difference on the income account (this represents the income for the year)

include the balance on the income account as a current asset in the balance sheet.

Example 11.6

Salman started a business on 1 April 20-7.

On that date he also agreed to act as an agent for Kohli & Company. Salman was to be paid a commission six monthly in arrears on all goods sold for Kohli & Company.

Commission of $120 was received by cheque on 1 October 20-7 and $135 was received by cheque on 2 April 20-8.
(a) Write up the commission received account in Salman's nominal ledger for the year ended 31 March 20-8.
(b) Prepare a relevant extract from Salman's income statement for the year ended 31 March 20-8.
(c) Prepare a relevant extract from Salman's balance sheet at 31 March 20-8.

Before attempting to answer the question it may be helpful to consider the problem by the use of a diagram.

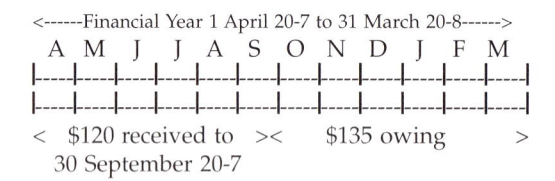

```
          <------Financial Year 1 April 20-7 to 31 March 20-8------>
          A   M   J   J   A   S   O   N   D   J   F   M
          |---+---+---+---+---+---+---+---+---+---+---+---|
          |---+---+---+---+---+---+---+---+---+---+---+---|
          <  $120 received to  ><    $135 owing        >
             30 September 20-7
```

The diagram shows that the income received does not match the period covered by the financial year, so it is necessary to add the amount not yet received at the end of the year.

(a)
Salman
Nominal Ledger
Commission received account

Date	Details	Folio	$	Date	Details	Folio	$
20-8				20-7			
Mar 31	Income statement		255	Oct 1	Bank		120
				20-8			
				Mar 31	Balance	c/d	135
			255				255
20-8							
Apl 1	Balance	b/d	135				

(b)
Salman
Extract from Income Statement for the year ended 31 March 20-8

	$
Gross profit	xxx
Add Commission received	255

(c)
Salman
Extract from Balance Sheet at 31 March 20-8

	$
Current assets	
Income accrued	135

- The commission receivable relating to the financial year ended on 31 March 20-8 amounts to $255, which is the total received plus the amount due but not yet received.

Other Payables and other Receivables

- The commission received would be listed with the other items of income in the income statement and added to the gross profit.
- The commission due but not yet received would appear in the balance sheet as a current asset under the description of income accrued. Alternatively, it could be included in the other receivables (in this case a note to the balance sheet would show the breakdown of this figure).

Prepaid income

Where an item of income is prepaid, it means that a person had paid for a benefit or service from the business, but this has not been provided by the business at the end of the financial year.

Once again, the accruals principle must be applied so that the amount transferred to the income statement represents the income for the accounting period covered by that statement. Any amount received during the financial year relating to a future accounting period must be deducted from the amount received so that only the income relating to the accounting period is transferred to the income statement.

The income account will now show a balance equal to the amount received in advance. To complete the double entry, this **balance is brought down on the credit side of the ledger account**. This balance will be included as a **current liability** in the **balance sheet** as the business has a liability to provide some service or benefit for which the business has already been paid.

The entries are summarised as follows:

During the year – credit the income account and debit the cash book with the amount received.

At the year end – debit the income account with any amount received in advance and carry down as a credit balance

debit the income account and credit the income statement with the difference on the income account (this represents the income for the year)

include the balance on the income account as a current liability in the balance sheet.

Example 11.7

Salman started a business on 1 April 20-7.

Salman rented premises until 1 July 20-7 when he purchased premises. On that date he rented out part of his premises to another trader at an annual rent of $1000, payable quarterly in advance.

The tenant paid rent of $250 by cheque on 1 July 20-7, 1 October 20-7, 31 December 20-7 and 30 March 20-8.

(a) Write up the rent received account in Salman's nominal ledger for the year ended 31 March 20-8.
(b) Prepare a relevant extract from Salman's income statement for the year ended 31 March 20-8.
(c) Prepare a relevant extract from Salman's balance sheet at 31 March 20-8.

> Before attempting to answer the question it may be helpful to consider the problem by the use of a diagram.
>
> ```
> <-----Financial Year 1 April 20-7 to 31 March 20-8------>
>   A   M   J   J   A   S   O   N   D   J   F   M
> |---|---|---|---|---|---|---|---|---|---|---|---|
>                                             A   M   J
> |---|---|---|---|---|---|---|---|---|---|---|---|
>   <         $1000 received to 30 June 20-8         >
> ```
>
> The diagram shows that the income received does not match the period covered by the financial year, so it is necessary to deduct that portion of the $1000 which falls outside the financial year ($250 relates to the following financial year).

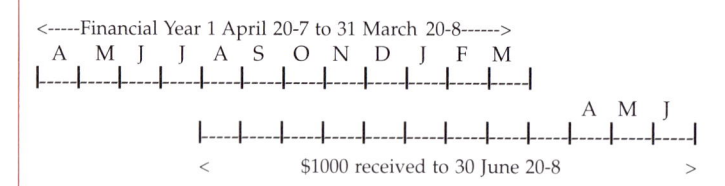

(a)

Salman
Nominal Ledger
Rent received account

Date	Details	Folio	$	Date	Details	Folio	$
20-8				20-7			
Mar 31	Income statement		750	July 1	Bank		250
				Oct 1	Bank		250
	Balance	c/d	250	Dec 31	Bank		250
				20-8			
				Mar 30	Bank		250
			1000				1000
				20-8			
				Apl 1	Balance	b/d	250

Other Payables and other Receivables

(b)
Salman
Extract from Income Statement for the year ended 31 March 20-8

	$
Gross profit	xxx
Add Rent received	750

(c)
Salman
Extract from Balance Sheet at 31 March 20-8

	$
Current liabilities	
Income prepaid	250

- The rent receivable relating to the financial year ended on 31 March 20-8 amounts to $750, which is the rent received for the period 1 July 20-7 to 31 March 20-8.
- The rent received would be listed with the other items of income in the income statement and added to the gross profit.
- The rent received in advance would appear in the balance sheet as a current liability under the description of income prepaid. Alternatively, it could be included in the other payables (in this case a note to the balance sheet would show the breakdown of this figure).

> **Test your understanding**
> 1. Explain why income received in advance is shown as a current liability in a balance sheet.
> 2. Explain why accrued income is shown as a current asset in a balance sheet.

Opening balances on income accounts

In the second and subsequent years of trading, a business may have opening balances on income accounts as well as opening balances on expense accounts. These must be considered when calculating the income relating to the particular financial year for which the accounts are prepared.

Example 11.8

Salman's financial year ends on 31 March.

He acts as an agent for Kohli & Company and is paid a commission six monthly in arrears on all goods sold for Kohli & Company.

On 1 April 20-8 the commission received account in Salman's nominal ledger showed a debit balance of $135.

During the year ended 31 March 20-9 he received cheques for commission as follows:

20-8 2 April $135
      1 October $145

At 31 March 20-9 commission due but not yet received amounted to $156.

Write up the commission received account in Salman's nominal ledger for the year ended 31 March 20-9.

> Before attempting to answer the question it may be helpful to consider the problem by the use of a diagram.
>
> ```
>                        <-----Financial Year 1 April 20-8 to 31 March 20-9---->
>                         A   M   J   J   A   S   O   N   D   J   F   M
>                        |---|---|---|---|---|---|---|---|---|---|---|---|
>        O   N   D   J   F   M
>       |---|---|---|---|---|---|---|---|---|---|---|---|---|---|---|---|---|---|
>       <      $280 received to 30 September 20-8      ><    $156 owing         >
> ```
>
> The diagram shows that the expenses paid do not match the period covered by the financial year, so it is necessary to –
>
> 1. deduct that portion of the $265 which falls outside the financial year ($120 was received during this financial year but related to the previous accounting period).
> 2. add the $156 owing at the end of present financial year.

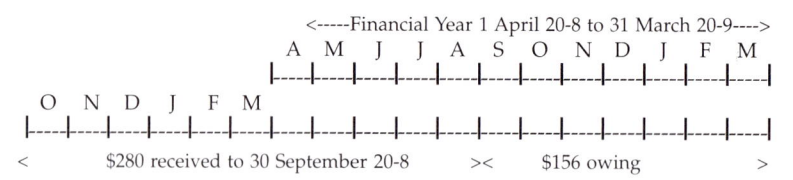

Salman
Nominal Ledger
Commission received account

Date	Details	Folio	$	Date	Details	Folio	$
20-8				20-8			
Apl 1	Balance	b/d	135	Apl 2	Bank		135
20-9				Oct 1	Bank		135
Mar 31	Income			20-9			
	statement		301	Mar 31	Balance	c/d	156
			436				436
20-9							
Apl 1	Balance	b/d	156				

Other Payables and other Receivables

Example 11.9

Salman's financial year ends on 31 March.

He rents part of his premises to another trader at an annual rent of $1000, payable quarterly in advance.

On 1 April 20-8 the rent received account in Salman's nominal ledger showed a credit balance of $250.

The tenant paid rent of $250 by cheque on 1 July 20-8 and 2 October 20-8. The rent due on 1 January 20-9 was not received until 2 April 20-9.

Write up the rent received account in Salman's nominal ledger for the year ended 31 March 20-9.

> Before attempting to answer the question it may be helpful to consider the problem by the use of a diagram.
>
> ```
> <--------Financial Year 1 April 20-8 to 31 March 20-9------------>
>    A    M    J    J    A    S    O    N    D    J    F    M
> |----|----|----|----|----|----|----|----|----|----|----|----|
>
> |----|----|----|----|----|----|----|----|----|----|----|----|
>  <    $250    ><      $500 received to     ><  $250 owing  >
>     received             31 December 20-8
>    last year
> ```
>
> The diagram shows that the expenses paid do not match the period covered by the financial year, so it is necessary to–
> 1. add the $250 due but not received at the end of the financial year
> 2. add the $250 received in the previous financial year as it falls within the present financial year.

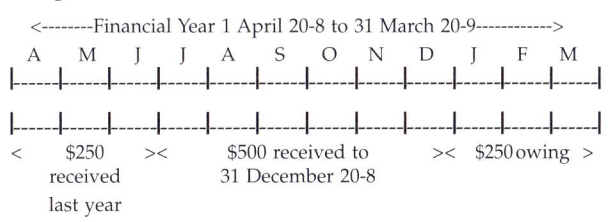

Salman
Nominal Ledger
Rent received account

Date	Details	Folio	$	Date	Details	Folio	$
20-8				20-8			
Mar 31	Income statement		1000	Apl 1	Balance	b/d	250
				July 1	Bank		250
				Oct 2	Bank		250
				20-9			
				Mar 31	Balance	c/d	250
			1000				1000
20-9							
Apl 1	Balance	b/d	250				

Test your understanding

1. Whabi & Company's financial year ends on 31 December. They act as agent for another business and receive a commission on goods sold.
   The following information is provided:

   20-6 Jan   1 Commission, $94, was owing to Whabi & Company
   　　 Dec 31 Commission, $1350, was received
   　　　　　　 Commission, $76, was owing to Whabi & Company
   20-7 Dec 31 Commission, $1480, was received

   For **each** of the years ended 31 December 20-6 and 31 December 20-7 state:
   (a) the amount shown for commission received in the income statement
   (b) the amount (if any) shown for commission received in the balance sheet, indicating whether it is a current asset or a current liability

POINTS TO REMEMBER

1. The expenses for an accounting period must be matched against the income of that particular period.
2. An accrual is an amount due in an accounting period which remains unpaid at the end of that period. A prepayment is an amount that has been paid or received in one accounting period which relates to a future period.
3. In the income statement an accrued expense is added to the total paid. The accrued amount is a current liability in the balance sheet.
4. In the income statement a prepaid expense is deducted from the total paid. The prepaid amount is a current asset in the balance sheet.
5. In the income statement accrued income is added to the total received. The accrued amount is a current asset in the balance sheet.
6. In the income statement income received in advance is deducted from the total received. The amount received in advance is a current liability in the balance sheet.

Other Payables and other Receivables

REVIEW QUESTIONS

1. Rupa made the following bank payments in the month of March 2008.

		$
March	6 Motor expenses – repairs	120
	12 Motor expenses – tyres	150

   The bill for repairs had been received in February and $120 had been accrued in the motor expenses account at the end of the month.

   Rupa received a bill for motor fuel for $80 on 219 March but the bill was not paid until 7 April.

Required

(a) Prepare the motor expenses account in Rupa's ledger for the month of March 2009. Show the amount transferred to the income statement for the month and the balance brought down on 1 April.

Mopsa has to pay $400 rent on her shop each month.

She was not able to pay all the rent due in March 2009 and $150 was outstanding on 1 April.

From 1 April, her landlord increased the rent to $450 each month.

On 27 April Mopsa made a payment of rent to her landlord of $500 in total.

Required

(b) Prepare the rent account in Mopsa's ledger for the month of April 2009. Show the amount to be transferred to the income statement for the month and balance brought down on 1 May.

Andrea does not include any accrual in her electricity account for electricity used, and invoiced, but not paid for at the end of the month.

Required

(c) Place a tick (✓) in one of the boxes below to show whether the amount for electricity in her income statement for the month will be

understated	
overstated	

[IGCSE 2009]

2. Susie is a trader. On 1 July 20-7 her inventory of stationery was valued at $110. During the year ended 30 June 20-8 the following transactions took place.

   20-7 September 1 Purchased stationery, $328, by cheque
   20-8 January 4 Purchased stationery, $95, in cash
   February 1 Received a cash refund, $15, for an overcharge by the stationery supplier

   Susie's inventory of stationery on 30 June 20-8 was valued at $187. Write up the stationery account in Susie's ledger for the year ended 30 June 20-8.

3. Amina Hassan's financial year ends on 30 April. She sublets part of her premises to Mariam Kamel.
   Amina provided the following information.

2001	$
May 1 Mariam owed 1 month's rent	60
July 1 Mariam paid rent for 15 months to 30 June 2002 by cheque	900

   Prepare the rent received account as it would appear in Amina Hassan's ledger for the year ended 30 April 2002. Show clearly the amount transferred to the income statement and the balance on 1 May 2002.

   [IGCSE 2002]

*4. The following extract shows transactions recorded in Ramon's cash book for the month of April 2007.

Other Payables and other Receivables

Ramon
Cash Book

Date	Details	Cash $	Bank $	Date	Details	Cash $	Bank $
Apl 1	Balance b/d	1100	2450	Apl 1	Rent		900
3	Sales	500		6	Electricity		120
12	Ahmed		1200	21	Drawings	800	
29	Ahmed		650	29	Wages	700	
				30	Balance c/d	100	3280
		1600	4300			1600	4300
May 1	Balance b/d	100	3280				

Additional information:
1. The balance on Ahmed's account in the ledger on 1 April was $2850 Dr.
2. Rent of $900 is payable quarterly in advance.
3. An electricity bill for $60 was accrued at 30 April.

Required

Write up the following accounts in Ramon's ledger for the month of April 2007.
Show the amounts transferred to Ramon's income statement for the month and any balances at 1 May.

(a) Sales account (b) Ahmed account (c) Rent account
(d) Electricity account (e) Drawings account (f) Wages account

[IGCSE 2007]

5. The following account appears in Ruth Tembe's nominal (general) ledger.

Business rates account

Date	Details	folio	$	Date	Details	folio	$
2008				2008			
Sept 30	Bank		1490	Aug 1	Balance	b/d	90
				2009			
				July 31	Income statement		1200
					Balance	c/d	200
			1490				1490
2009							
Aug 1	Balance	b/d	200				

Required

(a) Explain each of the entries in the business rates account as it appears in the nominal (general) ledger of Ruth Tempe. State where the double entry for each transaction would be made.
The first one has been completed as an example.
2008 Aug 1 Balance $90

    Explanation   *This is the amount owing for business rates for the previous financial year.*

    Double entry   *Debit business rates account for the year ended 31 July 2008*

2008 Sept 30 Bank $12490
2009 July 31 Income statement $1200

(b) (i) Explain the significance of the $200 shown at the end of the business rates account.
    (ii) State where this amount will appear in Ruth Tembe's balance sheet at 31 July 2009.

[IGCSE 2009]

6. Elmer Gantry is a self-employed builder whose financial year ends on 30 September. His trial balance drawn up on 30 September 2003 included the following balances.

	Dr $	Cr $
Revenue (sales)		100 000
Purchases	66 000	
Purchases returns		4 000
Inventory 1 October 2002	12 000	
Insurance	4 250	
Wages	6 000	
General expenses	1 000	
Motor expenses	2 600	
Rent	5 000	

You are given the following additional information.
1. On 30 September 2003 insurance prepaid was $250 and motor expenses due but unpaid were $400.

Other Payables and other Receivables

2. Inventory on 30 September 2003 was $9000.
   (a) Prepare Elmer Gantry's income statement for the year ended 30 September 2003.
   (b) (i) State what is meant by the accounting principle of accruals.
       (ii) Explain how the accruals principle is applied to insurance in Elmer's income statement.

   [Based on IGCSE 2003]

*7. Miriam is a business consultant. She provided the following information at the end of her first year on 30 September 20-4.

	$
Office expenses	7 250
Wages	27 500
Insurance	1 800
Property tax	800
Motor vehicle expenses	1 840
Fees received from clients	40 900
Commission received	5 600

The following information is also available.
1. The office expenses include stationery. On 30 September 20-4 the inventory of stationery was valued at $250.
2. It is estimated that half of the motor vehicle expenses relate to Miriam's personal use.
3. On 30 September 20-4
   Property tax due amounted to $160
   Office expenses due amounted to $45
   Commission receivable amounted to $250.
4. The insurance covers a period of 15 months to 31 December 20-4.
5. Bank charges, $115, have not been entered in the accounting records.

Prepare Miriam's income statement for the year ended 30 September 20-4.

Chapter 12

Depreciation and Disposal of Non-current Assets

In this chapter you will learn to:
- understand the nature and causes of depreciation
- understand the main methods of calculating depreciation
- make entries to record depreciation in the ledger
- make entries to record depreciation in the financial statements
- make entries to record disposal of non-current assets.

Introduction

As explained in Chapter 11, it is often necessary to include year-end adjustments in a set of financial statement. This ensures that the accounts provide a more accurate view of the profit or loss of the business and the financial position of the business.

Chapter 11 concentrated on accrued and prepaid expenses and income. This chapter focuses on the year-end adjustment made for depreciation of non-current assets.

Depreciation is an estimate of the loss in value of a non-current asset over its expected working life. Most of the non-current assets of a business lose value over a period of time they are used by the business. If the accounting records continue to show these assets at their cost prices then the accounts will provide misleading information. It is, therefore, necessary to record an estimate of the loss in value. The records can only show an *estimate* of the loss in value of a non-current asset because of depreciation. The *exact* amount will only be known when the asset is disposed of or sold. Buildings depreciate over time but land does not usually lose value (unless it is something like a well or mine when value is removed from the land).

Depreciation and Disposal of Non-current Assets

The purchase of a non-current asset is **capital expenditure** (see Chapter 10). The cost of a non-current asset is not charged as an expense in the year of purchase as it benefits the business for several years. **Matching** the capital expenditure against the sales it has helped the business to earn is done by an annual charge for depreciation. **This means that the cost of the non-current asset is spread over the years which benefit from the use of that asset**. The depreciation for the year is included in the expenses in the income statement, so the profit for the year is not overstated. This is an application of the **principle of prudence**. If the profit is overstated, the owner of a business may be tempted to withdraw more cash than the business can actually afford.

The **principle of prudence** is also applied in the balance sheet as the non-current assets are recorded at a figure less than the cost price (this is known as the **net book value** or the **written down value**). This overrides the **historical cost principle** as it ensures that the non-current assets are shown at more realistic values.

Depreciation is a **non-monetary expense** as it does not involve an outflow of money, nor does it provide a cash fund to use for the replacement of a non-current asset.

Causes of Depreciation

The four main causes of depreciation are explained below:

Physical deterioration

This is the result of "wear and tear" due to the normal usage of the non-current asset. It can also be because the asset falls into a poor physical state due to rust, rot, decay and so on.

Economic reasons

The non-current asset may become inadequate as it can no longer meet the needs of the business. It can also be because the non-current asset has become obsolete as newer and more efficient assets are now available.

Passage of time

This arises where a non-current asset, for example a lease, has a fixed life of a set number of years.

Depletion

This arises in connection with non-current assets such as wells and mines. The worth of the asset reduces as value is taken from the asset.

> **Test your understanding**
> 1. Explain the meaning of depreciation.
> 2. Explain how depreciation is an application of the accruals (matching) principle.
> 3. List four causes of depreciation of non-current assets.

Methods of Calculating Depreciation

There are several methods used to calculate the estimated loss in value of a non-current asset. Different types of non-current assets are often depreciated using different methods. The method selected should be the one which spreads the cost of the asset as fairly as possible over the periods which benefit from its use. Once a method has been selected for a particular non-current asset, it should be applied each year. This is an application of the **principle of consistency**.

In practice, many factors are considered before a depreciation method is selected. These are:

- How long is the asset expected to last?
- How much will the asset be sold for when it is put out of use?
- How can the benefits from the use of the asset be measured?

There are three main methods of depreciation:

- Straight line method
- Reducing balance method
- Revaluation method

These are explained below. There are several other methods, but they are outside the scope of the syllabus.

Straight line method of depreciation

This is also known as the **fixed instalment method**.

The formula used for calculating the annual depreciation using this method is:

Depreciation and Disposal of Non-current Assets

$$\frac{\text{Cost of asset}}{\text{Number of expected years of use}}$$

This expresses the annual depreciation as an amount of money. The answer to this formula is expressed as a percentage of the total cost.

This method applies the **same amount of depreciation or the same percentage rate each year**. The value of the asset can fall to nil if there is no residual value (see below).

This method is used where each year is expected to benefit equally from the use of the asset.

Example 12.1

Kavita's financial year ends on 30 June.

On 1 July 20-3 she purchased fixtures costing $25 000 and paid by cheque. She estimated that she would be able to use the fixtures for 4 years.

Calculate the annual depreciation charge
(a) as an amount of money
(b) as a percentage

(a) $\dfrac{\$25\,000}{4 \text{ years}} = \$6250$

(b) $\dfrac{\$6250}{\$25\,000} = 25\%$

Where it is estimated that the asset will have some value at the end of its working life, this must be included in the calculation. Such a value is known as a **residual value**. The formula then becomes:

$$\frac{\text{Cost of asset} - \text{Residual value}}{\text{Number of expected years of use}}$$

Example 12.2

Kavita's financial year ends on 30 June.

On 1 July 20-3 she purchased fixtures costing $25 000 and paid by cheque. She estimated that she would be able to use the fixtures for 4 years and then be able to sell them for $3000.

Calculate the annual depreciation charge
(a) as an amount of money
(b) as a percentage (based on the original cost)

(a) $\dfrac{\$25\,000 - \$3\,000}{4 \text{ years}} = \$5500$

(b) $\dfrac{\$5\,500}{\$25\,000} \times \dfrac{100}{1} = 22\%$

Reducing balance method of depreciation

This is also referred to as the **diminishing balance method**.

As the name implies, the amount of depreciation reduces each year. **The same percentage rate is applied, but it is calculated on a different value each year.** At the end of the first year the depreciation for that year is calculated on the cost of the asset. The depreciation for the following year is calculated (using the same percentage) on the cost of the asset less the depreciation previously written off. The figure of cost less depreciation is known as the **net book value** (or **written down value**) of the asset.

The value of the asset can never fall to nil as the depreciation is always calculated as a percentage of the net book value.

This method is used where the greater benefits from the use of the asset will be gained in the early years of its life. Assets depreciated by this method often have lower maintenance costs in the early years. This method is often used for those assets which quickly become out of data because of advancing technological progress.

Any residual value is taken into consideration when the percentage rate is selected.

Example 12.3

Kavita's financial year ends on 30 June.

On 1 July 20-3 she purchased fixtures costing $25 000 and paid by cheque. She estimated that she would be able to use the fixtures for 4 years and then be able to sell them for $3000.

Calculate the depreciation for **each** of the 4 years of the fixtures' working life using the reducing balance method at the rate of 40% per annum.

Depreciation and Disposal of Non-current Assets

	$
Cost	25 000
Depreciation for year ended 30 June 20-4 at 40%	10 000
Book value at 1 July 20-4	15 000
Depreciation for year ended 30 June 20-5 at 40%	6 000
Book value at 1 July 20-5	9 000
Depreciation for year ended 30 June 20-6 at 40%	3 600
Book value at 1 July 20-6	5 400
Deprecation for year ended 30 June 20-7 at 40%	2 160
Book value at 1 July 20-7	3 240

- Depreciation is usually expressed in units of whole dollars, so the amounts have been adjusted to avoid cents

Revaluation method of depreciation

This method is used where it is not practical, or is difficult, to keep detailed records of certain types of non-current assets. If detailed records are not available the previous two methods of depreciation cannot be calculated. Small items of equipment used in offices and laboratories, packing cases, loose tools etc. are usually depreciated using the revaluation method as no detailed records are kept for these assets.

The assets are valued at the end of each financial year. This value is compared with the value at the end of the previous financial year (or with the cost if it is the first year of ownership). **The amount by which the value of the asset has fallen is the depreciation for the year.**

Example 12.4

Kavita's financial year ends on 30 June.
    On 1 July 20-3 she purchased fixtures costing $25 000 and paid by cheque. She decided to revalue the fixtures at the end of each year.
    On 30 June 20-4 the fixtures were valued at $20 500.
    Calculate the depreciation for the year ended 30 June 20-4.

	$
Cost of fixtures on 1 July 20-3	25 000
Value of fixtures on 30 June 20-4	20 500
Depreciation for the year ended 30 June 20-4	4 500

> **Test your understanding**
> 1. Explain the straight line method of depreciation.
> 2. Explain how, using the reducing balance method, the *amount* of depreciation decreases each year even though the same *percentage rate* is applied.
> 3. State when the revaluation method is used to depreciate non-current assets.

Recording Depreciation in the Ledger

Recording depreciation using the straight line method and the reducing balance method.

The procedure for entering depreciation calculated using the straight line method and the reducing balance method is exactly the same.

Each type of non-current asset has two ledger accounts:
- an account for recording the cost of the asset (the asset account)
- an account for recording the depreciation (the provision for depreciation of asset account)

The asset account always has a debit balance and the provision for depreciation always has a credit balance. These two accounts must always be considered together. The difference between the balances of these accounts represents the net book value of the asset.

The entries are summarised as follows:

During the year – when the asset is purchased
　　debit the asset account and credit either the cash book or the supplier's account with the cost price

At the year end – debit the income statement and credit the provision for depreciation account with the depreciation for the year

　　balance the provision for depreciation account and carry down as a credit balance

　　balance the asset account if there have been any transactions during the year and carry down as a debit balance

Example 12.5

Kavita's financial year ends on 30 June.

Depreciation and Disposal of Non-current Assets

On 1 July 20-3 she purchased fixtures costing $25 000 and paid by cheque. She estimated that she would be able to use the fixtures for 4 years and then be able to sell them for $3000.

Kavita decided to use the reducing balance method of depreciation at 40% per annum.

Make the entries in Kavita's nominal ledger accounts for **each** of the years ended 30 June 20-4, 20-5, 20-6 and 20-7.

Kavita
Nominal Ledger
Fixtures account

Date	Details	Folio	$	Date	Details	Folio	$
20-3 July 1	Bank		25 000				

Provision for depreciation of fixtures account

Date	Details	Folio	$	Date	Details	Folio	$
20-4 June 30	Balance	c/d	10 000	20-4 June 30	Income statement		10 000
			10 000				10 000
20-5 June 30	Balance	c/d	16 000	20-4 July 1	Balance	b/d	10 000
				20-5 June 30	Income statement		6 000
			16 000				16 000
20-6 June 30	Balance	c/d	19 600	20-5 July 1	Balance	b/d	16 000
				20-6 June 30	Income statement		3 600
			19 600				19 600
20-7 June 30	Balance	c/d	21 760	20-6 July 1	Balance	b/d	19 600
				20-7 June 30	Income statement		2 160
			21 760				21 760
				20-7 July 1	Balance	b/d	21 760

173

- The asset account was not balanced at the end of each year as there is only one entry in the account.
- Before the transfer to the income statement can be made each year it is necessary to calculate the depreciation for the year. The calculations have been shown in **Example 12.3**.
- The difference between the balance on the asset account and the balance on the provision for depreciation account on the same date represents the net book value of the fixtures on that date.
- If the straight line method of depreciation had been selected the entry in the fixtures account would be exactly the same.
- If the straight line method of depreciation had been selected the entries in the provision for depreciation of fixtures account would be very similar. The transfer to the income statement would be $5500 each year, so the totals and balances on the account would differ to those shown earlier.

> **Test your understanding**
> 1. Referring to **Example 12.5**:
>   (a) State the total amount of depreciation up to 30 June 20-6.
>   (b) State the net book value of the fixtures on 30 June 20-7.
> 2. Explain why the asset account and the provision for depreciation account of that asset should both be referred to when the asset is being considered.

Where a non-current asset is purchased *during* the financial year a business may decide to charge depreciation from the date of purchase. This means that in the first year of ownership only a proportion of the annual depreciation will be charged to the income statement.

Example 12.6

Kavita's financial year ends on 30 June.
On 1 July 20-4 she purchased a motor vehicle costing $9000 and paid by cheque. On 1 April 20-5 an additional motor vehicle costing $8000 was purchased and paid for by cheque.
She decided to use the straight line method of deprecation at 20% per annum, depreciation to be calculated from the date of purchase.

Depreciation and Disposal of Non-current Assets

Make the entries in Kavita's nominal ledger accounts for the year ended 30 June 20-5.

Kavita
Nominal Ledger
Motor vehicles account

Date	Details	Folio	$	Date	Details	Folio	$
20-4 July 1	Bank (A)		9 000	20-5 June 30	Balance	c/d	17 000
20-5 Apl 1	Bank (B)		8 000				
			17 000				17 000
20-5 July 1	Balance	b/d	17 000				

Provision for depreciation of fixtures account

Date	Details	Folio	$	Date	Details	Folio	$
20-5 June 30	Balance	c/d	2 200	20-5 June 30	Income statement (A) 1800 (B) 400		2 200
			2 200				2 200
				20-5 July 1	Balance	b/d	2 200

Sometimes a business may decide to ignore the date of purchase when calculating depreciation. This means that a whole year's depreciation will be charged on all the assets held at the end of the financial year.

Recording depreciation using the revaluation method

The cost of the asset and the depreciation are recorded in the same account.

The entries are summarised as follows:

During the year – when the asset is purchased
debit the asset account and credit either the cash book or the supplier's account with the cost price.

At the year end – credit the asset account with the value of the asset at that date and carry down as a debit balance;

transfer the difference on the account to the income statement as this is the depreciation for the year.

Example 12.7

Kavita's financial year ends on 30 June.

On 1 July 20-3 she purchased fixtures costing $25 000 and paid by cheque. She decided to revalue the fixtures at the end of each year.

On 30 June 20-4 the fixtures were valued at $20 500.

Make the entries in the fixtures account in the nominal ledger for the year ended 30 June 20-4.

Kavita
Nominal Ledger
Fixtures account

Date	Details	Folio	$	Date	Details	Folio	$
20-3 July 1	Bank		25 000	20-4 June 30	Balance Income statement	c/d	20 500 4 500
			25 000				25 000
20-4 July 1	Balance	b/d	20 500				

Recording Depreciation in the Financial Statements

Recording depreciation in the income statement

The depreciation for the year for each type of asset is credited to the provision for depreciation account in the nominal ledger and is debited to the income statement. This reduces the business's profit for the year. As depreciation is a non-monetary expense, it is usually shown after the monetary expenses in the income statement.

If the business is a manufacturing business, depreciation of assets used in the manufacturing process will be debited to the manufacturing account rather than the income statement (see Chapter 20). This increases the cost of manufacturing which, in turn, reduces the profit for the year.

Depreciation and Disposal of Non-current Assets

Recording depreciation in the balance sheet

It is usual to show the total cost of each type of non-current asset less the total depreciation written off up to the date of the balance sheet (referred to as **depreciation to date** or **accumulated depreciation**). The difference between these figures is the net book value.

Example 12.8

Kavita's financial year ends on 30 June.

On 1 July 20-3 she purchased fixtures costing $25 000 and paid by cheque. She estimated that she would be able to use the fixtures for 4 years and then be able to sell them for $3000.

Kavita decided to use the reducing balance method of depreciation at 40% per annum.

(a) Prepare a relevant extract from Kavita's income statement for **each** of the years ended 30 June 20-4 and 30 June 20-5.
(b) Prepare a relevant extract from Kavita's balance sheet at 30 June 20-4 and at 30 June 20-5

(a)
Kavita
Extract from Income Statement for the year ended 30 June 20-4

	$
Expenses – Depreciation of fixtures	10 000

Kavita
Extract from Income Statement for the year ended 30 June 20-5

	$
Expenses – Depreciation of fixtures	6 000

(b)
Kavita
Extract from Balance Sheet at 30 June 20-4

	Cost $	Depreciation to date $	Book value $
Non-current assets			
Fixtures	25 000	10 000	15 000

Kavita
Extract from Balance Sheet at 30 June 20-5

	$	$	$
Non-current assets	Cost	Depreciation to date	Book value
Fixtures	25 000	16 000	9 000

As explained earlier in Chapters 8 and 9, the financial statements are prepared from a trial balance and its accompanying notes. In the trial balance, the balances on the asset accounts are shown in the debit column and the balances on the provision for depreciation accounts are shown in the credit column. One of the notes will indicate the depreciation to be charged for the current financial year.

The depreciation for the year will appear twice in the financial statements. It is an expense in the income statement: it is included in the balance sheet as part of the provision for depreciation (the depreciation for the year is added to the balance shown in the trial balance).

Example 12.9

Kavita's financial year ends on 30 June.

She depreciates her fixtures using the reducing balance method of depreciation at 40% per annum.

Her trial balance drawn up on 30 June 20-6 included the following:

	Dr $	Cr $
Fixtures	25 000	
Provision for depreciation of fixtures		16 000

(a) Prepare a relevant extract from Kavita's income statement for the year ended 30 June 20-6
(b) Prepare a relevant extract from Kavita's balance sheet at 30 June 20-6

(a)
Kavita
Extract from Income Statement for the year ended 30 June 20-6

	$
Expenses – Depreciation of fixtures	3 600

Depreciation and Disposal of Non-current Assets

(b)
Kavita
Extract from Balance Sheet at 30 June 20-6

Non-current assets	Cost $	Depreciation to date $	Book value $
Fixtures	25 000	19 600	5 400

- The deprecation relating to the current financial year is included as an expense in the income statement.
- In the balance sheet the total depreciation up to that date ($16 000 shown in the trial balance plus the depreciation for the year of $3600) are deducted from the cost price of the asset.

> **Test your understanding**
> 1. Explain why depreciation is a non-monetary expense.
> 2. Referring to **Example 12.9**, explain why the figure of $16 000 provision for depreciation does not actually appear in the financial statements.

Disposal of Non-current Assets

In Chapter 10 it was explained that, since the purchase of a non-current asset is **capital expenditure**, it is recorded in an account for the non-current asset rather than in the purchases account. Similarly, when a non-current asset is sold it is a **capital receipt** and is recorded in a special account known as a **disposal of non-current asset account** rather than in the sales account.

When a non-current asset is sold or disposed of, it must be removed from the ledger records. The cost of the asset and the depreciation on the asset are removed from the asset account and the provision for depreciation account and transferred to a disposal account. The proceeds of sale are also entered in this account. It is quite likely that this account will not balance. This is because the depreciation was only an estimate of the loss in value. Only when the asset is sold can the actual loss in value be calculated. The difference on the disposal account represents either a loss on disposal (when the actual depreciation proved to be more than the estimate) or a profit on disposal (when the actual depreciation proved to be less than the estimate).

The entries are summarised as follows:

On the date of sale – credit the asset account and debit the disposal of non-current asset account with the original cost price (of the asset being sold)

debit the provision for depreciation account and credit the disposal of non-current asset account with the total depreciation charged (on the asset being sold)

credit the disposal of non-current asset account and debit either the cash book or the debtor's account with the proceeds of sale

At the year end – transfer any difference on the disposal of non-current asset account to the income statement

Example 12.10

Kavita's financial year ends on 30 June.

On 1 July 20-3 she purchased fixtures costing $25 000 and paid by cheque. She decided to depreciate the fixtures using the reducing balance method.

On 1 July 20-7 the provision for depreciation of fixtures account showed a credit balance of $21 760.

Kavita sold all the fixtures on credit to Traders Ltd. for $3100 on 1 July 20-7.

Make the entries in Kavita's nominal ledger accounts for the year ended 30 June 20-8.

Kavita

Nominal Ledger

Fixtures account

Date	Details	Folio	$	Date	Details	Folio	$
20-3 July 1	Bank		25 000 _____ 25 000	20-7 July 1	Disposal		25 000 _____ 25 000

Depreciation and Disposal of Non-current Assets

Provision for depreciation of fixtures account

Date	Details	Folio	$	Date	Details	Folio	$
20-7 July 1	Disposal		21 760	20-7 July 1	Balance	b/d	21 760
			21 760				21 760

Disposal of fixtures account

Date	Details	Folio	$	Date	Details	Folio	$
20-7 July 1	Fixtures		25 000	20-7 July 1	Provision for depreciation Traders Ltd.		21 760 3 100
				20-8 June 30	Income statement		140
			25 000				25 000

- The difference on the disposal account remains in that account until the end of the financial year when it is transferred to the income statement.
- In this case the depreciation had been under-provided so there was a small loss of $140 to transfer to the income statement.
- If the total of the credit side of the account had exceeded the debit side, there would have been an over-provision of depreciation. The transfer to the income statement would have been shown on the debit of this account and on the credit of the income statement.

If only some of the assets of a particular type are being sold, it is important that only the entries relating to the assets being sold are removed from the ledger records.

Businesses may operate different policies in relation to depreciation where an asset is sold or disposed of part-way through the year. Some ignore depreciation in the year of sale; others charge depreciation up to the date of disposal of the asset. Once a method has been selected it should be employed **consistently**.

Points to Remember

1. Depreciation is an estimate of the loss in value of a non-current asset over its expected working life.
2. The main causes of depreciation are physical deterioration, economic reasons, passage of time and depletion.
3. The three main methods of calculating depreciation are straight line, reducing balance and revaluation.
4. Depreciation is shown as an expense in the income statement.
5. In the balance sheet the total depreciation to date is deducted from the cost of the asset.
6. When a non-current asset is sold it is removed from the ledger records by transfer to a disposal of non-current asset account.

Review Questions

1. (a) What is the reason for charging depreciation on capital expenditure in the income statement?
   Koala bought a printing press on 1 October 2004 for $40 000. She is preparing her financial statements for the year ended 30 September 2005 and needs to decide which method of depreciation should be used.
   She expects the printing press to have a useful life of ten years, and to be able to sell it at the end of that time for $4000.
   Using this information she could use the straight line method or the reducing (diminishing) balance method at 20% per annum.
   (b) Explain **each** of these methods of depreciation.
   (c) Calculate how much depreciation will be charged in Koala's income statement for the next three years under **each** of the two methods.
   Koala decides to use the reducing balance method of depreciation.

Depreciation and Disposal of Non-current Assets

(d) Show the entries in the provision for depreciation of machinery account for **each** of the three years ending 30 September 2005, 2006 and 2007.

(e) Explain to Koala the revaluation method of depreciation.

[Based on IGCSE 2005]

2. Smith has a business selling washing machines. He buys the goods from the manufacturers and sells them to stores and other suppliers.

He keeps full accounting records and his trial balance at 30 June 2005 is shown below.

Smith
Trial Balance at 30 June 2005

	Dr $	Cr $
Advertising	400	
Bank	3 200	
Carriage inwards	700	
Trade payables		8 600
Trade receivables	14 800	
Provision for depreciation of non-current assets		2 800
Drawings	24 000	
Fixtures & fittings	5 600	
General expenses	390	
Insurance	420	
Lighting and heating	600	
Motor vehicle	12 000	
Motor expenses	860	
Office expenses	280	
Rent	720	
Postage and stationery	180	
Purchases	75 600	
Revenue (sales)		102 000
Capital		40 000
Inventory at 1 July 2004	8 400	
Wages and salaries	5 250	
	153 400	153 400

The following additional information is available.
1. Inventory at 30 June 2005 was valued at $7100.
2. Motor expenses of $350 are to be accrued.

3. Depreciation of $700 for the year is to be charged.
4. Purchase invoices of $4000 have not been included but the goods are included in the closing inventory valuation.

Prepare Smith's income statement for the year ended 30 June 2005.

[IGCSE 2005]

*3. The financial year of Joe's engineering business ends on 31 August. On 1 September 2001 balances in Joe's ledger included the following.

	$
Equipment	40 000 Dr
Provision for depreciation of equipment	15 000 Cr

You are given the following further information.
1. Joe depreciates his equipment at the rate of 10% per annum on cost. Depreciation on new equipment is calculated from the date of purchase.
2. Additional equipment purchases during the year ended 31 August 2002 were:

	$
1 September 2001	30 000
1 March 2002	20 000

Both purchases were paid for by cheque.
3. There were no sales of equipment during the year.

(a) Make the entries required to record the above transactions in the equipment account and the provision for depreciation of equipment account in Joe's ledger.

(b) Complete the following extract to show how equipment appears in Joe's balance sheet at 31 August 2002.

Extract from Balance Sheet at 31 August 2002

Non-current assets	$ Cost	$ Accumulated Depreciation	$ Book value
Equipment	………..	………….….....	………..

Depreciation and Disposal of Non-current Assets

(c) Explain how the accounting principle of prudence is observed when Joe provides for the depreciation of his equipment.

[IGCSE 2002]

4. Solomon is a sole trader and his trial balance at 31 March 2008 was as follows.

	Dr $	Cr $
Bank	4 050	
Capital		35 000
Cash	250	
Carriage outwards	720	
Trade payables		2 400
Trade receivables	4 000	
Drawings	24 000	
Electricity	1 800	
Motor vehicle	9 600	
Motor expenses	1 380	
Provision for depreciation of motor vehicle		4 800
Purchases	28 800	
Revenue (sales)		47 500
Rent	6 000	
Inventory 1 April 2007	1 500	
Wages	8 600	
	90 700	90 700

The following additional information is available:

1. Inventory at 31 March 2008 was $1800.
2. A bonus of $400 is to be accrued in the wages account.
3. Depreciation on motor vehicle of $2400 is to be provided for the year.
4. Rent includes $1200 paid in advance.

Required

(a) Prepare Solomon's income statement for the year ended 31 March 2008.

(b) Write up Solomon's capital account for the year ended 31 March 2008.

(c) Suggest **two** ways in which Solomon could reduce his loss or increase his profit.

(d) Suggest **two** ways in which Solomon could increase the credit balance on his capital account.

[IGCSE 2008]

*5. Mustafa and Syed went into partnership on 1 April 2000. On that date they purchased equipment on credit from AB Ltd., for $10 000.

The partners decided to provide for a full year's depreciation on equipment in the year of purchase but no depreciation in the year of disposal. It was agreed that depreciation should be calculated on equipment owned at 31 March each year at a rate of 20% per annum, using the straight line method.

On 1 October 2001 half of the equipment was sold on credit to Zeta Ltd. for $3500.

(a) Prepare the following accounts in the ledger of Mustafa and Syed for **each** of the years ended 31 March 2001 and 31 March 2002.

(i) Equipment account
(ii) Provision for depreciation of equipment account
(iii) Disposal of equipment account

(b) On 1 April 2002 Mustafa stated:

"I suggest we change the method of depreciation of equipment to the reducing balance method for this financial year. My calculations show that if we do this the depreciation charge for the year will only be $315. This is much less than the depreciation under the straight line method, so our profits will increase."

State and explain **two** reasons why the partnership should **not** change to a different method of calculating depreciation.

[IGCSE 2002]

6. John Kamel is a sole trader whose financial year ends on 31 July.
(a) The following account appears in John's ledger.

Depreciation and Disposal of Non-current Assets

187

Disposal of motor vehicle account

Date	Details	Folio	$	Date	Details	Folio	$
2003 Mar 12	Motor vehicles		5 000	2003 Mar 12	Provision for depreciation		3 000
					XY Garages		1 500
				July 31	Income statement		500
			5 000				5 000

Explain **each** entry in the disposal of motor vehicles account as it appears in John Kamel's ledger.

(b) On 1 August 2001 John Kamel purchased a machine costing $8600 on credit from Superlooms. He decided to depreciate the machine using the reducing balance method at the rate of 60% per annum.

(i) Write up the provision for depreciation of machinery account in John's ledger for **each** of the **two** years ending 31 July 2002 and 31 July 2003.

(ii) When preparing the income statement for the year ended 31 July 2003, John Kamel included depreciation of machinery at 60% of the cost price instead of 60% of the book value of the machinery.

Calculate how this error would affect John's profit for the year ended 31 July 2003. Show your workings.

[IGCSE 2003]

7. Tony and Alice Mundondo started a business on 1 March 2007 supplying and repairing computers. On that date they purchased a motor vehicle, $9500, on credit from Valley Motors. They purchased a further motor vehicle, $10 800, on 1 July 2008 and paid by cheque.

They decided to depreciate the motor vehicles at 20% per annum using the straight line (equal instalment) method. The depreciation was to be calculated from the date of purchase. No depreciation was to be charged in the year of disposal of a motor vehicle.

Required

(a) Write up the following accounts in the ledger of Tony and Alice Mundondo for **each** of the years ended 29 February 2008 and 28 February 2009:
   (i) Motor vehicles account
   (ii) Provision for depreciation of motor vehicles account

(b) Prepare a relevant extract from the non-current assets section of Tony and Alice Mundondo's balance sheet at 28 February 2009.

(c) On 31 March 2009 Tony and Alice Mundondo decided that the motor vehicle purchased in 2007 was too small. On that date they purchased a larger motor vehicle from Valley Motors who agreed to accept the original motor vehicle in part exchange.

Tony and Alice Mundondo opened an account in the ledger to record the disposal of the motor vehicle.

Complete the following table to indicate the ledger accounts to be debited and credited to record the disposal of the motor vehicle on 31 March 2009.

	account to be debited	account to be credited
(i) eliminating original cost of motor vehicle from ledger		
(ii) eliminating accumulated depreciation from ledger		
(iii) recording part exchange allowance made by Valley Motors		

(d) (i) Explain the revaluation method of depreciation.
   (ii) State one type of non-current asset which is suitable for depreciation using the revaluation method.

[IGCSE 2009]

Chapter 13 Bad Debts and Provisions for Doubtful Debts

> **In this chapter you will learn to:**
> - understand the nature of bad debts and bad debts recovered
> - make entries to record bad debts and bad debts recovered
> - understand the purpose of a provision for doubtful debts
> - make entries to record creating and maintaining a provision for doubtful debts.

Introduction

When goods are sold on credit the customer is allowed to pay for the goods at a later date. There is always a risk that the customer may not pay for those goods. **A bad debt is an amount owing to a business which will not be paid by the debtor**. This may be because the debtor has disappeared, has gone out-of-business, or because he is unable to pay.

If all reasonable steps to obtain payment have failed the debt is **written off** as a bad debt.

The account of the debtor is closed by transferring the amount written off to the bad debts account. At the end of the year, the total of the bad debts account is transferred to the income statement where it is regarded as an expense for the year.

The entries are summarised as follows:

When the debt is written off – credit the debtor's account and debit the bad debts account

At the year end – credit the bad debts account and debit the income statement

Writing off bad debts is an example of the application of the principle of **prudence**. If a debt cannot be regarded as an asset it is written off so that the assets are not overstated. The amount of the bad debt is regarded as a loss for the year so must be included in the income statement otherwise the profit for the year will be overstated.

Bad Debts Recovered

A bad debt recovered arises when a debtor pays some, or all, of the amount owed, after the amount was written off as a bad debt.

As the account of the debtor has been closed the amount received is debited in the cash book and credited to a bad debts recovered account. An alternative method is to re-instate the debt by crediting the bad debts recovered account and debiting the debtor with the amount previously written off. The amount received would then be entered by debiting the cash book and crediting the debtor. The advantage of this method is that all the transactions relating to the debtor appear in the debtor's account.

At the end of the year the bad debts recovered account can either be transferred to the credit of the income statement (as income for the year) or transferred to the credit of the bad debts account (where it reduces the bad debts written off during the year). The effect on the profit for the year is the same in both cases.

The entries are summarised as follows:

When the amount is received – debit the cash book and credit the bad debts recovered account

Or debit the cash book and credit the debtor debit the debtor and credit bad debts recovered

At the year end – debit the bad debts recovered account and credit the income statement **or** credit the bad debts account

Example 13.1

Sachin is a trader who sells goods on credit. He offers customers a cash discount of 2% if accounts are paid within 30 days.

Sachin's financial year ends on 31 December.

Sachin sold goods, $400, on credit to Bhuvan's Stores on 1 February 20-2. The account was settled by cheque on 28 February 20-2. On this date Bhuvan's Stores purchased further goods, $150, on credit. After many

Bad Debts and Provisions for Doubtful Debts

attempts to recover the amount due, Sachin wrote off Bhuvan's Stores account as a bad debt on 30 December 20-2.

Sachin received a cheque from Bhuvan's Stores for $150 on 31 October 20-3.

During the year ended 31 December 20-3 Sachin wrote off bad debts totalling $820.

Write up the following accounts in Sachin's ledgers for **each** of the years ended 31 December 20-2 and 20-3 – Bhuvan's Stores account, bad debts account, and bad debts recovered account.

Sachin
Sales Ledger
Bhuvan's Stores account

Date	Details	Folio	$	Date	Details	Folio	$
20-2				20-2			
Feb 1	Sales		400	Feb 28	Bank		392
28	Sales		150		Discount		8
			___	Dec 30	Bad debts		150
			550				550

Nominal Ledger
Bad debts account

Date	Details	Folio	$	Date	Details	Folio	$
20-2				20-2			
Dec 30	Bhuvan's Stores		150	Dec 31	Income statement		150
			150				150
20-3				20-3			
Dec 31	Debtors written off		820	Dec 31	Income statement		820
			820				820

Bad debts recovered account

Date	Details	Folio	$	Date	Details	Folio	$
20-3				20-3			
Dec 31	Income statement		150	Oct 31	Bank (Bhuvan's Stores)		150
			___				
			150				150

- The words "debtors written off" have been used as no individual names, dates and amounts details have been provided.
- Alternatively, the debt could have been reinstated by debiting Bhuvan's Stores account and crediting bad debts recovered. The cheque would then be debited to the bank and credited to Bhuvan's Stores account.
- Alternatively the bad debts recovered account could have been transferred to the credit of the bad debts account. This would result in $670 being transferred from bad debts to the income statement on 31 December 20-3.

Reducing the possibility of bad debts

The only certain way of avoiding bad debts is not to sell goods on credit. In practice, this is not always an option. All possible steps must be taken to avoid bad debts. Before allowing credit to a new customer, credit references should be obtained – one from the customer's bank and one from a present or previous supplier. A credit limit is usually fixed for each customer, which places an upper limit on the amount the customer can owe at any one time (this credit limit can be reviewed periodically). The establishing of a credit limit and the later monitoring of the debtor's account is known as **credit control**.

Invoices and month-end statements of account should be issued promptly. The sales ledger accounts should be carefully monitored. Any overdue accounts should be investigated and the debtors contacted by letters and telephone calls if necessary. No further goods should be supplied until the amount due is paid. A more extreme measure involves taking legal action against the debtor, but sometimes the amount of the debt is too small to justify costly legal proceedings.

Some businesses may make use of factoring and invoice discounting, but these are outside the scope of the syllabus.

> **Test your understanding**
> 1. Explain how writing off bad debts is an application of the principle of prudence.
> 2. List **three** ways in which the possibility of bad debts may be reduced.

Bad Debts and Provisions for Doubtful Debts

Provision for Doubtful Debts

A provision for doubtful debts is an estimate of the amount which a business will lose in a financial year because of bad debts.

At the end of their financial year, many businesses try to anticipate the amount which will be lost because of bad debts. This ensures that the profit for the year is not overstated and the amount of trade receivables in the balance sheet is shown at a realistic level. This is an application of the principle of **prudence**. By maintaining a provision for doubtful debts, a business also observes the principle of **accruals**. The amount of sales for which the business is unlikely to be paid is regarded as an expense of the year in which those sales are made (rather than an expense of the year in which the debt is actually written off).

In order to make a provision for doubtful debts, it is necessary to estimate the amount of bad debts. The amount of the provision may be established by:
- Looking at each individual debtor's account and estimating which ones will not be paid.
- Estimating, on the basis of past experience, the percentage of the total amount owing by debtors that will not be paid.
- Considering the length of time debts have been outstanding by means of an ageing schedule. A provision of a higher percentage may be made on older debts (the longer a debt is outstanding the greater the risk it may become a bad debt).

> Test your understanding
> 1. Explain the meaning of a provision for doubtful debts.
> 2. Explain how maintaining a provision for doubtful debts is an application of both the principle of accruals and the principle of prudence.

Creating a provision for doubtful debts

Once it is decided to create a provision for doubtful debts and the amount or percentage has been decided, this can be recorded in the books. These entries are made at the end of the financial year.

The entries are summarised as follows:
- debit the income statement and credit the provision for doubtful debts account.
- in the balance sheet deduct the balance on the provision for doubtful debts account from the trade receivables.

Example 13.2

Sachin's financial year ends on 31 December.

During the year ended 31 December 20-4 he wrote off bad debts totalling $950.

On 31 December his trade receivables amounted to $25 000. He decided to create a provision for doubtful debts of 4% of the trade receivables.

(a) Write up the bad debts account and the provision for doubtful debts account in Sachin's nominal ledger for the year ended 31 December 20-4.
(b) Prepare a relevant extract from Sachin's income statement for the year ended 31 December 20-4.
(c) Prepare a relevant extract from Sachin's balance sheet at 31 December 20-4.

(a)

Sachin
Nominal Ledger
Bad debts account

Date	Details	Folio	$	Date	Details	Folio	$
20-4 Dec 31	Debtors written off		950	20-4 Dec 31	Income statement		950
			950				950

Provision for doubtful debts account

Date	Details	Folio	$	Date	Details	Folio	$
				20-4 Dec 31	Income statement		1 000

Bad Debts and Provisions for Doubtful Debts

- The words "debtors written off" have been used in the bad debts account as no individual names, dates and amounts have been provided.
- The provision has been calculated at 4% of $25 000.

(b)
Sachin
Extract from Income Statement for the year ended 31 December 20-4

	$
Expenses – Bad debts	950
Provision for doubtful debts	1 000

(c)
Sachin
Extract from Balance Sheet at 31 December 20-4

	$	$
Current assets		
Trade receivables	25 000	
Less Provision for doubtful debts	1 000	24 000

- Only the amount which is actually expected to be received from the trade receivables is added to the other current assets in the balance sheet.

Adjusting a provision for doubtful debts

In future years it may be decided to maintain the provision for doubtful debts at the same percentage of the trade receivables. If the amount owing has increased the provision needs to be increased and vice versa. If the original provision for doubtful debts was based on an amount of money rather than a percentage, it may be decided that this amount needs to be changed. This adjustment to the provision for doubtful debts is made at the end of the financial year.

The entries are summarised as follows:

- debit the provision for doubtful debts account with the *new* provision and carry down as a credit balance.
- transfer the difference on the provision for doubtful debts account to the income statement.
- in the balance sheet deduct the balance on the provision for doubtful debts account (the *new* provision) from the trade receivables.

Example 13.3

Increasing a provision for doubtful debts

Sachin's financial year ends on 31 December.

On 31 December 20-4 Sachin created a provision for doubtful debts of $1000.

During the year ended 31 December 20-5 Sachin wrote off bad debts totalling $990.

On 31 December 20-5 his trade receivables amounted to $28 000. He decided to maintain the provision for doubtful debts at the rate of 4% of the trade receivables.

(a) Write up the bad debts account and the provision for doubtful debts account in Sachin's nominal ledger for the year ended 31 December 20-5.
(b) Prepare a relevant extract from Sachin's income statement for the year ended 31 December 20-5.
(c) Prepare a relevant extract from Sachin's balance sheet at 31 December 20-5.

(a)

Sachin
Nominal Ledger
Bad debts account

Date	Details	Folio	$	Date	Details	Folio	$
20-5 Dec 31	Debtors written off		990	20-5 Dec 31	Income statement		990
			990				990

Provision for doubtful debts account

Date	Details	Folio	$	Date	Details	Folio	$
20-5 Dec 31	Balance	c/d	1 120	20-4 Dec 31	Income statement		1 000*
				20-5 Dec 31	Income statement		120
			1 120				1 120
				20-6 Jan 1	Balance	b/d	1 120

Bad Debts and Provisions for Doubtful Debts

- The words "debtors written off" have been used in the bad debts account as no individual names, dates and amounts have been provided.
- The item indicated with * was entered in the account on 31 December 20-4 at the end of the previous financial year.
- The new provision has been calculated at 4% of $28 000.

(b)
Sachin
Extract from Income Statement for the year ended 31 December 20-5

	$
Expenses – Bad debts	990
Provision for doubtful debts	120

- Only the amount by which the provision needs to be increased is included in the expenses in the income statement.

(c)
Sachin
Extract from Balance Sheet at 31 December 20-5

	$	$
Current assets		
Trade receivables	28 000	
Less Provision for doubtful debts	1 120	26 880

- The amount of the provision for doubtful debts at 31 December 20-5 (the balance on the provision account) is deducted from the trade receivables to show the amount expected to be received.

Example 13.4

Reducing a provision for doubtful debts

Sachin's financial year ends on 31 December.

On 31 December 20-5 Sachin's provision for doubtful debts amounted to $1120.

On 31 December 20-6 his trade receivables amounted to $24 000. He decided to maintain the provision for doubtful debts at the rate of 4% of the trade receivables.

(a) Write up the provision for doubtful debts account in Sachin's nominal ledger for the year ended 31 December 20-6.

(b) Prepare a relevant extract from Sachin's income statement for the year ended 31 December 20-6.
(c) Prepare a relevant extract from Sachin's balance sheet at 31 December 20-6.

(a)

Sachin
Nominal Ledger
Provision for doubtful debts account

Date	Details	Folio	$	Date	Details	Folio	$
20-6 Dec 31	Income statement Balance	c/d	160 960 1 120	20-6 Jan 1 20-7 Jan 1	Balance Balance	b/d b/d	1 120 1 120 960

- The new provision has been calculated at 4% of $24 000.

(b)

Sachin
Extract from Income Statement for the year ended 31 December 20-6

	$
Gross profit	xxx
Add reduction in provision for doubtful debts	160

- The surplus provision is added to the gross profit in the income statement.
- Any bad debts would be included in the expenses in the income statement in the usual way.

(c)

Sachin
Extract from Balance Sheet at 31 December 20-6

	$	$
Current assets		
Trade receivables	24 000	
Less Provision for doubtful debts	960	23 040

- The amount of the provision for doubtful debts at 31 December 20-6 (the balance on the provision account) is deducted from the trade receivables to show the amount expected to be received.

Bad Debts and Provisions for Doubtful Debts

POINTS TO REMEMBER

1. A bad debt is an amount owing to a business which will not be paid by the debtor. Bad debts are shown as an expense in the income statement.
2. A bad debt recovered occurs when a debtor pays some, or all, or the debt after it has been written off. Bad debts recovered are added to the gross profit in the income statement.
3. A provision for doubtful debts is an estimate of the amount which a business will lose in a financial year because of bad debts.
4. The amount required to create or increase a provision for doubtful debts is shown as an expense in the income statement. Any surplus provision is added to the gross profit in the income statement.
5. The provision for doubtful debts is deducted from the trade receivables in the balance sheet.

REVIEW QUESTIONS

*1. K Dhoni is a business consultant.
    The following trial balance is provided at 30 September 20-1.

	$	$
Capital		94 000
Drawings	12 250	
Premises	82 000	
Office equipment	19 000	
Provision for depreciation of office equipment		1 900
Trade receivables	5 000	
Loan (repayable 20-9)		10 000
Bad debts	100	
Provision for doubtful debts		150
Income from clients		75 300

Insurance	2 400	
Printing and stationery	3 150	
Wages	47 000	
Office expenses	2 950	
Rent received		5 400
Cash	200	
Bank	12 700	
	186 750	186 750

The following additional information is supplied.

1. At 30 September 20-1 –   rent received in advance amounted to $1800

   insurance prepaid amounted to $600

   printing expenses owing amounted to $150

   loan interest owing amounted to $500.

2. The office equipment is being depreciated at the rate of 10% per annum using the straight line method.

3. The provision for doubtful debts is maintained at 4% of the trade receivables.

(a) Prepare the income statement of K Dhoni for the year ended 30 September 20-1.

(b) Prepare the balance sheet of K Dhoni at 30 September 20-1.

*2. Maria van Zyl maintains a provision for doubtful debts.

Required

(a) Name **two** accounting principles which Maria is applying by maintaining a provision for doubtful debts.

Maria van Zyl provides the following information.

	$
Trade receivables at 1 August 2004	33 000
Trade payables at 31 July 2005	30 000

Bad Debts and Provisions for Doubtful Debts

Maria maintains a provision for doubtful debts at 3% of the trade receivables at the end of each financial year.

Required

(b) Write up the provision for doubtful debts account in Maria's ledger for the year ended 31 July 2005.

Mark van Zyl, Maria's brother, is also a trader. His financial year ends on 31 August. Maria advises Mark to create a provision for doubtful debts.

Required

(c) State **two** ways in which Mark could decide on the amount of his provision for doubtful debts.

One of Mark's debtors owes $2000. This has been outstanding since May 2002. Mark is unable to trace this debtor.

Required

(d) Indicate how **each** of the following will be affected if Mark does not write off this debt.

The first one has been completed as an example.

1 Gross profit for the year ended 31 August 2005

| Effect | Overstated | Understated | No effect |

Reason   Bad debts are not entered in the trading account section of the income statement and so do not affect the gross profit.

2 Net profit for the year ended 31 August 2005

| Effect | Overstated | Understated | No effect |

Reason   ....

3 Current assets at 31 August 2005

| Effect | Overstated | Understated | No effect |

Reason   ....

[IGCSE 2005]

3. Suzi Iyambo is a sole trader whose financial year ends on 31 January.

   (a) The following account appears in Suzi's ledger.

   John Karunda account

Date	Details	Folio	$	Date	Details	Folio	$
2002				2002			
Apl 1	Sales		1000	Apl 30	Bank		1000
May 6	Bank			Dec 1	Cash		850
	(dishonoured			2003			
	cheque)		1000	Jan 3	Bad debts		150
			2000				2000

   Explain **each** entry in John Karunda's account as it appears in Suzi Iyambo's ledger.

   (b) Suzi maintains a provision for doubtful debts. On 1 February 2002 there was a credit balance of $900 on the provision for doubtful debts account.

   At 31 January 2003 Suzi's trade receivables amounted to $40 000, and she decided to maintain the provision for doubtful debts at 2% of the trade receivables.

   Write up the provision for doubtful debts account in Suzi's ledger for the year ended 31 January 2003.

   (c) State **four** ways in which Suzi Iyambo could reduce the risk of bad debts.

   [IGCSE 2003]

4. James Kanu is a trader who sells goods on credit. He offers his credit customers a cash discount of 3% provided the account is paid within 30 days. He has applied the accounting principle of prudence and maintains a provision for doubtful debts. The provision amounted to $150 on 1 February 2008.

Bad Debts and Provisions for Doubtful Debts

Required

(a) State two effects on his financial statements of applying the principle of prudence.

(b) Name one other accounting principle which James Kanu is applying by maintaining a provision for doubtful debts.

James Kanu's transactions during the financial year ended 31 January 2007 included the following.

2006
Feb   4 Sold goods, $900, on credit to J Ukata
Mar 1 J Ukata paid his account by cheque after deducting the cash discount to which he was entitled
          He purchased further goods, $80, on credit
Dec 31 Received cash, $35, from W Blanco whose debt had been written off in June 2005

2007
Jan 31 As J Ukata could not be found his account was written off
          James Kanu increased the provision for doubtful debts by $50

Required

(c) Write up the following accounts in James Kanu's ledger for the year ended 31 January 2007.
   (i) J Ukata account
  (ii) Bad debts account
 (iii) Bad debts recovered account
 (iv) Provision for doubtful debts account

(d) Assuming that James Kanu did **not** maintain a provision for doubtful debts, state how **each** of the following would be affected.

Where the item is not affected write "No effect". Where the item is affected insert the amount by which it is overstated or understated.

The first has been completed as an example.

Item	Overstated $	Understated $
(i) Gross profit for the year ended 31 January 2007	No effect	No effect
(ii) Net profit for the year ended 31 January 2007	....	....
(iii) Total of current assets in balance sheet at 31 January 2007	....	....

[IGCSE 2007]

5. The following trial balance was extracted from the books of Amir Sadiq at 31 March 2003.

	$	$
Capital		33 000
Drawings	2 500	
Buildings at cost	20 000	
Fixtures and equipment at valuation	3 400	
Motor vehicles at cost	8 000	
Provision for depreciation of motor vehicles		3 250
Provision for doubtful debts		200
Trade receivables	7 500	
Trade payables		6 700
Bank overdraft		2 880
Motor vehicle expenses	1 240	
General expenses	2 030	
Wages	11 940	
Insurance	1 470	
Carriage inwards	700	
Discount received		250
Revenue (sales)		92 100
Purchases	68 500	
Sales returns	1 200	
Inventory 1 April 2002	9 900	
	138 380	138 380

Additional information

1 At 31 March 2003: Inventory was valued at $10 200
Wages outstanding amounted to $1080
Insurance prepaid amounted to $210.

Bad Debts and Provisions for Doubtful Debts

2 During the year ended 31 March 2003 Amir took goods costing $300 for his own use. No entries had been made in the accounting records.
3 The provision for doubtful debts is to be maintained at 2% of the trade receivables.
4 Motor vehicles are to be depreciated at 20% per annum using the reducing balance method.
5 Fixtures and equipment were valued at $2800 on 31 March 2003. No fixtures and equipment were bought or sold during the year.

Required

(a) Prepare the income statement of Amir Sadiq for the year ended 31 March 2003.
(b) Prepare the balance sheet of Amir Sadiq at 31 March 2003.
(c) (i) Explain what is meant by the going concern principle.
    (ii) State the basis on which inventory should be valued when the going concern principle is applied.

[Based on IGCSE 2003]

6. Morag MacDonald provides a range of business services for small retail organisations. Her financial year ends on 31 December. She provided the following information for the year ended 31 December 2008.

	$
Fees from clients	75 050
Property tax paid	1 800
Repairs and maintenance	2 930
Rent received from tenant	2 750
Wages	45 000
Stationery and office supplies	1 790
Insurance	1 680

Additional information
1 On 31 December 2008:

	$
Fees due from clients	9 000
Wages owing	2 000

Insurance prepaid							240
Inventory of stationery and office supplies							35
Rent prepaid by tenant							150

2 Office equipment is depreciated using the reducing balance method at 50% per annum.
   On 1 January 2008 the office equipment account had a balance of $10 800 and the provision for depreciation of office equipment account had a balance of $8100.
3 A provision for doubtful debts is maintained at 2 ½ % of the fees due from clients at the end of each financial year.
   On 1 January 2008 the provision for doubtful debts amounted to $250.

Prepare the income statement of Morag MacDonald for the year ended 31 December 2008.

[IGCSE 2009]

7. Miriam Rajah is a trader. Her financial year ends on 31 January. Miriam employs a bookkeeper to maintain her financial records.
The following account appears in Miriam Rajah's ledger:

Provision for doubtful debts account

Date	Details	Folio	$	Date	Details	Folio	$
2008				2007			
Jan 31	Income statement		50	Feb 1	Balance	b/d	650
	Balance	c/d	600				
			650				650
				2008			
				Feb 1	Balance	b/d	600

(a) State **one** reason why Miriam Rajah should maintain a provision for doubtful debts.
(b) (i) Explain the following entries in the provision for doubtful debts account as it appears in Miriam Rajah's ledger.
      2007 February 1 Balance
      2008 January 31 Income statement
   (ii) Explain the significance of the $600 shown at the end of the account.
[IGCSE 2008]

Chapter 14 Bank Reconciliation Statements

In this chapter you will learn to:
- understand the purpose of bank reconciliation
- understand why the bank account may not agree with the bank statement
- understand the stages of bank reconciliation
- update the cash book
- prepare a bank reconciliation statement
- understand the advantages of bank reconciliation.

Introduction

A bank will send a statement at regular intervals to its customers detailing the transactions that have taken place during the period covered by the statement and showing the bank balance at the end of the period. This is similar to the **statement of account** issued by its suppliers to the customers who have purchased goods on credit.

A bank statement is a copy of the customer's account in the books of the bank. This is a record of transactions as they affect the bank. When money is paid into the bank the customer's account will be credited as this is the amount owed by the bank to the customer and when money is taken out of the bank, the customer's account will be debited as this reduces the amount owed by the bank to the customer. A positive bank balance will appear as a credit balance and an overdrawn balance as a debit balance.

When the entries on a bank statement are compared to those in the bank account in the cash book it will be found that they are recorded on opposite sides of the account. The bank account is a record of transactions as they affect the business. Money paid into the bank is debited (the bank is a debtor for this amount) and money withdrawn from the bank is credited (the bank is a creditor for this amount).

It is important to compare the bank statement and the bank account in the cash book. If the two balances disagree, it is necessary to **reconcile** them to explain why the differences have arisen.

> **Test your understanding**
> 1. State why bank reconciliation should be carried out.
> 2. Explain why money paid into the bank appears on the debit of the bank account but on the credit of the bank statement.

Reasons why the Bank Account and the Bank Statement may Differ

Differences between the two records usually occur because of:
- The different times at which the same items are recorded
- The business not recording certain items in the cash book

Timing Differences

These are usually due to:
1. **Cheques not yet presented**
   These are cheques that have been paid by the business and entered on the credit of the cash book, but which do not appear on the bank statement. This may be because the payee has not paid the cheque into his bank or because the cheque is still in the banking system and has not yet been deducted from the business's account.
2. **Amounts not yet credited**
   These are cash and cheques that have been paid into the bank and entered on the debit side of the cash book, but which do not appear on the bank statement. It usually takes a few days before the money paid into the bank is recorded in the customer's account.

Items not recorded in the cash book

It often happens that the business does not record certain items until the bank statement is received. These include:

Bank Reconciliation Statements

1. **Bank charges and bank interest**
   The bank may deduct an amount from the customer's account to cover the cost of running the account and for any interest charged on overdrafts and loans.
2. **Dishonoured cheques**
   A cheque paid into the bank may be returned because the drawer did not have sufficient funds in the account (this has been already explained in Chapter 4).
3. **Amounts paid directly into the bank**
   These are **credit transfers, standing orders** and **direct debits** where a person has instructed their bank to pay an amount of money directly into the bank account of the business.
4. **Amounts paid directly by the bank to others**
   These include credit transfers, standing orders and direct debits which the business has instructed the bank to pay directly from the account of the business.

Any other differences between the two records must be investigated. **Errors made by the business** should be corrected and **errors made by the bank** should be notified to the bank.

The differences between the bank account in the cash book and the bank statement are summarised as follows:

Items in cash book not in bank statement	Items in bank statement but not in cash book
Cheques not yet presented Amounts not yet credited Errors in cash book	Bank charges and bank interest Dishonoured cheques Standing orders Credit transfers Direct debits Errors on bank statement

Test your understanding
1. Explain the term "cheque not yet presented".
2. Explain the term "dishonoured cheque".
3. Give an example of an expense which may be paid by standing order.

Stages of Bank Reconciliation

1. Compare the bank account in the cash book with the bank statement

The debit side of the bank account should be compared with the credit side of the bank statement and the credit side of the bank account compared with the debit side of the bank statement. Put a tick (✓) against those items which appear in both records.

2. Update the cash book

Enter in the cash book any items which appear on the bank statement but which have not yet been entered in the cash book.
- (a) Items debited on the bank statement (e.g. bank charges, credit transfers paid by the bank etc.) should be credited to the bank account in the cash book.
- (b) Items credited on the bank statement (e.g. credit transfers and direct debits paid into the bank) should be debited to the bank account in the cash book.

3. Correct any errors in the cash book.

4. Balance the cash book and carry down the balance

This balance is the correct bank balance. If it is the end of the financial year, this is the balance which should appear in the balance sheet.

5. Prepare a bank reconciliation statement

This should show why the balance on the up-dated cash book does not agree with the balance shown on the bank statement.
- (a) Start with the balance shown on the bank statement.
- (b) Add any items which appear on the debit side of the cash book but which do not appear on the bank statement (e.g. amounts not yet credited).
- (c) Deduct any items which appear on the credit side of the cash book but which do not appear on the bank statement (e.g. cheques not yet presented).

Bank Reconciliation Statements

(d) Make any adjustments for bank errors by adding amounts debited in error by the bank and deducting amounts credited in error by the bank.

(e) The total of this calculation should equal to the updated bank balance in the cash book.

It is possible to start the bank reconciliation statement with the updated bank account balance. In this case, it is necessary to reverse the items (b), (c) and (d) listed above.

A bank reconciliation statement does not form part of the double entry records of the business. It is a statement which shows that, on a certain date, the bank account and the bank statement balances were reconciled.

Example 14.1

The bank columns of Fatima's cash book for the month of April 20-8 are given below.

Cash Book (Bank columns only)

Date	Details	Folio	$	Date	Details	Folio	$
20-8				20-8			
April 1	Balance		2970	April 10	Purchases		234
14	J Dhatwani		420	19	B Malukani		110
26	ABC Stores		217	29	TeeDee Co.		1372
28	Sales		1460	30	Dobhal Ltd.		517
					Balance	c/d	2834
			5067				5067
20-8							
May 1	Balance	b/d	2834				

Fatima's bank statement for the month of April 20-8 is given below.

REGIONAL BANK LTD
West District

Account: Fatima Goyal

Account No: 987654
Date: 30 April 20-8

Date	Details	Debit	Credit	Balance
20-8		$	$	$
April 1	Balance			2970 Cr
13	Cheque No 2388	243		2727 Cr
19	Credit No 6983		420	3147 Cr
20	Credit Transfer (Dividend)		150	3297 Cr
24	Cheque No 2389	110		3187 Cr
30	Bank charges	95		3092 Cr

It is discovered that Fatima has made an error on 10 April and recorded purchases as $234, when the correct figure was $243.

(a) Make any additional entries that are required in Fatima's cash book. Balance the bank account and bring down the balance on 1 May 20-8.

(b) Prepare a bank reconciliation statement at 30 April 20-8.

The first thing to do is to compare the entries in the cash book with those on the bank statement. Place a tick (✓) against the items appearing in both the records.

The cash book and the bank statement should now look like this:

Cash Book (Bank columns only)

Date	Details	Folio	$	Date	Details	Folio	$
20-8				20-8			
April 1	Balance		✓ 2970	April 10	Purchases		234
14	J Dhatwani		✓ 420	19	B Malukani		✓ 110
26	ABC Stores		217	29	TeeDee Co.		1372
28	Sales		1460	30	Dobhal Ltd.		517
					Balance	c/d	2834
			5067				5067
20-8							
May 1	Balance	b/d	2834				

Bank Reconciliation Statements

REGIONAL BANK LTD
West District

Account: Fatima Goyal   **Account No**: 987654
                                              Date: 30 April 20-8

Date	Details	Debit	Credit	Balance
		$	$	$
20-8				
April 1	Balance			2970 Cr ✓
13	Cheque No 2388	243		2727 Cr
19	Credit No 6983		420 ✓	3147 Cr
20	Credit Transfer (Dividend)		150	3297 Cr
24	Cheque No 2389	110 ✓		3187 Cr
30	Bank charges	95		3092 Cr

It is now possible to up-date the bank account in the cash book. Firstly, the error on 10 April must be corrected. Items appearing in the debit column of the bank statement which have not been ticked off (excluding 13 April which has now been corrected in the bank account) must be credited in the bank account. Items appearing in the credit column of the bank statement which have not been ticked off must be debited in the bank account.

(a)

Cash Book (Bank columns only)

Date	Details	Folio	$	Date	Details	Folio	$
20-8				20-8			
May 1	Balance		2834	May 1	Correction		
	Dividend		150		of error		9
					Bank charges		95
					Balance	c/d	2880
			2984				2984
20-8							
May 1	Balance	b/d	2880				

The bank reconciliation statement can now be prepared.

(b)

Fatima
Bank Reconciliation Statement at 30 April 20-8

	$	$
Balance shown on bank statement		3092
Add Amounts not yet credited – ABC Stores	217	
Sales	1460	1677
		4769
Less Cheques not yet presented – TeeDee Co.	1372	
Dobhal Ltd.	517	1889
Balance shown in cash book		2880

It is important to remember that the bank columns are actually part of the main three column cash book – not a separate ledger account. Examination questions usually avoid giving an extract from a complete cash book to avoid presenting candidates with a large amount of details which are not necessary to complete the bank reconciliation.

> **Test your understanding**
> 1. On 31 May a trader's bank account showed a debit balance of $250. On the same day his bank statement showed a credit balance of $198. The cash book was up-dated and the new balance was $141.
> In the trader's balance sheet on 31 May:
> (a) Under what heading will bank be shown?
> (b) What amount will be entered for bank?

Bank Reconciliation when there is a Bank Overdraft

Example 14.1 showed how to up-date the cash book and prepare a bank reconciliation statement when there is a positive bank balance. Exactly same principles are followed when there is a bank overdraft. In this case, it is important to take great care with the arithmetic calculations and it is helpful to place brackets around overdrawn amounts. A bank overdraft will appear as a credit balance in the bank account in the cash book of the business and as a debit balance on the bank statement.

Bank Reconciliation Statements

215

Example 14.2

On 31 July 20-8 the bank account in Fatima's cash book showed an overdrawn balance of $1121. On the same date her bank statement showed a debit balance of $1091.

When comparing the cash book and the bank statement it was found that the following items appeared only in the cash book:
1. A cheque paid to PJ Motors for $163 on 29 July
2. Cash sales amounting to $1010 paid into the bank on 31 July.

The following items appeared only on the bank statement and not in the cash book:
1. Rent received paid directly into the bank $190
2. Bank charges of $213
3. A credit balance on 1 July was shown as $2100 instead of $1200.

(a) Make any additional entries that are required in Fatima's cash book. Balance the bank account and bring down the balance on 1 May 20-8.

(b) Prepare a bank reconciliation statement at 31 July 20-8.

The comparison of the cash book with the bank statement has already been completed and the differences are shown above, so it is possible to start with the updating of the cash book.

(a)

Cash Book (Bank columns only)

Date	Details	Folio	$	Date	Details	Folio	$
20-8				20-8			
Aug 1	Rent received		190	Aug 1	Balance	b/d	1121
	Balance	c/d	1144		Bank charges		213
			1334				1334
				20-8			
				Aug 1	Balance	b/d	1144

(b)

Fatima
Bank Reconciliation Statement at 31 July 20-8

	$
Balance shown on bank statement	(1091)
Add Amounts not yet credited – Sales	1010
	(81)
Less Cheques not yet presented – PJ Motors	163
	(244)
Less Bank error	900
Balance shown in cash book	(1144)

Advantages of Bank Reconciliation

There are several advantages of reconciling the balance on the bank statement with that shown on the bank account in the cash book. These are:

1. After up-dating the bank account an accurate bank balance is available.
2. Errors in the bank account or on the bank statement can be identified.
3. Assists in discovering fraud and embezzlement.
4. Amounts not credited by the bank can be identified.
5. Cheques not yet presented can be identified.
6. Any "stale" cheques (these are usually those which are over 6 months old, which will not be met by the bank) can be identified and written back into the bank account.

POINTS TO REMEMBER

1. The purpose of bank reconciliation is to explain the differences between the bank balance shown in the cash book and the balance on the bank statement.
2. Most of the differences between the balances are caused by differences in the time at which items are recorded and because

Bank Reconciliation Statements

some items cannot be recorded in the cash book until the bank statement is received.
3. The cash book should be updated by entering those items which appear on the bank statement but not in the cash book.
4. The bank reconciliation statement shows the balance on the bank statement adjusted for amounts not yet credited, cheques not yet presented and any bank errors. The final figure should agree with the balance shown in the bank account in the cash book.

Review Questions

1. Tarek Wahid is a sole trader who keeps full double entry records including a three column cash book.
   On 1 April 2006 his cash book showed the following debit balances:

	$
Cash	125
Bank	6750

   Tarek's transactions for the month of April 2006 included the following:

   April 5 Cheque for $230, received from Asmaa El Zein in March, was dishonoured by the bank

   10 Received a cheque from Mohammed Riyas in settlement of his account of $480, after deducting cash discount of 2 ½%

   16 Paid cheques totalling $9980 for a new motor vehicle costing $9900, and repairs to existing motor vehicle costing $80

   24 Paid Salma Abbas a cheque for $546 to settle the amount due after deducting cash discount of $14

   29 Cash sales amounted to $2150

   30 Paid all the cash into the bank except for $100

Required

(a) Enter the above transactions in Tarek Wahid's cash book. Balance the cash book at 30 April and bring down the balances on 1 May 2006.

On 30 April 2006 Tarek Wahid obtained a statement from his bank and compared it with the bank column in his cash book.

The bank balance shown in the cash book differed from that shown on the bank statement because:

1 the cheque paid to Salma Abbas had not yet been presented for payment
2 the cash paid into the bank had not yet been credited to Tarek's account

Required

(b) Explain why items are recorded on the opposite side of the cash book to that on which they appear on the bank statement.
(c) Prepare a statement to calculate the balance which should have appeared on the bank statement on 30 April 2006.
(d) State the bank balance that should be shown in the balance sheet of Tarek Wahid at 30 April 2006. State whether it is an asset or a liability.

[IGCSE 2006]

*2. On 31 January 2003 Mary, a trader, obtained a statement from her bank and compared it with the bank account in her cash book.

The bank balance shown in the cash book was an overdraft of $1780. This differed from the balance shown on the bank statement because:

1. a cheque for $270 payable to David had not yet been presented for payment
2. cash paid into the bank amounting to $800 had not yet been credited to Mary's account.

Prepare a bank reconciliation statement to show the balance which appeared on the bank statement on 31 January 2003.

[IGCSE 2003]

*3. (a) (i) State two items of information given in a bank statement.

Bank Reconciliation Statements

(ii) Give **two** reasons for drawing up a bank reconciliation statement.

On 31 October 2000 the cash book (bank columns) and bank statement of Sara Perez were as follows.

Cash Book (bank columns)

			$				$
Oct 24	Balance	b/d	5203	Oct 27	Paris Fashions		2069
25	Fine Fabrics		242	28	Thai Exports		240
26	Super Satins		1150	31	Balance	c/d	5264
30	Sales		1078				
			7573				7573
Nov 1	Balance	b/d	5264				

Bank Statement 31 October 2000

		Dr	Cr	Balance
		$	$	$
Oct 24	Balance			5203 Cr
25	Fine Fabrics		242	5445
	Super Satins		1150	6595
27	Cheque 185673	2069		4526
	S.O. Motor insurance	26		4500
28	S.O. Rent	25		4475
31	Bank charges	88		4387
	Dishonoured cheque (Fine Fabrics)	242		4145

The following errors were discovered.
1. The debit side of the bank column in the cash book had been undercast.
2. The bank had debited a standing order for payment of rent for $25 to Sara's business account instead of her personal account.

(b) Make any additional entries that are required in the cash book of Sara Perez. Calculate a new bank balance at 31 October 2000. Bring down the balance on 1 November 2000.
(c) Prepare a bank reconciliation statement at 31 October 2000.
(d) State the bank balance that should be shown in the balance sheet of Sara Perez at 31 October 2000. State whether it is an asset or a liability.

[IGCSE 2000]

4. The balance shown in the bank column in Zafira's cash book at 30 April 2005 was $620 debit.
   She compares her cash book with the bank statement at 30 April. She finds the following items were included on the bank statement but are not yet in the cash book.

	$
Bank charges	15
Direct debit paid for insurance	40
Bank interest received	20
Bank (credit) transfer from customer, Aisha	130
Dishonoured cheque, Yanni	65

   ### Required

   (a) Write up the cash book at 30 April 2005 and bring down the updated balance.

   At 30 April 2005 Zafira discovers the following:
   1. she has recorded a receipt in her cash book of $310 but has not yet deposited the money at the bank.
   2. she has written a cheque for $250 and entered it in the cash book but it has not yet been paid by the bank.

   ### Required

   (b) Prepare the bank reconciliation statement at 30 April 2005.
   Zafira's bank statement shows a balance which is different from the bank reconciliation statement.

   ### Required

   (c) Suggest **two possible errors** which may have caused this difference.

   [IGCSE 2005]

5. Jane Sharma is a trader. Her financial year ends on 30 April.
   The bank columns of her cash book for the month of April 2008 were as follows:

Bank Reconciliation Statements

Cash Book (bank columns only)

2008			$	2008			$
April 1	Balance	b/d	2210	April 9	Mashatu Stores		436
12	Lobatse Traders		314	16	General expenses		125
30	Cash		500	28	Ghanzi & Co		390
				30	Balance	c/d	2073
			3024				3024
May 1	Balance	b/d	2073				

Jane Sharma's business bank statement for April 2008 was as follows:

Bank Statement at 30 April 2008

Date 2008	Details	Debit $	Credit $	Balance $
April 1	Balance		2120	2120 Cr
10	AB Insurance	360		1760
11	Dividend (credit transfer)		62	1822
17	Mashatu Stores	436		1386
18	Lobatse Traders		314	1700
21	General expenses	125		1575
29	Lobatse Traders (dishonoured)	314		1261
30	Bank charges	11		1250

The following errors were discovered:
1. The cash book balance brought forward on 1 April should have been $2120.
2. The bank had credited dividend received, $62, to Jane Sharma's business account instead of her personal account.

Required
(a) State **two** reasons, other than finding errors, why Jane Sharma should reconcile her cash book with the statement received from the bank.
(b) Update Jane Sharma's cash book. Bring down the updated cash book balance on 1 May 2008.
(c) Prepare a bank reconciliation statement for Jane Sharma at 30 April 2008.
(d) State the bank balance that should be shown in the balance sheet of Jane Sharma at 30 April 2008. State whether it is an asset or a liability.

[IGCSE 2008]

Chapter 15 — Journal Entries and Correction of Errors

In this chapter you will learn to:
- understand the use of the journal as a book of prime entry
- prepare journal entries
- correct errors using journal entries and suspense accounts
- calculate the effect of correcting errors on the profit or loss
- demonstrate the effect of correcting errors on the balance sheet.

Introduction

Chapter 7 explained how all transactions are recorded in a book of prime entry (book of original entry) *before* they are entered in the ledger. It also described how sales and purchases on credit, and sales and purchases returns are entered in the sales, purchases and returns journals before being posted to the ledger. Chapters 4 and 5 explained how transactions involving cash or cheques etc. are entered in the cash book and the petty cash book before being posted to the ledger. There is one other book of prime entry which is known as the **journal** or **general journal**.

The journal is not a part of the double entry bookkeeping. It is regarded as a diary in which transactions are noted before they are entered in the ledger. **Anything which is not entered in one of the books of prime entry must be entered in the journal before being recorded in the ledger**.

A journal entry shows:

    The date of the transaction
    The name of the account to be debited and the amount
    The name of the account to be credited and the amount
    A narrative

Journal Entries and Correction of Errors

The narrative consists of a brief explanation of what is being recorded and why the entry is being made. This is useful because it is impossible to remember the reason for every entry and the entries in the journal sometimes involve "out of the ordinary" transactions.

The layout of the journal is as follows:

Journal

Date	Details	Folio	Debit $	Credit $

The items usually recorded in the journal are:
- Opening entries
- Purchase and sale of fixed assets
- Non-regular transactions such as year-end transfers
- Correction of errors

Opening Journal Entries

As the name suggests, these entries are made when the business starts (or when the business first keeps accounting records). An opening journal entry lists the assets owned by the business (shown in the debit column), the liabilities owed by the business (shown in the credit column) and the capital of the business (also shown in the credit column).

After the journal entry has been prepared, the items are posted to the appropriate ledger accounts.

Example 15.1

Chandra started business on 1 November 20-4. He did not maintain any accounting records during his first year of trading.

On 1 November 20-5 he was able to provide the following information about his business:

Assets   premises $56 000, fixtures $19 400, motor vehicle $12 500, inventory $3100, trade receivables $4700, cash $200
Liabilities   trade payables $5600, bank overdraft $2300.

Prepare an opening journal entry for Chandra at 1 November 20-5.

Chandra
Journal

Date	Details	Folio	Debit $	Credit $
20-5 Nov 1	Premises		56 000	
	Fixtures		19 400	
	Motor vehicle		12 500	
	Inventory		3 100	
	Trade receivables		4 700	
	Cash		200	
	Trade payables			5 600
	Bank			2 300
	Capital			88 000
			95 900	95 900
	Assets, liabilities and capital to open the books			

- It is usual to show the debit entries first.
- It is usual to slightly indent the credit entries.
- It is usual to draw a line after each separate journal entry.
- The capital was inserted as the difference between the assets and the liabilities.
- The items would be posted to the appropriate ledger accounts from this journal entry, the assets being debited and the liabilities and capital being credited. The folio number column would be completed to indicate that the posting had been completed.
- No names and amounts of individual debtors and creditors were provided in this question. In practice, these will be known and an account opened for each individual debtor and creditor.

Journal Entries and Correction of Errors

> **Test your understanding**
> 1. Name **three** transactions for which a journal entry would be made.
> 2. In connection with a journal entry:
>   (a) explain the meaning of a narrative
>   (b) explain why a narrative is necessary.

Purchase and Sale of Non-current Assets

As the purchase and sale of non-current assets are not recorded in one of the other books of prime entry they should be entered in the journal before being posted to the ledger.

After the journal entry has been completed, the transaction is posted to the appropriate ledger accounts.

Example 15.2

Chandra's financial year ends on 31 October.
Prepare the journal entries to record the following transactions on 1 September 20-6.

> Purchased additional fixtures, $1300, on credit from Office Supplies
> Sold the motor vehicle (cost $12 500) for $7400 on credit to Used Vehicles Ltd.

Chandra
Journal

Date	Details	Folio	Debit $	Credit $
20-6 Sept 1	Fixtures 　　Office Supplies Purchase of fixtures on credit		1 300	1 300
	Disposal of motor vehicle 　　Motor vehicles Used Vehicles Ltd. 　　Disposal of motor vehicle Transfer of motor vehicle to disposal account and sale of motor on credit		12 500 7 400	 12 500 7 400

Cont.

Cont.

Oct 31	Income statement	5 100	
	Disposal of motor vehicle		5 100
	Loss on disposal transferred to profit and loss		

Non-Regular Transactions

As explained earlier, any transactions which cannot be recorded in another book of prime entry are recorded in the journal. These often consist of transactions which are not occurring regularly and year-end transfers to the income statement. The transaction is posted to the appropriate ledger accounts after the journal entry is completed.

Example 15.3

Chandra's financial year ends on 31 October. Prepare journal entries to record the following.

On 30 September 20-6 he wrote off $50 owing by Ansari Stores as a bad debt.

At 31 October 20-6 Chandra's ledger accounts include the following –

    Purchases for the year $39 000
    Bad debts for the year $190
    Insurance $1500, which includes a prepayment of $300
    Inventory at 1 November 20-5 $3100.

On 31 October 20-6:

    Inventory was valued at $3900.
    Fixtures are to be depreciated by $2070
    A provision for doubtful debts is to be created of $250.

Journal Entries and Correction of Errors

Chandra
Journal

Date	Details	Folio	Debit $	Credit $
20-6 Sept 30	Bad debts Ansari Stores Writing off bad debt		50	50
Oct 31	Income statement Purchases Transfer of purchases for the year to the income statement		39 000	39 000
	Income statement Bad debts Transfer of total bad debts written off to the income statement		190	190
	Income statement Insurance Transfer of insurance for the year to the income statement		1 200	1 200
	Income statement Inventory Transfer of opening inventory to the income statement		3 100	3 100
	Inventory Income statement Transfer of closing inventory to the income statement		3 900	3 900
	Income statement Provision for depreciation of fixtures Annual depreciation charge transferred to the income statement		2070	2070
	Income statement Provision for doubtful debts Creation of provision for doubtful debts		250	250

> **Test your understanding**
> 1. Prepare a journal entry to record **each** of the following transactions.
>   (a) Goods costing $200 taken by the business owner for personal use.
>   (b) Drawings, $5000, transferred from drawings account to capital account.
>   (c) The profit for the year, $15 000, transferred from the income statement to the capital account.

Correction of Errors

Errors made in the recording of the day-to-day transactions can be divided into those which are not revealed by the trial balance and those which result in the trial balance not balancing.

Errors which are not shown by a trial balance

Chapter 3 explained the six errors which can be made which will not be revealed by the trial balance. These are:

Error of commission
Error or complete reversal
Error of omission
Error of original entry
Error of principle
Compensating errors

When such errors are discovered, they should be corrected by means of a journal entry before making entries in the appropriate ledger accounts.

Students often find it is useful to prepare working notes in the form of ledger accounts before attempting an examination question which requires complex journal entries.

Example 15.4

Chandra's financial year ends on 31 October.
The totals of the trial balance prepared on 31 October 20-7 agreed, but the following errors were later discovered.

Journal Entries and Correction of Errors

(a) The purchase of stationery, $30, had been debited to the purchases account.
(b) A cheque, $500, received from K Singh had been credited to the account of H Singh.
(c) The wages account had been under-cast by $100 and the purchases account had been over-cast by $100.

Prepare the necessary journal entries to correct these errors.

Chandra
Journal

	Date	Details	Folio	Debit $	Credit $
(a)	20-7 Oct 31	Stationery Purchases Error in posting stationery to purchases now corrected		30	30
(b)		H Singh K Singh Error in posting cheque to wrong personal account now corrected		500	500
(c)		Wages Purchases Wages under-cast and purchases over-cast, now corrected		100	100

Errors which affect a trial balance

Chapter 3 explained the types of errors which may occur that result in the totals of the trial balance not balancing. A check list was also provided for locating errors.

If the errors are not found immediately, the trial balance is balanced by inserting the difference between the two sides in a **suspense account**. This is regarded as a temporary account in which the difference on the trial balance is held until the errors are discovered. As the errors are found, they are corrected by means of a journal entry. The appropriate entries are then made in the ledger accounts. When all the errors have been found and corrected, the suspense account will close automatically.

Once a suspense account is opened, draft financial statements can be prepared even if all the errors have not been discovered. In this case, the balance on the suspense account will appear in the balance sheet (as an asset if it is a debit balance and as a liability if it is a credit balance).

Example 15.5

Chandra's financial year ends on 31 October.

The totals of the trial balance prepared on 31 October 20-8 failed to agree. The difference of $260 was a shortage on the debit side. This was entered in a suspense account.

The following errors were later discovered.
(a) The purchases account had been over-cast by $110.
(b) No entry had been made for office expenses, $20, paid in cash.
(c) Credit sales, $630, to Anil had been correctly entered in the sales account but debited as $360 in Anil's account.
(d) Capital introduced by Chandra, $5000 (paid into the bank), has been debited to the capital account and credited to the bank account
(e) A cheque, $200, received from a debtor, Yuvraj, has been correctly entered in the bank account, but no other entry has been made.
(f) Sales returns, $150, have been correctly entered in the debtor's account but have been credited to the purchases returns account.

Prepare the necessary journal entries to correct these errors.
Write up the suspense account in Chandra's ledger.

Journal Entries and Correction of Errors

Chandra
Journal

	Date	Details	Folio	Debit $	Credit $
(a)	20-8 Oct 31	Suspense Purchases Purchases over-cast, now corrected		110	110
(b)		Office expenses Cash Omission of cash paid for office expenses, now corrected		20	20
(c)		Anil Suspense Sales, $630, incorrectly entered in Anil's account as $360, now corrected		270	270
(d)		Bank Capital Capital introduced debited to capital and credited to bank, now corrected		10 000	10 000
(e)		Suspense Yuvraj Cheque received from Yuvraj entered only in the bank, now corrected		200	200
(f)		Sales returns Purchases returns Suspense Sales returns incorrectly credited to purchases returns, now corrected		150 150	300

231

Chandra
Nominal Ledger
Suspense account

Date	Details	Folio	$	Date	Details	Folio	$
20-8				20-8			
Oct 31	Difference on trial balance		260	Oct 31	Anil		270
	Purchases		110		Sales returns		150
	Yuvraj		200		Purchases returns		150
			570				570

- An entry was required in the suspense account to correct errors (a), (c), (e) and (f) as all these affected the balancing of the trial balance.
- No entry was required in the suspense account to correct errors (b) and (d) as these did not affect the balancing of the trial balance.
- Error (f) required two accounts to be debited – the sales returns and the purchases returns – with the corresponding credits in the suspense account in order to correct the error.
- Where an entry has been reversed (as in error (d)) it is necessary to double the amount of the error in order to correct it and to restore the accounts to the correct amount.

> **Test your understanding**
> 1. Explain when it is necessary to open a suspense account.
> 2. It is found that machinery repairs have been debited to the machinery account. Explain:
>   (a) the type of error that has been made.
>   (b) whether a correcting entry is required in the suspense account, give reason.

Effect on Profit of Correcting Errors

If errors are discovered after the income statement has been prepared, it may be necessary to amend the figure of profit. Any corrections made to items appearing in the trading account section of the income statement will affect both the gross profit and the net profit. Any corrections made to items appearing in the profit and loss account section of the income statement will affect the net profit.

Journal Entries and Correction of Errors

Example 15.6

Chandra's financial year ends on 31 October.

The totals of the trial balance prepared on 31 October 20-8 failed to agree. The difference was entered in a suspense account and draft financial statements were prepared. The net profit was $15 000.

The following errors were later discovered.

(a) The purchases account had been over-cast by $110.
(b) No entry had been made for office expenses, $20, paid in cash.
(c) Credit sales, $630, to Anil had been correctly entered in the sales account but debited as $360 in Anil's account.
(d) Capital introduced by Chandra, $5000 (paid into the bank), has been debited to the capital account and credited to the bank account.
(e) A cheque, $200, received from a debtor, Yuvraj, has been correctly entered in the bank account, but no other entry has been made.
(f) Sales returns, $150, have been correctly entered in the debtor's account but have been credited to the purchases returns account.

Prepare a statement to show the corrected profit for the year ended 31 October 20-8.

Chandra
Statement of corrected profit for the year ended 31 October 20-8

	$	$
Profit for the year from income statement		15 000
Add Purchases over-cast		110
		15 110
Less Office expenses omitted	20	
Sales returns understated	150	
Purchases returns overstated	150	320
Corrected profit for the year		14 790

- Errors (c), (d) and (e) do not affect the calculation of the profit.
- If the purchases are over-cast, the profit will be understated and therefore $110 must be added.
- If expenses have been omitted, the profit will be overstated and therefore $20 must be deducted.

- If the sales returns have been understated, the profit will be overstated and so $150 must be deducted.
- If the purchases returns have been overstated, the profit will also be overstated and therefore $150 must be deducted.

Effect on Balance Sheet of Correcting Errors

If errors are discovered and corrected after the preparation of financial statements, the balance sheet may have to be amended. If the profit for the year has been corrected this will affect the capital section of the balance sheet, but other items may also need to be amended.

Example 15.7

Chandra's financial year ends on 31 October.

The totals of the trial balance prepared on 31 October 20-8 failed to agree. The difference was entered in a suspense account and draft final accounts were prepared.

The following errors were later discovered.
(a) The purchases account had been over-cast by $110.
(b) No entry had been made for office expenses, $20, paid in cash.
(c) Credit sales, $630, to Anil had been correctly entered in the sales account but debited as $360 in Anil's account.
(d) Capital introduced by Chandra, $5000 (paid into the bank), has been debited to the capital account and credited to the bank account.
(e) A cheque, $200, received from a debtor, Yuvraj, has been correctly entered in the bank account, but no other entry has been made.
(f) Sales returns, $150, have been correctly entered in the debtor's account but have been credited to the purchases returns account.

The corrected profit for the year ended 31 October 20-8 was $14 790.

Explain how correcting **each** of the above errors will affect the balance sheet at 31 October 20-8.

Errors (a), (b), and (f) do not affect items within the balance sheet directly, but are used in the calculation of the corrected profit for the year. The profit which is added to the capital in the balance sheet will need to be amended to the correct figure of $14 790.

Journal Entries and Correction of Errors

To correct error (c) the figure for trade receivables in the current assets section of the balance sheet will have to be increased by $270.

To correct error (d) the capital figure will have to be increased by $10 000. The figure for bank in the current assets section of the balance sheet will also have to be increased by $10 000.

To correct error (e) the figure for trade receivables in the current assets section of the balance sheet will have to be reduced by $200.

> **Test your understanding**
> No entries have been made for goods, $500, sold on credit to Mitali.
> 1. State the type of error made.
> 2. State what correcting entries are required.
> 3. State the effects on the profit for the year after correcting this error.

Points to Remember

1. A journal can be regarded as a diary in which transactions are noted before they are entered in the ledger.
2. A narrative is a brief explanation of what is being recorded in the journal entry and why the entry is being made.
3. Journal entries are made to open the accounting records, to record the purchase and sale of non-current assets, to record non-regular transactions, and to correct errors.
4. A suspense account is opened if a trial balance fails to balance. This means that the draft financial statements can be prepared.
5. Errors affecting the balancing of the trial balance are corrected by making an entry in the suspense account.

Review Questions

1. Loretti started a business on 1 April 2006. On that day he introduced the following into the business:

   Inventory $12 000, office furniture $1500 and cash $2500, of which $200 was kept on hand for petty cash and the balance, $2300, was paid into a business bank account.

   On the same day his cousin, Hassan, paid $3000 into the business bank account as a loan to the business.

   Required

   (a) Show the opening journal entry to record these transactions. A narrative is not required.

   On 31 March 2007 Loretti's ledger included the following:
   - Purchases for the year $65 000
   - Sales returns for the year $2100

   On 31 March 2007 Loretti decided to:
   - Depreciate his office furniture by $150
   - Create a provision for doubtful debts of $320

   Required

   (b) Prepare journal entries to record the above year-end transfers to the income statement. Narratives should be shown.

   [Based on IGCSE 2006]

*2. (a) (i) In connection with journal entries, explain what is meant by the term 'narrative'.

   (ii) Explain why a narrative should be shown as part of a journal entry.

   (b) Ruth provides the following information.
   1. Ruth took goods costing $60 for her own use.
   2. An invoice was received from PJ Motors for $15 600. This included $600 for repairs to a motor vehicle, and $15 000 for the purchase of an additional motor vehicle.

Journal Entries and Correction of Errors

3. It was discovered that the purchase of stationery, $20, had been debited to the purchases account. This error should now be corrected.

Prepare the necessary journal entries to record the above. Narratives are required.

[IGCSE 2004]

3. (a) Give one reason for preparing a trial balance.

The following list of balances was taken from the books of Ismail Khan, a sole trader, on 30 April 2007.

	$
Revenue (sales)	125 000
Inventory	14 500
Purchases	76 000
Bank overdraft	2 300
Machinery	9 000
Trade receivables	1 700
Trade payables	2 800
Expenses	37 500
Capital	15 500
Drawings	8 000

(b) Prepare Ismail's trial balance at 30 April 2007. Include a suspense account to show any difference.

After the trial balance had been prepared, the following errors were found.
1. Cash sales of $2000 had been paid into the bank but had not been posted to the sales account.
2. Drawings of $900 had been correctly entered in the cash book but posted to the drawings account as $500.
3. The cash account of $500 has been omitted from the list of balances.

(c) Give the journal entries, with narratives, required to correct **each** error.
(d) State the balance on the suspense account after these journal entries have been posted to the ledger.

[IGCSE 2007]

*4. Maria Matsa's financial year ends on 30 September. The trial balance prepared on 30 September 2002 showed a shortage on the credit side of $788. Maria entered this in a suspense account and then prepared a draft income statement.

The following errors were later discovered.
1. $50 cash spent on stationery was entered in the cash book but not in the stationery account.
2. The sales journal was under-cast by $1000.
3. $240 received from Abdul Ahmed, a customer, had been credited to the account of Abdulla Ahmed, another customer, in the sales ledger.
4. The total of the discount received column in the cash book of $14 had been debited to the discount allowed account in the general ledger.
5. $95 cash paid to Joe Jones, a creditor, had been credited to his account in the purchases ledger.

(a) Prepare the entries in Maria Matsa's journal to correct the above errors. Narratives are **not** required.
(b) Prepare the suspense account in Maria Matsa's ledger to show the required amendments. Start with the balance arising from the difference on the trial balance.
(c) For **each** error 1–5 state how the draft profit for the year will be affected when the errors are corrected. If the error does not affect the draft profit for the year write 'no effect'. The first one has been completed as an example.

Error 1 Decrease by $50.
Error 2 ....
Error 3 ....
Error 4 ....
Error 5 ....

[IGCSE 2002]

5. On 1 July 2008 Michael Ong started to maintain a set of double entry records. A trial balance drawn up on 30 September 2008 failed to balance. Michael entered the difference on the trial balance in a suspense account.

Journal Entries and Correction of Errors

Required

(a) State **one** reason why it is necessary to open a suspense account when the totals of a trial balance fail to agree.

The following errors were later discovered:

1. Goods returned to J Chan, $20, had been incorrectly entered in the account of J Chua, another supplier.
2. A cheque for the sale of equipment, $400, had been debited to the bank account, but no other entry had been made.
3. Goods for Michael's own use, $100, had been debited to both the purchases account and the drawings account.
4. On 15 September 2008, $50 had been received from W Lee. This amount was incorrectly debited to the bad debts account and credited to W Lee's account. W Lee's account had been written off as a bad debt on 30 June 2008.

Required

(b) Complete the following table to show the entries required to correct the above errors.

The first one has been completed as an example.

	Account(s) to be debited	$	Account(s) to be credited	$
1	J Chan	20	J Chan	20
2	....	....	....	....
3	....	....	....	....
4	....	....	....	....

[IGCSE 2008]

6. (a) When is it necessary to open a suspense account?
   (b) On checking his sales ledger, a trader found the following errors had been made.
      1. Cash received from Tarek El Sayed was correctly entered in the cash book but had been credited to the account of Tarek El Sherif.
      2. A cheque received from Susan Zafar was correctly entered in the cash book but had been debited to Susan Zafar's account.

Only one of the above errors will require a correcting entry in the suspense account. State which one and give a reason for your answer.

(c) Mary Manake is a sole trader. She has very little knowledge of bookkeeping, but attempted to prepare a trial balance and a set of final accounts.

The balance sheet she prepared is shown as follows:

Balance Sheet at 30 April 2004

	$
Non-current assets at cost	40 000
Depreciation	8 000
	32 000
Inventory	8 500
Trade receivables	6 100
	46 600
Capital at 1 May 2003	34 000
Profit for the year	8 440
	42 440
Drawings	7 300
	35 140
Trade payables	5 200
Bank overdraft	2 010
	42 350
Suspense account (difference on trial balance)	4 250
	46 600

When the books were checked the following matters were discovered.

1. No adjustment has been made for expenses prepaid at 30 April 2004 amounting to $30.
2. The bank statement received on 30 April 2004 showed that the bank had debited the business's bank account with $70 for interest charged on the overdraft. No adjustment has been made for this in Mary Manake's books.
3. The total of the discount received column in the cash book, amounting to $150, has not been transferred to the discount

Journal Entries and Correction of Errors

received account in the ledger. Because of this, discount received does not appear in either the trial balance or the income statement.

4. Non-current assets costing $5000 had been sold during the year ended 30 April 2004. Depreciation of $500 had been provided up to the date of sale. The amount received for the assets, $4100, had been correctly entered in the cash book, but no other entries had been made.

Taking the above items into account, prepare a corrected balance sheet for Mary Manake at 30 April 2004.

The balance sheet should be shown using a suitable form of presentation, showing the different types of assets and liabilities, and the net current assets. The calculation of the corrected profit for the year should also be shown, either within the balance sheet, or as a separate calculation.

[IGCSE 2004]

7. Ahmed Shafik's financial year ends on 31 January. The totals of his trial balance on 31 January 2005 failed to agree. Ahmed entered the difference on the trial balance in a suspense account.

Required
(a) Explain why it is necessary to open a suspense account when the totals of a trial balance fail to agree.

The following errors were later discovered:
1. Commission received, $390, was entered in the cash book but not in the commission received account.
2. $400 paid to Mutua, a supplier, had been credited to the account of Mutola, another supplier.
3. The purchase of stationery, $20, was credited to the cash book and debited to the purchases account.
4. No entry had been made for cash discount, $215, allowed to Lima, a debtor, for prompt payment.
5. The total of the sales returns journal, $420, had been credited to the purchases returns account as $240.

Required

(b) Prepare entries in Ahmed's journal to correct the above errors. Narratives are **not** required

Before the errors were discovered Ahmed calculated that he had made a profit for the year of $16 000.

Required

(c) Prepare a statement to show the effect of correcting the errors 1-5 on Ahmed's original profit for the year and calculate the corrected profit.

If the error does not affect the original profit for the year write "No effect".

The first correction has been completed as an example.

Ahmed Shafik
Statement of corrected profit for the year ended 31 January 2005

	Effect on profit		$
Profit for the year before corrections			16 000
	−	+	
	$	$	
Error 1	390		
Error 2			
Error 3			
Error 4			
Error 5	___	___	
	___	___	___
Corrected profit for the year			___

[IGCSE 2005]

Chapter 16 Control Accounts

In this chapter you will learn to:
- understand the nature and purpose of control accounts
- identify and use the books of prime entry as sources of information for control accounts
- prepare a sales ledger control account
- prepare a purchases ledger control account.

Introduction

Control accounts are also known as **total accounts**. If the trial balance fails to balance and the error cannot be readily located, it is necessary to check all the accounting records. This can take a considerable amount of time. The checking process can be speeded up if a control account for the sales ledger (which contains the accounts of the debtors) and a control account for the purchases ledger (which contains the accounts of the creditors) have been prepared. These accounts act as a check on the individual accounts within these ledgers. Like the trial balance, however, these accounts can only check the arithmetical accuracy: errors such as omission and commission will not be revealed by a control account.

Advantages of Control Accounts

Where a full set of accounting records is maintained, it is usual to prepare a control account for the sales ledger and the purchases ledger. The advantages of preparing these accounts are as follows:
1. They can assist in locating errors when the trial balance fails to balance.
2. They are proof of the arithmetical accuracy of the ledgers they control.

3. The balances on these accounts are regarded as being equal to the total of the trade receivables and the total of the trade payables, so this information is available immediately.
4. Draft financial statements can be prepared quickly because of the balances provided by the control accounts.
5. They help to reduce fraud as the control accounts are prepared by someone who has not been involved in making the entries in those particular ledgers.
6. They provide a summary of the transactions affecting the debtors and creditors for each financial period.

> **Test your understanding**
> 1. Name the account which summarises all the sales ledger accounts.
> 2. Name the account which summarises all the purchases ledger accounts.
> 3. State **three** reasons for preparing control accounts.

Sales Ledger Control Account

This is also referred to as a **total trade receivables account**. This account resembles the account of a debtor, but instead of containing transactions concerned with just one person or business it contains transactions relating to *all* the debtors. A typical sales ledger control account appear as follows:

Nominal Ledger
Sales ledger control account

Date	Details	Folio	$	Date	Details	Folio	$
	Balance	b/d			Sales returns		
	Sales				Cash		
	Bank				Bank		
	(dishonoured cheque)				Discount allowed		
	Bank/Cash (refunds)				Bad debts		
	Interest charged				Balance	c/d	
	Balance	b/d					

Control Accounts

As this account acts as a check on the individual debtors' accounts, it should be prepared independently and information in the individual debtors' accounts must *not* be used. (An error in the sales ledger would not be revealed if the control account is prepared from the accounts in that ledger.) **The information to prepare a sales ledger control account is obtained from the books of prime entry**. The sources of information are summarised as follows:

Item	Source of information
Sales	Sales journal
Sales returns	Sales returns journal
Cash and cheques received from debtors	Cash book
Discounts allowed to debtors	Cash book
Dishonoured cheques	Cash book
Refunds to debtors	Cash book
Bad debts written off	Journal
Interest charged on overdue accounts	Journal

The sales ledger control account is drawn up at the end of the financial period (often monthly) and balanced. The total of the balances on all the individual debtor's accounts should agree with the balance on the control account. If they differ, it indicates that there is an error in one of the debtor's accounts or an error in the control account, so further checks are required.

Example 16.1

Shweta maintains a full set of accounting records and prepares control accounts at the end of each month.
    She provides the following information.

			$
20-8 March	1	Sales ledger control account balance	1200 debit
March	31	Totals for the month:	
		Sales journal	4890
		Sales returns journal	250
		Cheques received from debtors	3892
		Discount allowed to debtors	8
		Cash received from debtors	120
		Cash refunds to debtors	19
		Cheque received (included in the above figure) later dishonoured	80
		Bad debts written off	94

Prepare Shweta's sales ledger control account for the month of March 20-8.

Shweta
Nominal Ledger
Sales ledger control account

Date	Details	Folio	$	Date	Details	Folio	$
20-8				20-8			
Mar 1	Balance	b/d	1 200	Mar 31	Sales returns		250
31	Sales		4 890		Cash		120
	Bank				Bank		3 892
	(dishonoured cheque)		80		Discount allowed		8
	Cash				Bad debts		94
	(refunds)		19		Balance	c/d	1 825
			6 189				6 189
20-8							
Apl 1	Balance	b/d	1 825				

Purchases Ledger Control Account

This is also known as a **total trade payables account**. This account resembles the account of a creditor, but instead of containing transactions concerned with just one person or business it contains transactions relating to *all* the creditors. A typical purchases ledger control account appear as follows:

Control Accounts

Nominal Ledger
Purchases ledger control account

Date	Details	Folio	$	Date	Details	Folio	$
	Purchases returns				Balance	b/d	
	Cash				Purchases		
	Bank				Interest charged		
	Discount received				Bank/Cash (refunds)		
	Balance	c/d					
					Balance	b/d	

This account serves a similar purpose to the sales ledger control account. It acts as a check on the individual creditors' accounts and must be prepared independently and *not* from information in the individual creditors' accounts. **The information to prepare a purchases ledger control account is obtained from the books of prime entry.** The sources of information are summarised as follows:

Item	Source of information
Purchases	Purchases journal
Purchases returns	Purchases returns journal
Cash and cheques paid to creditors	Cash book
Discounts received from creditors	Cash book
Refunds from creditors	Cash book
Interest charged on overdue accounts	Journal

Like the sales ledger control account, the purchases ledger control account is drawn up at the end of the financial period (often monthly) and balanced. The total of the balances on all the individual creditor's accounts should agree with the balance on the control account. If they differ it indicates that there is an error in one of the creditor's accounts or the control account, so further checks are required.

Example 16.2

Shweta maintains a full set of accounting records and prepares control accounts at the end of each month.
She provides the following information.

			$
20-8 March	1	Purchases ledger control account balance	1880 credit
March	31	Totals for the month:	
		Purchases journal	4230
		Purchases returns journal	180
		Cheques paid to creditors	3900
		Discount received from creditors	104
		Cheque refunds from creditors	100
		Interest charged on overdue account	12

Prepare Shweta's purchases ledger control account for the month of March 20-8.

Shweta
Nominal Ledger
Purchases ledger control account

Date	Details	Folio	$	Date	Details	Folio	$
20-8				20-8			
Mar 31	Purchases returns		180	Mar 1	Balance		1 880
	Bank		3 900	31	Purchases		4 230
	Discount received		104		Bank (refunds)		100
	Balance	c/d	2 038		Interest charged		12
			6 222				6 222
				20-8			
				Apl 1	Balance	b/d	2 038

Test your understanding

1. Explain why the information used for preparing control accounts must be obtained from books of prime entry.
2. State the source of information for **each** of the following:
   (a) purchases returns
   (b) discount allowed
   (c) bad debts

Control Accounts

Balances on Both Sides of a Control Account

Occasionally a debtor's account may show a credit balance. This may occur due to the following factors:

- an overpayment by the debtor
- the debtor returning goods after paying the account
- the debtor paying in advance for the goods
- cash discount not being deducted before payment was made.

In the sales ledger control account it is usual to keep any credit balance separate from the debit balance. The control account will, therefore, have two balances—the usual debit balance representing money owing *by* debtors, and the more unusual credit balance representing money owing *to* debtors. Any credit balance is entered on the debit side of the control account and carried down as a credit balance. The account can then be balanced in the usual way.

Example 16.3

Shweta maintains a full set of accounting records and prepares control accounts at the end of each month.

She provides the following information.

				$
20-8	April	1	Sales ledger control account balance	1825 debit
	April	30	Totals for the month:	
			Sales journal	4910
			Sales returns journal	210
			Cheques received from debtors	4788
			Discount allowed to debtors	12
			Interest charged on overdue account	10
			Sales ledger credit balances	115

Prepare Shweta's sales ledger control account for the month of April 20-8.

Shweta
Nominal Ledger
Sales ledger control account

Date	Details	Folio	$	Date	Details	Folio	$
20-8				20-8			
Apl 1	Balance	b/d	1 825	Apl 30	Sales returns		210
30	Sales		4 910		Bank		4 788
	Interest charged		10		Discount allowed		12
	Balance	c/d	115		Balance	c/d	1 850
			6 860				6 860
20-8				20-8			
May 1	Balance	b/d	1 850	May 1	Balance	b/d	115

In a similar way, a creditor's account can show a debit balance. This may occur due to the following factors:

- an overpayment to the creditor
- returning goods to the creditor after paying the account
- paying the creditor in advance for the goods
- cash discount not being deducted before payment was made.

As in the sales ledger control account, the debit balance and the credit balance are shown separately in the purchases ledger control account. The purchases ledger control account will, therefore, have two balances - the usual credit balance representing money owing *to* creditors, and the more unusual debit balance representing money owing *by* creditors. Any debit balance is entered on the credit side of the control account and carried down as a debit balance. The account can then be balanced in the usual way.

> **Test your understanding**
> 1. Explain how it is possible for a debtor's account to have a credit balance.

Control Accounts

Contra entries in Control Accounts

These are also known as **inter-ledger transfers** or **set-offs**.

It may happen that a business sells goods to another business and also buys different goods from that business. This means that there will be two ledger accounts for that business – one in the sales ledger and the other in the purchases ledger.

Rather than each business sending the other a cheque to cover the amount due, they may agree to set one account off against the other. Any remaining amount will be settled by one business issuing a cheque.

Example 16.4

Shweta provides the following information.

20-8 May 15 Sold goods, $190, on credit to Mansingh Road Stores
        22 Bought goods, $320, on credit from Mansingh Road Stores
        30 The balances of the two accounts for Mansingh Road Stores were set-off and Shweta sent a cheque for the remaining balance.

Record the above transactions in the account for Mansingh Road Stores in the sales ledger and the account for Mansingh Road Stores in the purchases ledger.

Shweta
Sales Ledger
Mansingh Road Stores account

Date	Details	Folio	$	Date	Details	Folio	$
20-8 May 15	Sales		190	20-8 May 30	Purchases ledger		190
			190				190

Purchases Ledger
Mansingh Road Stores account

Date	Details	Folio	$	Date	Details	Folio	$
20-8				20-8			
May 30	Sales ledger Bank		190 130 320	May 22	Purchases		320 ___ 320

- A journal entry would be made for the transfer of $190 on 30 May as it is a non-regular transaction.
- As the transfer of $190 on 30 May affected both the accounts in sales ledger and purchases ledger, it would affect both the sales ledger control account and the purchases ledger control account.
- The sales ledger control account would be credited with the contra entry and the purchases ledger control account would be debited with the contra entry (the source of information being the journal).

> **Test your understanding**
> 1. In connection with control accounts, explain the meaning of a contra entry.

POINTS TO REMEMBER

1. The main purpose of control accounts is to assist in locating errors in the sales ledger and the purchases ledger.
2. A sales ledger control account resembles the account of a debtor but contains transactions affecting all debtors.
3. A purchases ledger control account resembles the account of a creditor but contains transactions affecting all creditors.
4. The information to prepare control accounts is obtained from the books of prime entry.
5. It is possible to have a balance on each side of a control account.
6. If a business is both a customer and a supplier, a contra entry may be made to transfer a balance from the sales ledger account to the purchases ledger account.

Control Accounts

REVIEW QUESTIONS

1. Amina Nawaz has a large number of debtors. She is considering preparing monthly control accounts for her sales ledger. She believes that this will help to locate errors if the trial balance fails to balance.

   Required

   (a) State **three** advantages to Amina of preparing a sales ledger control account other than the location of errors.
   (b) Explain what is meant by a contra entry in connection with control accounts.
   (c) State where the following items will appear in a sales ledger control account. If the item will not appear in a sales ledger control account write "No entry".
   The first one has been completed as an example.

Item	Entry in sales ledger control account
(i) Sales returns	Credit
(ii) Bad debts	....
(iii) Provision for doubtful debts	....
(iv) Interest charged on overdue account	....

   [IGCSE 2006]

*2. Ruth Tembe is a trader. She employs a bookkeeper who maintains a full set of accounting records.

   Ruth Tembe's bookkeeper prepares a purchases ledger control account and a sales ledger control account at the end of every month.

   On 1 July 2009 the balances brought down on the purchases ledger control account were as follows:

	$
Debit balance	15
Credit balance	3680

The bookkeeper provided the following information for the month ended 31 July 2009.

	$
Cheques paid to suppliers	4650
Cheques received from customers	5660
Discounts allowed	75
Discounts received	90
Returns to suppliers	30
Returns to customers	41
Credit purchases	4800
Transfer from a purchases ledger account to a sales ledger account	105

Required

Select the relevant figures and prepare Ruth Tembe's purchases ledger control account for the month ended 31 July 2009. There is only one balance on the account at the end of the month.

[IGCSE 2009]

3. Mohammed Hanif maintains a full set of books or prime (original) entry and prepares a sales ledger control account and a purchases ledger control account at the end of every month.

He provided the following information for the month of April 2009.

	$	
April 1 Sales ledger balances	4100	debit
Sales ledger balances	72	credit
April 30 Totals for the month:		
Sales journal	5300	
Sales returns journal	320	
Cash sales	3900	
Cheques received from debtors	3850	
Cheque received from a debtor (included in the cheques received shown above) later dishonoured	65	
Cash received relating to a bad debt written off in September 2007	250	

Control Accounts

Discount allowed	150
Increase in provision for doubtful debts	60
Transfer from a purchases ledger account to a sales ledger account	240

Required

(a) Select the relevant figures and prepare Mohammed Hanif's sales ledger control account for the month ended 30 April 2009. There is only one balance on the account at the end of the month.

(b) State **one** reason why it is possible to have a credit balance brought down on a sales ledger control account.

(c) State where **each** of the following items will appear in a purchases ledger control account. If the item will not appear in a purchases ledger control account write "No effect".

The first one has been completed as an example.

Item	Entry in purchases ledger control account
(i) Purchases returns	Debit
(ii) Cash purchases	....
(iii) Discount received	....
(iv) Interest charged by supplier on overdue account	....

[IGCSE 2009]

4. Susan Sawka maintains a full set of books of prime (original) entry and writes up a purchases ledger control account and a sales ledger control account at the end of every month.

On 1 March 2006 the balances brought down on Susan's purchases ledger control account were as follows:

	$
Debit balance	120
Credit balance	9500

Susan Sawka provided the following information for the month ended 31 March 2006.

	$
Cash purchases	1660
Credit purchases	7420
Returns to credit suppliers	135
Returns by credit customers	210
Cheques paid to credit suppliers	8780
Cheques received from credit customers	9360
Discounts allowed	240
Discounts received	20
Transfer from a purchases ledger account to a sales ledger account	380

Required

(a) Select the relevant figures and prepare Susan Sawka's purchases ledger control account for the month ended 31 March 2006. There is only one balance on the account at the end of the month.

(b) State **two** reasons why it is possible to have a debit balance on a purchases ledger control account.

(c) Explain why the information used to write up Susan's purchases ledger control account is obtained from books of prime (original) entry and **not** from the purchases ledger.

[IGCSE 2006]

5. Ian Selkirk is a sole trader who maintains a full set of accounting records. He divides his ledger into three sections – general ledger, purchases ledger and sales ledger.

(a) State and explain **one** advantage of dividing the ledger into these three sections.

(b) Name **two** accounts which would appear in the general ledger.

(c) Ian Selkirk prepares control accounts for his purchases and sales ledgers at the end of each month.

On 1 April 2003 the balances brought down on the control accounts were:

	$
Purchases ledger control account	1960 credit
Sales ledger control account	1750 debit
Sales ledger control account	100 credit

Control Accounts

Totals of the journals for April 2003 were:

	$
Purchases journal	4190
Sales journal	5150
Purchases returns journal	135
Sales returns journal	270

The cash book for April 2003 showed:

	$
Cheques received from debtors	4990
Cheques paid to creditors	3830
Cheque paid to debtor in respect of overpayment	100
Discount allowed	110
Discount received	180

The journal entries for April 2003 showed:

	$
Bad debts written off	74

Prepare Ian Selkirk's purchases ledger control account and sales ledger control account for the month of April 2003. Bring down the balances on 1 May 2003.

[IGCSE 2003]

*6. David Odoyo maintains a full set of books of account. He prepares a purchases ledger control account and a sales ledger control account at the end of every month.
   (a) State **two** advantages of control accounts.
   (b) State where David will obtain the relevant figure for **each** of the following items which appear in his sales ledger control account.
      (i) credit sales
      (ii) discount allowed
      (iii) bad debts
   (c) On 1 October 2002 David's sales ledger control account had two balances
      $4345 debit
      $130 credit

Assuming that there are no errors, explain **one** reason why a credit balance may occur on a sales ledger control account.

(d) On 1 October 2002 the balance brought down on David's purchases ledger control account was $2950, which agreed with the total of the creditors' balances in the purchases ledger.
He supplied the following information for the month ending 31 October 2002.

	$
Purchases on credit	5050
Returns to suppliers	135
Cheques paid to suppliers	4120
Cash discount received from suppliers	85
Cash received from a supplier for an overpayment by David	100

Prepare David Odoyo's purchases ledger control account for the month ended 31 October 2002.

[IGCSE 2002]

7. Abdul Aziz maintains a full set of books of prime (original) entry and prepares a purchases ledger control account and a sales ledger control account at the end of every month.

(a) On 1 September 2004 the balances brought down on Abdul's sales ledger control account were:

	$
Debit balance	5688
Credit balance	194

He supplied the following information for the month ending 30 September 2004.

	$
Credit sales	7650
Cash sales	2900
Returns by credit customers	356
Cheques received from credit customers	5430

Control Accounts

Cheques received from credit customer (included in the total cheques received) dishonoured by the bank	280
Discounts allowed	264
Provision for doubtful debts 1 September 2004	300
Bad debts written off	250

Select the relevant figures and prepare Abdul's sales ledger control account for the month ended 30 September 2004. There is only one balance on the account at the end of the month.
(b) Select **one** of the items listed in (a) above that should **not** be included in the sales ledger control account and explain why it does not appear.
(c) On 1 October 2004 the debit balance brought down on Abdul's sales ledger control account disagreed with the list of balances in the sales ledger by $280. It is found that the cheque dishonoured by the bank has not been recorded in the personal account of the debtor.
What is the total of the list of balances in the sales ledger?
(d) State where Abdul will obtain the relevant figure for **each** of the following items which appear in his purchases ledger control account.
   (i) credit purchases
   (ii) discounts received
   (iii) refunds from credit suppliers
(e) State **two** advantages to Abdul of preparing control accounts.

[IGCSE 2004]

Chapter 17 Incomplete Records

In this chapter you will learn to:
- prepare an opening and closing statement of affairs
- calculate net profit or net loss from changes in capital
- calculate sales, purchases, bank balance and gross profit from incomplete information
- apply margin, mark-up and stock turnover calculations to arrive at missing figures.

Introduction

When a full set of accounting records is maintained the owner of the business has all the information available about the assets, liabilities, revenues and expenses of the business. This makes the preparation of financial statements relatively easy. Sometimes businesses, small businesses in particular, do not maintain a full set of accounting records. This means that a trial balance cannot be drawn up and the financial statements cannot be prepared until a certain amount of preparatory calculations have been carried out. Much depends on the records and information available as to whether a full set of fincncial statements can be prepared.

Statement of Affairs

If the only records available are those relating to the assets and liabilities of the business it is not possible to prepare an income statement. **These assets and liabilities are listed in a statement of affairs which is similar to a balance sheet**. When a list of assets and liabilities is prepared without the use of a set of double entry records it is known as a statement of affairs rather than a balance sheet.

Incomplete Records

If the assets, liabilities and capital of the business are known and no further information is available, the only way in which the profit can be measured is to compare the change in the capital over the financial period. Capital increases when a profit is made and decreases when a loss is incurred. The basic formula for calculating profit is:

| Closing capital | − | Opening capital | = | Profit |

Part of the difference between the two capital figures may be caused by drawings made by the owner. If drawings have taken place during the period, the formula must be modified to:

| Closing capital | − | Opening capital | + | Drawings | = | Profit |

If additional capital has been introduced during the period, this will also account for some of the difference between the two capital figures. The formula must be modified to:

| Closing capital | − | Opening capital | + | Drawings | − | Capital introduced | = | Profit |

An alternative way to calculate profit is to construct a capital account and insert the missing figure of profit:

Capital account

Date	Details	Folio	$	Date	Details	Folio	$
Year 1				Year 1			
Dec 31	Drawings		xxx	Jan 1	Balance	b/d	xxx
	Balance	c/d	xxx	Dec 31	Bank		xxx
					Profit		?
							xxx
				Year 2			
				Jan 1	Balance	b/d	xxx

- The dates of 1 January and 31 December have been used for convenience. The first and last days of the financial year of the particular business are used in practice.

Calculating profit by comparing the change in the capital is very unsatisfactory. Only an estimate of the net profit is possible: it is not possible to show details about gross profit, sales, purchases, expenses and so on. It is not possible to analyse the results and informed decisions about the future cannot be made.

> **Test your understanding**
> 1. Explain the meaning of a statement of affairs.
> 2. State the circumstances in which a statement of affairs is prepared.
> 3. State why it is not satisfactory to measure profit by changes in capital.

Example 17.1

Vijay is a sole trader. He has not kept a full set of double entry records, but is able to provide the following information about his assets and liabilities.

	1 May 20-8 $	30 April 20-9 $
Premises at cost	30 000	30 000
Equipment at cost	9 000	9 000
Motor vehicle at cost	8 000	8 000
Inventory	14 000	16 000
Trade receivables	8 500	9 400
Trade payables	8 000	9 200
Bank	1 200	–
Bank overdraft	–	900
Other payables	–	100
Other receivables	120	130

During the year ended 30 April 20-9 Vijay purchased additional equipment for the business, costing $7000, out of his personal funds. This is in addition to the equipment listed above. His cash drawings during the year amounted to $7000, and he also took goods costing $3000 for personal use.

On 30 April 20-9 it was decided that *all* the equipment should be depreciated by 10%, and the motor vehicle should be depreciated by 25%.

Incomplete Records

It was also decided to create a provision for doubtful debts of 2% of the trade receivables.

    (a) Prepare a statement of affairs of Vijay at 1 May 20-8.
    (b) Prepare a statement of affairs of Vijay at 30 April 20-9.
    (c) Calculate Vijay's profit for the year ended 30 April 20-9.

(a)

Vijay
Statement of Affairs at 1 May 20-8

	$	$	$
Non-current assets			Cost
Premises			30 000
Equipment			9 000
Motor vehicle			8 000
			47 000
Current assets			
Inventory		14 000	
Trade receivables		8 500	
Other receivables		120	
Bank		1 200	
		23 820	
Current liabilities			
Trade payables		8 000	
Net current assets			15 820
			62 820
Financed by			
Capital			
Balance			62 820
			62 820

(b)
Vijay
Statement of Affairs at 30 April 20-9

	$ Cost	$ Depreciation to date	$ Book value
Non-current assets			
Premises	30 000	–	30 000
Equipment	16 000	1 600	14 400
Motor vehicle	8 000	2 000	6 000
	54 000	3 600	50 400

	$	$	$
Current assets			
Inventory		16 000	
Trade receivables	9 400		
Less Provision for doubtful debts	188	9 212	
Other receivables		130	
		25 342	
Current liabilities			
Trade payables	9 200		
Other payables	100		
Bank overdraft	900	10 200	
Net current assets			15 142
			65 542
Financed by			
Capital			
Balance			65 542
			65 542

- In (a) and (b) the capital figure has been inserted to make the statement of affairs balance.

(c)
Vijay
Calculation of profit for the year ended 30 April 20-9

	$	$
Capital at 30 April 20-9		65 542
Less Capital at 1 May 20-8		62 820
		2 722
Add Drawings – cash	5 000	
goods	3 000	8 000
		10 722
Less Capital introduced		7 000
Profit for the year		3 722

Incomplete Records

(c) Alternative presentation

Vijay
Capital account

Date	Details	Folio	$	Date	Details	Folio	$
20-9				20-8			
Apl 30	Drawings		5 000	May 1	Balance		62 820
	Purchases		3 000	20-9			
	Balance	c/d	65 542	Apl 30	Equipment		7 000
					Profit		3 722
			73 542				73 542
				20-9			
				May 1	Balance	b/d	65 542

- The profit is inserted as a "missing figure" in order to balance the account.

If no instructions are provided to the contrary, the profit calculation can be shown *within* the closing statement of affairs. In this case the net profit or net loss will be inserted to make the statement of affairs balance.

Example 17.2

Vijay is a sole trader. He has not kept a full set of double entry records. A statement of affairs on 1 May 20-8 was shown in **Example 17.1**.

Assume that the calculation of the profit is to be shown within the statement of affairs on 30 April 20-9. The first section of the statement of affairs on 30 April 20-9 would be as shown in **Example 17.1**. The last section of the statement of affairs is shown as follows:

	$	$	$
Financed by			
Capital			
Opening balance			62 820
Plus Capital introduced			7 000
Profit for the year			3 722
			73 542
Less Drawings (5000 + 3000)			8 000
			65 542

> **Test your understanding**
> 1. Manan is a trader. The following information is provided: capital 1 January 20-5 $40 000, capital 31 December 20-6 $50 000, profit for the year $8500, capital introduced during the year $5000. Calculate, by means of a capital account, Manan's drawings for the year.

Even when a business has not maintained the double entry records it is sometimes able to provide information in addition to details of the assets and liabilities. If details of money received and paid are available, it is possible to calculate the sales, purchases and expenses. This means that, after various calculations, a set of financial statements can be prepared.

Example 17.3

Anjali is a sole trader. She maintains a bank account, but not a full set of double entry records. She provided the following information.

	1 July 20-4 $	30 June 20-5 $
Premises at cost	60 000	60 000
Equipment (cost $22 500)	18 000	?
Inventory	28 100	29 800
Trade receivables	23 800	26 800
Trade payables	19 700	20 200
Other payables (accrued general expenses)	200	–
Other receivables (prepaid general expenses)	–	340
Bank	12 700	?

Summary of receipts and payments for the year:

Receipts	$	Payments	$
Receipts from debtors	331 600	Payments to creditors	249 400
Cash sales	12 000	General expenses	19 620
		Drawings	38 400
		Wages	40 000
		Property tax	3 800
		Insurance	1 900
		Equipment	8 000

Incomplete Records

During the year ended 30 June 20-5 Anjali took goods costing $4000 for her own use.

On 30 June 20-5 equipment should be depreciated by 10% on the cost of equipment owned at that date. On that date, it was decided to create a provision for doubtful debts of 2½% of the trade receivables.

Prepare the income statement of Anjali for the year ended 30 June 20-5 and a balance sheet at 30 June 20-5.

> Before attempting to answer a question of this nature it is necessary to calculate the following:
> 1. Opening capital
> 2. Sales for the year
> 3. Purchases for the year
> 4. Closing bank balance

Calculations

1. Opening capital

Statement of Affairs at 1 July 20-4

	$ Cost	$ Depreciation to date	$ Book value
Non-current assets			
Premises	60 000		60 000
Equipment	22 500	4 500	18 000
	82 500	4 500	78 000
Current assets			
Inventory		28 100	
Trade receivables		23 800	
Bank		12 700	
		64 600	
Current liabilities			
Trade payables	19 700		
Other payables	200	19 900	
Net current assets			44 700
			122 700
Financed by			
Capital			122 700
			122 700

2. Sales for the year
(i) Credit sales

The amount received from the debtors is not necessarily equal to the actual sales. Some of the money received is to settle the amount owed by debtors at the start of the year (for goods sold in the previous financial year). Money is owed by the debtors at the end of the year for goods sold during the present financial year.

The credit sales can be calculated as follows:

	$
Receipts from debtors	331 600
Less trade receivables 1 July 20-4	23 800
	307 800
Plus trade receivables 30 June 20-5	26 800
Credit sales for the year	334 600

Alternatively, the credit sales can be calculated by inserting a "missing figure" in a total trade receivables account:

Total trade receivables account

Date	Details	Folio	$	Date	Details	Folio	$
20-4				20-5			
July 1	Balance	b/d	23 800	June 30	Bank		331 600
20-5					Balance	c/d	26 800
June 30	Sales*		334 600				
			358 400				358 400
20-5							
July 1	Balance	b/d	26 800				

(ii) Total sales

	$
Credit sales	334 600
Cash sales	12 000
Total sales	346 600

Incomplete Records

3. Purchases for the year
(i) Credit purchases

The amount paid to the creditors is not necessarily equal to the actual purchases. Some of the money paid is to settle the amount owed to creditors at the start of the year (for goods bought in the previous financial year). Money is owed to the creditors at the end of the year for goods bought during the present financial year.

The credit purchases can be calculated as follows:

	$
Payments to creditors	249 400
Less trade payables 1 July 20-4	19 700
	229 700
Plus trade payables 30 June 20-5	20 200
Credit purchases for the year	249 900

Alternatively, the credit purchases can be calculated by inserting a "missing figure" in a total trade payables account:

Total trade payables account

Date	Details	Folio	$	Date	Details	Folio	$
20-5				20-4			
June 30	Bank		249 400	July 1	Balance	b/d	19 700
	Balance	c/d	20 200	20-5			
				June 30	Purchases*		249 900
			269 600				269 600
				20-5			
				July 1	Balance	b/d	20 200

(ii) Total purchases

As there are no cash purchases the total purchases are equal to the credit purchases calculated above.

4. Closing bank balance

The bank balance on 1 July 20-4 is given together with details of receipts and payments. A summary of the bank account can be prepared to calculate the closing bank balance. It is not usually necessary to itemise all the transactions (unless this is required by an examination question).

Bank account

Date	Details	Folio	$	Date	Details	Folio	$
20-4				20-5			
July 1	Balance	b/d	12 700	June 30	Total payments		361 120
20-5							
June 30	Total receipts		343 600				
	Balance	c/d	4 820				
			361 120				361 120
				20-5			
				July 1	Balance	b/d	4 820

Anjali
Income Statement for the year ended 30 June 20-4

	$	$	$
Revenue (sales)			346 600
Less Cost of sales			
Opening inventory		28 100	
Purchases	249 900		
Less Goods for own use	4 000	245 900	
		274 000	
Less Closing inventory		29 800	244 200
Gross profit			102 400
Less General expenses		19 080	
Wages		40 000	
Property tax		3 800	
Insurance		1 900	
Provision for doubtful debts		670	
Depreciation of equipment		3 050	68 500
Profit for the year			33 900

- The figures for revenue (sales) and purchases have come from previous calculations.
- The general expenses have been calculated $19 620 - $200 - $340.
- The provision for doubtful debts has been calculated at 2½% of $26 800.
- The depreciation of equipment has been calculated at 10% of ($22 500 + $8000).

Incomplete Records

Anjali
Balance Sheet at 30 June 20-5

	$ Cost	$ Depreciation to date	$ Book value
Non-current assets			
Premises	60 000		60 000
Equipment	30 500	7 550	22 950
	90 500	7 550	82 950
Current assets			
Inventory		29 800	
Trade receivables	26 800		
Less Provision for doubtful debts	670	26 130	
Other receivables		340	
		56 270	
Current liabilities			
Trade payables	20 200		
Bank overdraft	4 820	25 020	
Net current assets			31 250
			114 200
Financed by			
Capital			
Opening balance			122 700
Plus profit for the year			33 900
			156 600
Less Drawings			42 400
			114 200

- The depreciation to date on equipment has been calculated $4500 + $3050.
- The figure for bank overdraft has come from a previous calculation.
- The drawings have been calculated $38 400 + $4000.

> **Test your understanding**
> 1. A trader's financial year ends on 31 May. The following information is provided – cash purchases $4000, cheques paid to creditors $23 300, trade payables at 1 June 20-7 $2500, trade payables at 31 May 20-8 $3100. Calculate the purchases for the year.

When a business allows its debtors a cash discount if the account is paid within the set time limit this will affect the calculation of the credit sales. Similarly, any discount received from creditors will affect the calculation of the credit purchases.

Example 17.4

Anjali is a sole trader. She maintains a bank account, but not a full set of double entry records. She provided the following information.

	1 July 20-4 $	30 June 20-5 $
Trade receivables	23 800	26 800
Trade payables	19 700	20 200

During the year ended 30 June 20-5 receipts from debtors totalled $331 600 (after the deduction of $8200 cash discount). $249 400 was paid to creditors (after the deduction of $6780 cash discount).

Calculate the credit sales and credit purchases for the year ended 30 June 20-5.

Total trade receivables account

Date	Details	Folio	$	Date	Details	Folio	$
20-4				20-5			
July 1	Balance	b/d	23 800	June 30	Bank		331 600
20-5					Discount		
June 30	Sales*		342 800		allowed		8 200
					Balance	c/d	26 800
			366 600				366 600
20-5							
July 1	Balance	b/d	26 800				

Total trade payables account

Date	Details	Folio	$	Date	Details	Folio	$
20-5				20-4			
June 30	Bank		249 400	July 1	Balance	b/d	19 700
	Discount			20-5			
	received		6 780	June 30	Purchases*		256 680
	Balance	c/d	20 200				
			276 380				276 380
				20-5			
				July 1	Balance	b/d	20 200

Incomplete Records

- The amounts shown above for sales and purchases would appear in the trading account section of the income statement.
- The amounts for discount allowed and discount received would appear in the profit and loss account section of the income statement.

Margin, Mark-up and Inventory Turnover

When dealing with incomplete records, it is sometimes necessary to use percentages to calculate missing information.

Margin and mark-up

These both measure the gross profit as a percentage.

The margin is the gross profit measured as a percentage of selling price

The mark-up is the gross profit measured as a percentage of the cost price

Example 17.5

A trader's sales for the year were $20 000 and the cost of goods sold was $15 000.

Calculate:
(a) the margin
(b) the mark-up.

(a) The margin $\dfrac{\text{Gross profit}}{\text{Sales}} \times \dfrac{100}{1} = \dfrac{\$5\ 000}{\$20\ 000} \times \dfrac{100}{1} = 25\%$

(b) The mark-up $\dfrac{\text{Gross profit}}{\text{Cost of sales}} \times \dfrac{100}{1} = \dfrac{\$5\ 000}{\$15\ 000} \times \dfrac{100}{1} = 33.33\%$

Applying either margin or mark-up, it is possible to calculate any one unknown figure in the trading account section of an income statement.

Example 17.6

The financial year of North West Traders ends on 30 November. The following information is provided.

	$
Inventory 1 December 20-3	4 600
Inventory 30 November 20-4	5 200
Revenue (sales)	72 000

The mark-up is at a standard rate of 25%.
Calculate, by means of a trading account section of an income statement, the purchases for the year ended 30 November 20-4.

North West Traders
Income Statement for the year ended 30 November 20-4

	$	$
Revenue (sales)		72 000
Less Cost of sales		
Opening inventory	4 600	
Purchases	58 200 (d)	
	62 800 (c)	
Less Closing inventory	5 200	57 600 (b)
Gross profit		14 400 (a)

- An outline statement was prepared and the figures for revenue (sales), opening inventory and closing inventory were inserted, with gaps left for purchases, cost of sales and gross profit.
- The gross profit was calculated. The mark-up is 25% so the gross profit is 25% of the cost of sales, so the selling price equals 125%. The gross profit is 25/125 of the revenue (sales) which is 1/5 or 20% of $72 000. The gross profit is, therefore, $14 400. (a)
- The cost of sales was inserted as the difference between the revenue (sales) and the gross profit. Alternatively, it can be calculated at 100/125 of the revenue (sales) which is 4/5 or 80% of $72 000. The cost of sales is, therefore, $57 600. (b)
- The purchases figure was calculated by working "backwards" from the cost of sales. The cost of sales plus the opening inventory amounted to $62 800 (c). This figure less the opening inventory equals the purchases of $58 200. (d)

Incomplete Records

> **Test your understanding**
> 1. Differentiate between margin and mark-up.
> 2. A trader purchased goods for $4000 and sold them for $5000. Calculate the percentage margin and the percentage mark-up.

Rate of inventory turnover

It is sometimes necessary to use calculations relating to the rate of inventory turnover in order to calculate an unknown figure in the trading account section of an income statement. **The rate of inventory turnover is the number of times a business replaces its inventory in a given period of time**. The importance of this calculation is explained in detail in Chapter 22.

The formula for calculating the rate of inventory turnover is:

$$\frac{\text{Cost of sales}}{\text{Average inventory}}$$

Example 17.7

M Parmar is a trader. The financial year ends on 31 October. The following information is provided.

	$
Inventory 1 November 20-1	12 000
Inventory 31 October 20-2	8 000

The margin is at a standard rate of 20%.
The rate of inventory turnover is 15 times a year.
Calculate, by means of the trading account section of an income statement, the purchases for the year ended 31 October 20-2.

M Parmar
Income statement for the year ended 31 October 20-2

	$	$
Revenue (sales)		187 500 (e)
Less Cost of sales		
Opening inventory	12 000	
Purchases	146 000 (c)	
	158 000 (b)	
Less Closing inventory	8 000	150 000 (a)
Gross profit		37 500 (d)

- An outline of the statement was prepared and the figures of opening inventory and closing inventory were inserted, with gaps left for revenue (sales), purchases, cost of sales and gross profit.
- The average inventory was calculated.

$$\text{Average inventory} = \frac{\text{opening inventory} + \text{closing inventory}}{2}$$

$$= \frac{12\,000 + 8\,000}{2} = \$10\,000$$

- The cost of sales was calculated.

$$\text{Rate of inventory turnover} = \frac{\text{Cost of sales}}{\text{Average inventory}}$$

$$= \frac{\text{Cost of sales}}{10\,000} = 15$$

The cost of sales is, therefore $150 000.

- The cost of sales was inserted in the statement. (a)
- The purchases figure was calculated by working "backwards" from the cost of sales. (b) and (c)
- The gross profit was calculated. The margin is 20% so the gross profit is 20% of the revenue (sales). The selling price equals 100%, the gross profit equals 20%, so the cost of sales equals 80%. The gross profit is 20/80 of the cost of sales which is 1/4 or 25% of $150 000. The gross profit is $37 500. (d)
- The revenue (sales) figure was calculated by working "backwards". The gross profit plus the cost of sales equals the sales (revenue). (e)

Incomplete Records

POINTS TO REMEMBER

1. A statement of affairs is similar to a balance sheet and is prepared when a full set of accounting records is not maintained.
2. Profit can be measured from the change in the capital over a period of time, taking into consideration drawings and capital introduced.
3. The amount received from debtors does not necessarily equal the credit sales: the amount paid to creditors does not necessarily equal the credit purchases.
4. When a record of money paid and received is available as well as the assets and liabilities, it is possible to prepare a set of financial statements after calculating sales and purchases (and possibly the capital and the bank balances).
5. Gross profit can be expressed as margin (on selling price) and as mark-up (on cost price).
6. The rate of inventory turnover is the number of times a business replaces its inventory in a given period of time.

REVIEW QUESTIONS

*1. Rebecca Tan is a trader. Her financial year ends on 30 June. She does not keep many financial records, but is able to provide the following information.

Assets and liabilities on 30 June 2005 were as follows.

	$
Equipment at cost	13 900
Motor vehicle at cost	7 500
Trade receivables	5 200
Trade payables	4 800
Inventory	7 250
Bank overdraft	250
Other receivables	122
Other payables	146

The following adjustments should be made on 30 June 2005.

The motor vehicle should be depreciated by 20% on cost.
The equipment should be revalued at $12 700.
A provision for doubtful debts of 2% of the trade receivables should be created.

Required

(a) Draw up a statement of affairs for Rebecca Tan at 30 June 2005 showing the total capital at that date.

Candidates who are not familiar with a statement of affairs may present their answer in the form of a balance sheet on 30 June 2005 showing the total capital of the business.

On 1 July 2004 Rebecca Tan's capital was $27 000.

On 2 July 2004 she introduced a further $5000 as capital.

During the year ended 30 June 2005 Rebecca Tan made the following drawings.

	$
Cash	3150
Goods	1250

Required

(b) Using the capital you calculated in (a) and the information provided above, calculate Rebecca Tan's profit (or loss) for the year ended 30 June 2005.
Your answer may be in the form of either a capital account or an arithmetic calculation.

[IGCSE 2005]

2. Leroy is a trader. He does not maintain a full set of accounting records, but was able to provide the following information on 1 June 20-8.

	$
Fixtures and fittings at valuation	6 000
Motor vehicle at cost	14 000
Inventory	3 800

Incomplete Records

	$
Trade receivables	4 250
Trade payables	2 950
Long term loan from Lenders Ltd	5 000
Other receivables	360
Bank overdraft	2 410

During the year ended 31 May 20-9 he borrowed a further $3500 from Lenders Ltd. He took $2000 from the bank for personal use.

On 31 May 20-9 it was decided that the motor vehicle should be depreciated by 20% on cost and that the fixtures and fittings should be valued at $5600.

On 31 May 20-9 the inventory was valued at $4100, the trade receivables totalled $4660, the trade payables totalled $3140 and there was $380 in the bank.

(a) Prepare a statement of affairs of Leroy on 1 June 20-8 showing the total capital at that date.
(b) Prepare a statement of affairs of Leroy on 31 May 20-9 showing the total capital at that date.
(c) Prepare a capital account for Leroy for the year ended 31 May 20-9 showing the profit or loss for the year.

*3. A summary of William's cash book for the year ended 31 March 2005 showed the following.

Date			$	Date			$
1 April 2004	Balance	b/d	730	Year ended 31 March 2005	Payments to suppliers, expenses and drawings		14 750
Year ended 31 Mar 2005	Cash and credit deposits from customers		15 270	31 March 2005	Balance	c/d	1 250
			16 000				16 000
1 April 2005	Balance	b/d	1 250				

You are given the following additional information:

		$
Trade receivables	at 1 April 2004	3 140
	at 31 March 2005	4 080

Cash sales all deposited at the bank (already included in the deposits for the year shown above)	2 680
Inventory at 1 April 2004	1 780
Inventory at 31 March 2005	1 920

An analysis of cheque payments shows the following:

	$
Purchases from suppliers	9 560
Carriage inwards	280
Rent	600
Electricity	360
Motor expenses	800
Insurance	580
Wages paid to staff	1 370
Drawings (William)	1 200
	14 750

Required

(a) Calculate William's total credit sales for the year. Show your workings.
(b) Prepare William's income statement for the year ended 31 March 2005.
(c) Calculate William's gross profit margin for the year, to **two** decimal places.
(d) William has forgotten to deposit $90 cash sales at the bank on 31 March 2005. He wishes to adjust his accounts for this amount by adding $90 to the sales.
  (i) What would be the effect on his gross profit?
  (ii) Calculate William's revised gross profit margin to **two** decimal places. Show your workings.

[IGCSE 2005]

4. Mohan is a sole trader who does not maintain a full set of accounting records. He was able to provide the following information.

On 1 May 20-8:	$
Fixtures (cost $31 000)	24 800
Motor vehicle (cost $15 000)	9 000

Incomplete Records

Inventory	19 600
Trade receivables	17 300
Bank	9 750
Trade payables	16 450

For the year ended 20 April 20-9:

	$
Receipts – From credit customers	458 800
Payments – To credit suppliers	371 820
For motor expenses	15 070
For general expenses	25 500
For new fixtures	4 000
For Mohan's personal use	20 000

On 30 April 20-9:

	$
Inventory	23 080
Trade receivables	21 500
Trade payables	15 510

Fixtures should be depreciated by 10% per annum on the cost of fixtures held at the end of the year. The motor vehicle should be depreciated by 25% per annum on cost.

(a) Prepare the income statement of Mohan for the year ended 30 April 20-9.
(b) Prepare the balance sheet of Mohan at 30 April 20-9.
Show all calculations.

5. Pradeep is a trader. The following information is provided.

	$
Inventory at cost on 1 August 20-5	1 600
For the year ended 31 July 20-6	
Purchases	39 200
Sales	48 000

On the evening of 31 July 20-6 a fire destroyed a quantity of goods. The cost of the goods salvaged from the fire was $700.

Pradeep marks up the goods by 25% on cost when calculating the selling price.

Calculate, by means of a trading account section of an income statement, the cost of the goods which were destroyed.

*6. Jane Joda started a business on 1 April 2003. Since that time Jane has not maintained any financial records.

She is able to provide the following information relating to her second year of trading.

	$
Inventory 1 April 2004	9 500
Inventory 31 March 2005	17 500
Purchases	22 000
Cash sales	6 600
Credit sales	?

The gross profit margin is 20%.

Calculate, by means of a trading account section of an income statement, the value of Jane Joda's credit sales for the year ended 31 March 2005.

[IGCSE 2005]

7. The following trial balance was extracted from the books of Saleem Ahmed at 31 July 2006.

	$	$
Capital		62 000
Drawings	7 200	
Premises at cost	38 000	
Fixtures at valuation	7 800	
Equipment at cost	5 000	
Provision for depreciation of equipment		950
Provision for doubtful debts		130
Trade receivables	9 000	
Bad debts recovered		170
Trade payables		7 970
Bank		4 755

Incomplete Records

Inventory 1 August 2005	10 260	
Revenue (sales)		89 500
Purchases	65 700	
Sales returns	1 100	
Carriage outwards	210	
Discount allowed	600	
Discount received		610
Administration expenses	21 215	
	166 085	166 085

Additional information

1. During the year ended 31 July 2006 Salem took goods costing $1260 for his own use. No entries had been made in the accounting records.
2. The provision for doubtful debts is to be maintained at 2% of the trade receivables.
3. Equipment is to be depreciated at 10% per annum using the reducing balance method.
4. Fixtures were valued at $7250 on 31 July 2006. No fixtures were bought or sold during the year ended 31 July 2006.
5. Because of illness, Salem was unable to value the inventory on 31 July 2006. Saleem's gross profit margin is 25%.

Required

Prepare the income statement of Salem Ahmed for the year ended 31 July 2006.

The value of the inventory on 31 July 2006 should be clearly shown in the income statement.

[IGCSE 2006]

8. Suzan Hamouda has been in business for two years but has not maintained a full set of accounting records. All purchases and sales are made on credit terms.

Suzan Hamouda is able to provide the following information:

	$
At 1 October 2007	
amounts owing by customers	5 000
amounts owing to suppliers	4 500

For the year ended 30 September 2008
cheques received from customers	58 114
cheques paid to suppliers	45 930
discounts received	470
discounts allowed	1 186
bad debts written off	900

At 30 September 2008
amounts owing by customers	4 800
amounts owing to suppliers	5 200

Required

(a) Calculate Suzan Hamouda's credit sales and credit purchases for the year ended 30 September 2008.
Your answer may be in the form of ledger accounts or calculations.

(b) Suzan sells all her goods at a mark-up of 20%.
Explain the difference between mark-up and margin.

On 1 October 2007 Suzan Hamouda's inventory was valued at $7800.
During the year ended 30 September 2008 Suzan Hamouda took goods costing $200 for her own use. No adjustments have been made for these goods.

Required

(c) Using your answers to (a) and the above information calculate, by means of a trading account section of an income statement, the value of Suzan Hamouda's inventory on 30 September 2008.

[IGCSE 2008]

Chapter 18 Accounts of Clubs and Societies

> **In this chapter you will learn to:**
> - prepare a receipts and payments account and understand its purpose
> - prepare a trading account section of an income statement of a club or society
> - prepare an income and expenditure account and understand its purpose
> - understand and calculate the accumulated fund of a club or society
> - prepare a balance sheet of a club or society
> - understand the difference between the accounts of a business and those of a club or society
> - record subscriptions in the accounts of a club or society.

Introduction

This chapter concentrates on the accounts of **non-trading organisations** such as clubs and societies. The main aim of these organisations is to provide some facilities and services for their members: making a profit is not the main objective. Examples of such organisations include youth clubs, sports clubs, amateur dramatic groups, golf clubs, scout groups etc. In some case a full set of double entry records is written up each year, but it is more usual to find that only a record of money received and paid is maintained.

The main source of income of a society is **subscriptions**. These are the amounts members pay usually annually, to use the facilities provided by the society.

A person is appointed to act as treasurer and be responsible for collecting any money due to the society and for paying money owed by the society. At the end of the financial year the treasurer will usually present financial statements to the members. These financial statements may consist of a **receipts and payments account**, possibly a **trading account section of an income statement**, an **income and expenditure account** and a **balance sheet**.

Preparation of a Receipts and Payments Accounts

This is regarded as a **summary of the cash book** for the financial year. All money received is debited and all money paid is credited. The account is balanced and the balance carried down to become the opening balance for the following financial year. This account does not usually distinguish between cash and bank transactions, so the balance may represent actual cash, money in the bank, or a combination of the two. A debit balance is an asset and represents money owned by the society whereas a credit balance is a liability and represents a bank overdraft.

A receipts and payments account, just like a cash book, records all money received and paid. It is important to remember that:
- no adjustments are made for accruals and prepayments.
- no distinction is made between capital receipts and revenue receipts.
- no distinction is made between capital expenditure and revenue expenditure.
- non-monetary items such as depreciation are not included.

Example 18.1

The Apollo Athletics Club was formed some years ago to provide various sporting facilities for its members. The club also has a shop where members can purchase sportswear.

On 1 August 20-7 the club had $2200 in the bank. The treasurer provided the following list of receipts and payments for the year ended 31 July 20-8.

	$
Subscriptions received	5860
Receipts from shop sales	3960
Purchases of goods for resale	2130
Wages – shop assistant	1300
athletics coach	2700
Rates and insurance	328
General expenses	1120
Purchase of new sports equipment	2950
Athletics competition – entrance fees received	1100
cost of prizes	660

Accounts of Clubs and Societies

All receipts are paid into the bank and all payments are made by cheque.

Prepare the receipts and payments account of the Apollo Athletics Club for the year ended 31 July 20-8.

Apollo Athletics Club
Receipts and Payments Account for the year ended 31 July 20-8

Receipts			$		Payments	$
20-7				20-8		
Aug 1	Balance	b/d	2 200	July 31	Purchases	2 130
20-8					Wages – shop assistant	1 300
July 31	Subscriptions		5 860		athletics coach	2 700
	Receipts from				Rates & insurance	328
	shop		3 960		General expenses	1 120
	Competition				Sports equipment	2 950
	entrance fees		1 100		Competition prizes	660
					Balance c/d	1 932
			13 120			13 120
20-8						
Aug 1	Balance	b/d	1 932			

> **Test your understanding**
> 1. Name **three** financial statements the treasurer of a club may prepare at the end of the financial year.
> 2. Explain the term "subscriptions" in connection with a club or society.
> 3. Explain the purpose of a receipts and payments account.

Preparation of a Trading Account Section of an Income Statements of a Club or Society

Although buying and selling is not the main purpose of a club or society, many do carry out a trading activity. Many clubs operate a shop or a café where goods are bought and sold. At the end of the financial year a **trading account section of an income statement** should be prepared for each separate trading activity to show the profit earned on that activity.

The trading account of a club or society is prepared in exactly the same way as that for a business. Any expenses which arise as a result of running the trading activity such as wages of café assistants, depreciation of café equipment etc. should be added to the cost of the goods sold in order to calculate the correct profit or loss.

In a business, the gross profit is calculated in the trading account and then transferred to the profit and loss account: in a club or society the profit on a trading activity is calculated in the trading account and then transferred to the income and expenditure account (see later in this chapter).

Example 18.2

The Apollo Athletics Club was formed some years ago to provide various sporting facilities for its members. The club also has a shop where members can purchase sportswear.

The treasurer provided the following information for the year ended 31 July 20-8.

	$
Receipts from shop sales	3960
Purchases of goods for resale	2130
Shop inventory 1 August 20-7	240
Shop inventory 31 July 20-8	310
Wages of shop assistant	1300

Prepare the shop income statement of the Apollo Athletics Club for the year ended 31 July 20-8.

Accounts of Clubs and Societies

Apollo Athletics Club
Shop Income Statement for the year ended 31 July 20-8

	$	$
Revenue (sales)		3960
Less Cost of sales		
Opening inventory	240	
Purchases	2130	
	2370	
Less Closing inventory	310	
Cost of goods sold	2060	
Wages of shop assistant	1300	3360
Profit on shop (transferred to Income and Expenditure Account)		600

> **Test your understanding**
> 1. Explain when it is necessary for a club or society to prepare a trading account section of an income statement as part of the financial statements.

Preparation of an Income and Expenditure Account

An income and expenditure account compares the gains of the club with the expenses of running the club. If the gains are more than the expenses the difference is referred to as a **surplus** or **excess of income over expenditure** (this is known as the net profit in a business). If the gains are less than the expenses the difference is referred to as a **deficit** or **excess of expenditure over income** (this is known as the net loss in a business).

An income and expenditure account is prepared using the same principles as those applied in the preparation of a **profit and loss account** of a trading business.

It is important to remember that:
- adjustments must be made for accruals and prepayments
- capital receipts and capital expenditure are not included
- only revenue receipts and revenue expenditure are included
- non-monetary items such as depreciation are included
- assets and liabilities at the beginning and end of the financial year are not included.

Where the club or society holds a fund-raising activity, the income and the expenses of that activity should be set off against each other in the income and expenditure account. In this way, the profit or loss on that particular activity can be calculated.

Example 18.3

The Apollo Athletics Club was formed some years ago to provide various sporting facilities for its members. The club also has a shop where members can purchase sportswear.

The following receipts and payments account was prepared for the year ended 31 July 20-8.

Receipts and Payments Account for the year ended 31 July 20-8

Receipts			$	Payments		$
20-7				20-8		
Aug 1	Balance	b/d	2 200	July 31	Purchases	2 130
20-8					Wages – shop assistant	1 300
July 31	Subscriptions		5 860		athletics coach	2 700
	Receipts from				Rates & insurance	328
	shop		3 960		General expenses	1 120
	Competition				Sports equipment	2 950
	entrance fees		1 100		Competition prizes	660
					Balance c/d	1 932
			13 120			13 120
20-8						
Aug 1	Balance	b/d	1 932			

The treasurer also provided the following additional information:

1. On 31 July 20-8:

    insurance prepaid amounts to $16

    wages of athletics coach outstanding amount to $400

    15 members still owe their annual subscription of $20 each for the current financial year

    8 members have paid their annual subscription of $20 each for the following financial year

    sports equipment is to be depreciated by $1715.

Accounts of Clubs and Societies

2. The profit on the Club's shop for the year ended 31 July 20-8 was $600 (calculated in the shop income statement).

Prepare the income and expenditure account of the Apollo Athletics Club for the year ended 31 July 20-8.

Apollo Athletics Club
Income and Expenditure Account for the year ended 31 July 20-8

	$	$
Income		
Subscriptions (5860 + 300 – 160)		6000
Profit on shop		600
Competition – entrance fees	1100	
cost of prizes	660	440
		7040
Expenditure		
Wages – athletics coach (2700 + 400)	3100	
Rates and insurance (328 – 16)	312	
General expenses	1120	
Depreciation of equipment	1715	6247
Surplus for the year		793

> **Test your understanding**
> 1. State the equivalent term used by a business for **each** of the following terms used by a club
>   (a) Deficit
>   (b) Income and expenditure account
> 2. Explain why a club should set off the expenses of any fund-raising activity against the income from that activity.

Preparation of a Balance Sheet of a Club or Society

The principles applied when preparing a balance sheet of a club or society are similar to those applied in the preparation of a balance sheet of a business. The balance sheet of a club or society shows non-current assets, current assets, long-term liabilities and current liabilities in exactly the same way as a balance sheet of a trading organisation.

The main difference is that there is **no capital in the balance sheet of a club or society** whereas a business is usually financed by an investment of capital from the owner(s). Members of a club or society do not invest money in the same way as the proprietor of a business. Because of this, the members are not entitled to make any drawings if a club or society makes a surplus. This means that these surpluses will accumulate within the organisation to form a capital fund known as the **accumulated fund**. If the club makes a deficit the accumulated fund will decrease. This **accumulated fund replaces capital in the balance sheet of a club or society**.

Example 18.4

The Apollo Athletics Club was formed some years ago to provide various sporting facilities for its members. The club also has a shop where members can purchase sportswear.

On 1 August 20-7 the following balances appeared in the books of the Club.

	$
Premises at cost	20 000
Equipment at cost	14 200
Provision for depreciation of equipment	5 680
Balance at bank	2 200
Shop inventory	240
Accumulated fund	30 960

The income and expenditure account for the year ended 31 July 20-8 showed a surplus of $793.

During the year ended 31 July 20-8 new equipment costing $2950 was purchased. The depreciation on equipment for the year amounted to $1715.

Accounts of Clubs and Societies

On 31 July 20-8:

	$
Balance at bank	1 932
Shop inventory	310
Insurance prepaid	16
Wages of athletics coach outstanding	400
Subscriptions owing by members	300
Subscriptions paid in advance by members	160

Prepare the balance sheet of the Apollo Athletics Club at 31 July 20-8.

Apollo Athletics Club
Balance Sheet at 31 July 20-8

	$ Cost	$ Depreciation to date	$ Book value
Non-current assets			
Premises	20 000	–	20 000
Equipment	17 150	7 395	9 755
	37 150	7 395	29 755
Current assets			
Shop inventory		310	
Subscriptions owing by members		300	
Other receivables		16	
Bank		1 932	
		2 558	
Current liabilities			
Other payables	400		
Subscriptions prepaid by members	160	560	
			1 998
			31 753
Financed by			
Accumulated fund			
Opening balance			30 960
Add Surplus for year			793
			31 753

- The subscriptions owing could have been included under other receivables and the subscriptions prepaid could have been included under the other payables. In this case a note to the balance sheet would show the breakdown of these figures.

Comparison of Accounting Terms Used by a Business and Those Used by a Club or Society

Business	Club or society
–	Receipts and payments account
Profit and loss account	Income and expenditure account
Profit for the year	Surplus
Loss for the year	Deficit
Capital	Accumulated fund

Test your understanding

1. State the term used by a business to describe the equivalent of the accumulated fund in a club.
2. Explain how **each** of the following will affect the accumulated fund of a club
   (a) surplus
   (b) deficit

Subscriptions

The receipts and payments account shows the amount of subscriptions *received* during the financial year, but the income and expenditure account shows the amount of subscriptions *relating* to the financial year. This means that the amount received must be adjusted for any subscriptions owed by members and any subscriptions paid in advance by members (see **Example 18.3**). The calculation of the amount relating to the financial year may be shown in the form of a ledger account known as a **subscriptions account**.

This may be regarded as the account of the members in the books of the organisation. Subscriptions owing by members will appear as a debit balance as they are a current asset to the club or society. Subscriptions paid in advance by members will appear as a credit balance as they are a current liability because the club or society has an obligation to provide a period of membership which has already been paid for. It is possible to have two balances on a subscriptions account as the account is for *all* the

Accounts of Clubs and Societies

members and some may have paid subscriptions in advance and some may not have paid their subscription.

At the end of the financial year the account is closed by a transfer to the income and expenditure account of the amount relating to that financial year.

Example 18.5

The Apollo Athletics Club was formed some years ago to provide various sporting facilities for its members.

On 1 August 20-7 there were no subscriptions owing by members and no members had paid their subscriptions in advance.

During the year ended 31 July 20-8 the club received subscriptions totalling $5860 from members. This included subscriptions of $20 each from 8 members for the following financial year. On 31 July 20-8 subscriptions of $20 each for the current financial year were still outstanding from 15 members.

During the year ended 31 July 20-9 the club received subscriptions from members totalling $6020. On 31 July 20-9 there were subscriptions outstanding of $120.

Prepare the subscriptions account in the books of the Apollo Athletics Club for **each** of the **two** years ended 31 July 20-8 and 31 July 20-9.

Apollo Athletics Club
Subscriptions account

Date	Details	Folio	$	Date	Details	Folio	$
20-8 July 31	Balance Income & Expenditure	c/d	160 6000 6160	20-8 July 31	Bank Balance	c/d	5860 300 6160
20-8 Aug 1	Balance	b/d	300	20-8 Aug 1	Balance	b/d	160
20-9 July 31	Income & Expenditure		6000 6300	20-9 July 31	Bank Balance	c/d	6020 120 6300
20-9 Aug 1	Balance	b/d	120				

Test your understanding

1. Explain why the amount received from members appears on the credit of a subscriptions account.
2. Explain why subscriptions prepaid by members are a current liability of a club.
3. Explain why the amount shown for subscriptions in a receipts and payments account is not necessarily the same as that shown in an income and expenditure account.

Calculation of Sales and Purchases

As the accounts of a club or society are often incomplete it is often necessary to calculate credit purchases (and sometimes credit sales if goods are sold on credit) before the preparation of the trading account.

The same principles applied when calculating these figures for a business which has not got a complete set of accounting records are followed (see Chapter 17).

Example 18.6

The Apollo Athletics club has a shop where members can purchase sportswear. All the sales are made for cash and all purchases are made on credit terms.

The treasurer provided the following information.

	$
Trade payables 1 August 20-5	155
Trade payables 31 July 20-6	215
Amount paid to creditors during the year ended 31 July 20-6	2980

Calculate the purchases for the year ended 31 July 20-6.

Accounts of Clubs and Societies

Apollo Athletics Club
Total trade payables account

Date	Details	Folio	$	Date	Details	Folio	$
20-6				20-5			
July 31	Bank		2980	Aug 1	Balance	b/d	155
	Balance	c/d	215	20-6			
				July 31	Purchases		3040*
			3195				3195
				20-6			
				Aug 1	Balance	b/d	215

* This represents the purchases for the year and will appear in the shop trading account.

Calculation of Accumulated Fund

It is sometimes necessary to calculate the accumulated fund of a club or society. This can be calculated by applying the same formula used to calculate the capital of a business.

In a business	Assets	= Capital	+	Liabilities
In a club or society	Assets	= Accumulated fund	+	Liabilities

Example 18.7

On 1 August 20-6 the assets and liabilities of the Apollo Athletics Club were as follows.

	$
Premises at cost	20 000
Equipment at cost	14 200
Provision for depreciation of equipment	4 260
Balance at bank	1 700
Shop inventory	285
Trade payables for shop supplies	215

Calculate the accumulated fund on 1 August 20-7.

Calculation of accumulated fund on 1 August 20-6

		$	$
Assets	Premises at cost		20 000
	Equipment at cost	14 200	
	Less Provision for depreciation	4 260	9 940
	Balance at bank		1 700
	Shop inventory		285
			31 925
Liabilities	Trade payables		215
Accumulated fund			31 710

Test your understanding

1. Explain why the amount shown for purchases in the café trading account of a club is not necessarily equal to the amount paid to credit suppliers.
2. State the formula for calculating accumulated fund.

Points to Remember

1. A club or society is often referred to as a non-trading organisation.
2. At the end of the financial year a club will usually prepare a receipts and payments account which is a summary of the cash book.
3. If a club carries out a trading activity it may be necessary to prepare a trading account section of an income statement at the end of the financial year.
4. At the end of the financial year a club will prepare an income and expenditure account which is similar to a profit and loss account.
5. The balance sheet of a club is very similar to that of a business except that the capital is replaced by the accumulated fund.
6. The main source of income for a club is the subscriptions received from its members for the use of the facilities provided by the club.

Accounts of Clubs and Societies

REVIEW QUESTIONS

1. (a) Explain the term 'accumulated fund' in connection with the accounts of a non-trading organisation.
   (b) The following balances appeared in the books of the Green Jackets Sports Club on 30 September 2002.

	$
Clubhouse	25 000
Equipment	5 400
Subscriptions prepaid by members	1 000
Refreshments inventory	1 020
Trade payables for refreshments	850
Cash	280
Bank overdraft	2 990
Other receivables – insurance prepaid	190

   Calculate the accumulated fund of the Green Jackets Sports Club at 30 September 2002. Show your workings.

   (c) On 1 October 2002 the Green Jackets Sports Club had prepaid insurance amounting to $190.

   On 1 December 2002 the Club paid $1200 by cheque for one year's insurance to 30 November 2003.

   Prepare the insurance account as it would appear in the ledger of the Green Jackets Sports Club for the year ended 30 September 2003. Show clearly the amount transferred to the income and expenditure account. Bring down the balance on 1 October 2003.

   (d) The Green Jackets Sports Club has 300 members who pay an annual subscription of $200.

   The following information is available.

   1. On 1 October 2002, 5 members had paid their subscriptions in advance for the financial year ending 30 September 2003.

2. During the year ended 30 September 2003, 280 members paid their annual subscription in full.
3. At 30 September 2003 subscriptions due from 15 members remained unpaid.

Prepare the subscriptions account as it would appear in the ledger of the Green Jackets Sports Club for the year ended 30 September 2003. Show clearly the amount transferred to the income and expenditure account. Bring down the balance on 1 October 2003.

[IGCSE 2003]

*2. The assets and liabilities of the Safat Judo Club on 1 February 2005 were as follows:

	$
Bank	3150 debit
Motor vehicle at valuation	2000
Subscriptions owed by members	250
Rent owing	50

The treasurer provided the following information for the year ended 31 January 2006:

Receipts during the year	$	Payments during the year	$
Subscriptions	10 650	Purchase of new motor vehicle	10 000
Proceeds of sale of motor vehicle	1 750	Competition prizes	210
		General expenses	2 645
Competition entrance fees	800	Travelling expenses	830
		Rent	2 600

The following information is also available:

1 The motor vehicle is used to take members to tournaments and competitions.

The motor vehicle owned on 1 February 2005 was sold in March 2005. No depreciation is provided for in the year of sale.

A new motor vehicle was purchased on the same day. On 31 January 2006 the new motor vehicle was valued at $8500.

Accounts of Clubs and Societies

2 On 31 January 2006:
subscriptions paid in advance by members amounted to $400;
rent prepaid amounted to $100.

Required

(a) Prepare the income and expenditure account of the Safat Judo Club for the year ended 31 January 2006.
(b) Prepare the balance sheet of the Safat Jude Club at 31 January 2006.

A member of the club is worried that the surplus or deficit in the income and expenditure account does not agree with the bank balance shown in the balance sheet at 31 January 2006.

Required

(c) State and explain **two** reasons for this difference.

[IGCSE 2006]

*3. The following terms are used in connection with non-trading organisations such as clubs.

Required

(a) Explain each of the following terms
 (i) Income and expenditure account
 (ii) Accumulated fund

The Siltones Music Society was formed some years ago. It has 40 members who each pay an annual subscription of $100.

On 1 April 2004 the Siltones Music Society had the following assets.

	$
Musical instruments (book value)	1200
Balance at bank	2210
Subscriptions due from members	1000
Rent of premises prepaid	280

The treasurer provided the following information relating to the year ended 31 March 2005. All receipts were paid into the bank and all payments were made by cheque.

	$	$
Subscriptions received from members		
for the year ended 31 March 2004	1000	
for the year ended 31 March 2005	4000	
for the year ending 31 March 2006	800	5800
Receipts from concert		1900
Expenses of concert		1250
Rent of premises		
for the year ended 31 March 2005	1400	
for the year ending 31 March 2006	420	1820
General expenses		215
Insurance		325
Proceeds of sale of musical instruments		700
Purchase of new musical instruments		3350

Required

(b) Prepare the receipts and payments account of the Siltones Music Society for the year ended 31 March 2005. Balance the account at 31 March and bring down the balance on 1 April 2005.

(c) Prepare the subscriptions account as it would appear in the ledger of the Siltones Music Society for the year ended 31 March 2005.

Show the amount transferred to the income and expenditure account.

Balance the account at 31 March and bring down the balance on 1 April 2005

[IGCSE 2005]

4. The Lobatse Rugby Club had the following assets and liabilities on 1 April 2008.

	$
Equipment at book value	4400
Cash at bank	3700
Subscriptions prepaid by members	100
Subscriptions owed by members	50
Accumulated fund	8050

Accounts of Clubs and Societies

The treasurer of the club prepared the following receipts and payments account for the year ended 31 March 2009.

2008			$	2008		$
April 1	Balance	b/d	3700	Mar 31	Transfer to bank deposit account	2000
2009					Equipment	1800
Mar 31	Subscriptions		2250		Secretarial expenses	210
	Interest received		100		Advertising	40
	Entrance fees for sports day		520		General expenses	490
					Rent	1530
					Sports day expenses	370
					Balance c/d	130
			6570			6570
2009						
April 1	Balance	b/d	130			

The treasurer supplied the following additional information.

1 On 31 March 2009:

	$
Subscriptions owing by members	200
Rent accrued	30
General expenses prepaid	20

2 The equipment is depreciated by 10% per annum on the value of equipment held at the end of each financial year.

Required

(a) Prepare the subscriptions account as it would appear in the ledger of the Lobatse Rugby Club for the year ended 31 March 2009.
Show the amount transferred to the income and expenditure account.
(b) Prepare the income and expenditure account of the Lobatse Rugby Club for the year ended 31 March 2009.
(c) Select one of the items appearing in the receipts and payments account which should **not** be included in the income and expenditure account and explain **why** it does not appear.

(d) Select one of the items appearing in the income and expenditure account which does **not** appear in the receipts and payments account and explain **why** it does not appear.

[IGCSE 2009]

5. The All Star Sports Club was formed on 1 August 2003.
The treasurer produced the following information for the year ended 31 July 2004.

Receipts	$	Payments	$
Subscriptions	14 600	Sports equipment	9 000
Snack bar sales	10 900	Snack bar supplies	7 850
Barbecue ticket sales	1 400	Barbecue expenses	750
		Staff wages:	
		Snack bar staff	2 100
		General staff	2 430
		Rent	2 160
		Insurance	1 660
		Repairs and maintenance	1 840
		General expenses	1 220

Additional information:

1. On 31 July 2004:

   10 members each owed the club $50 for their subscription for the current year.

   2 members had each paid $50 subscription for the year ending 31 July 2005.

2. On 31 July 2004:

	$
Trade payables for snack bar supplies	850
Inventory of snack bar supplies was valued at	1200
Rent prepaid amounted to	80
General expenses accrued amounted to	60

3. The sports equipment is to be depreciated using the straight line (equal instalment) method at 10% p.a. A full year's depreciation is charged in the year of purchase.

    (a) Prepare the snack bar income statement of the All Star Sports Club for the year ended 31 July 2004.

Accounts of Clubs and Societies

(b) Prepare the income and expenditure account of the All Star Sports Club for the year ended 31 July 2004.

(c) The All Star Sports Club has been given the opportunity to purchase the clubhouse and grounds in 2006. At the end of the first year the club has a bank overdraft of $2110. The treasurer is worried that the club will not have enough money to pay for the property.

Suggest **two** ways in which the club could raise a large sum of money for this purpose. [IGCSE 2004]

6. The accounts maintained by non-trading organisations such as clubs and societies often use different terms to those used in the accounts of a trading business.

Required

(a) Complete the following table to name the equivalent terms used by a non-trading organisation.
The first one has been completed as an example.

Trading business	*Non-trading organisation*
(i) Cash book	*Receipts and payments account*
(ii) Loss for the year	....
(iii) Capital	....
(iv) Profit and loss account	....

The treasurer of the El Nil Sailing Club maintains a full set of accounting records. The following account appears in the ledger of El Nil Sailing Club.

Subscriptions account

2005			$	2005			$
Aug 1	Balance	b/d	750	Aug 1	Balance	b/d	300
2006				2006			
July 31	Income & Expenditure		4500	July 31	Bank		5850
	Balance	c/d	900				
			6150				6150
				2006			
				Aug 1	Balance	b/d	900

Required

(b) (i) Explain each of the following entries in the subscriptions account as it appears in the ledger of El Nil Sailing club. State where the double entry for each transaction would be made.

The first one has been completed as an example.

2005 Aug 1 Balance $300

Explanation This is the total subscriptions paid by members during the financial year ended 31 July 2005 which relate to the following financial year.

Double entry Debit subscriptions account for the year ended 31 July 2005.

2005 Aug 1 Balance $750
2006 July 31 Bank $5850
2006 July 31 Income and expenditure $4500

(ii) Explain the significance of the $900 shown at the end of the subscriptions account and state where this amount will appear in El Nil Sailing Club's balance sheet at 31 July 2006.

The treasurer of El Nil Sailing Club provided the following information relating to the year ended 31 July 2006. All receipts were paid into the bank and all payments were made by cheque.

	$
Bank balance at 1 August 2005	6 300
Purchase of new boat	13 000
Repairs to boat	90
Proceeds of sale of old boat	280
Insurance	750
General expenses	560
Competition entrance fees received	690
Cost of competition prizes	420

Additional information

1 Details of the subscriptions are provided in the subscriptions account shown above.
2 At 31 July 2006 insurance prepaid amounted to $150 and general expenses outstanding amounted to $30.

Accounts of Clubs and Societies

Required

(c) Using the information above and the subscriptions account shown earlier in the question, prepare the receipts and payments account of El Nil Sailing Club for the year ended 31 July 2006.

[IGCSE 2006]

Chapter 19 Partnership Accounts

> **In this chapter you will learn to:**
> - recognise the advantages and disadvantages of partnerships
> - understand the purpose and contents of a partnership agreement
> - understand the entries necessary in connection with a loan from a partner
> - prepare a partnership profit and loss appropriation account and understand its purpose
> - prepare capital and current accounts in the ledger of a partnership
> - prepare a balance sheet of a partnership.

Introduction

The earlier chapters (except Chapter 18) related to businesses which were owned by only one person (a sole trader). Another very common form of business is a partnership. **A partnership is a business in which two or more people work together as owners with a view to making profits**. Normally, there cannot be more than 20 partners in a business.

Professional people such as accountants and solicitors often operate as partnerships. A large number of family businesses also run as partnerships. Sometime a new business is formed as a partnership: sometimes a partnership is formed when a sole trader wishes to expand his/her business: sometimes a partnership is formed when two or more sole traders agree to amalgamate their businesses.

A partnership business will maintain double entry records in the same way as a sole trader. At the end of the financial year, an income statement and a balance sheet are prepared. However, a partnership will prepare an extra account after the income statement. This is known as a **profit and loss appropriation account**.

Partnership Accounts

The Advantages and Disadvantages of Partnership Businesses

Before agreeing to enter into a partnership business a person must consider the likely advantages and disadvantages of such an arrangement. The advantages and disadvantages are summarised as follows:

Advantages	Disadvantages
Additional finance is available.	Profits have to be shared among the partners.
Additional knowledge, experience and skills are available.	Decisions have to be recognised by all partners.
The responsibilities are shared.	Decisions may take longer to put into effect.
The risks are shared.	One partner's actions on behalf of the business are binding on all the partners.
Discussions can take place before decisions are taken.	Disagreements can occur.
	All partners are responsible for the debts of the business.

> **Test your understanding**
> 1. Define a partnership.
> 2. Rahul is a sole trader. He forms a partnership with Anuradha. State
>   (a) **two** benefits this may have for Rahul
>   (b) **two** drawbacks this may have for Rahul.

Partnership Agreement

Although it is not legally necessary to draw up a partnership agreement when forming a partnership, it is advisable to do so. Drawing up an agreement can avoid misunderstandings and arguments later. The clauses of a partnership agreement cover many aspects of the business. Those relating to the accounting usually include the following:

Amount of capital invested by each partner.	Partners do not need to invest equal amounts.
How profits and losses are to be shared.	Profits and losses may be shared equally, in proportion to capital invested, or in some other ratio.
If interest on partners' capital is to be paid, and if so, at what rate.	This interest is a reward for investing in the business rather than elsewhere. If all partners invest the same amount it may not be necessary to pay interest. Where partners invest different amounts, interest can be a form of compensation to the person who has invested most capital.
If partners' salaries are to be paid, and if so, what amount.	If all partners share the work and responsibilities equally it may be not necessary to pay salaries. A salary can be a form of compensation where one partner has a greater share of the work and responsibilities.
If an upper limit is to be placed on partners' drawings, and if so, what amount.	The business will benefit if partners keep drawings as low as possible.
If interest on partners' drawings is to be charged, and if so, at what rate.	This is a method of discouraging partners from making drawings from the business (especially early in the financial year). Interest on the amount withdrawn is calculated from the date of withdrawal until the end of the financial year.
If interest on partners' loans is to be paid, and if so, at what rate.	If extra finance is required a partner may make a loan to the business. To compensate for the loss of interest they could otherwise earn, interest on the loan may be paid.

Loans from Partners

A partnership may borrow money from one of the partners if extra finance is required (particularly if it is needed for a fixed period of time). Loans from partners are **not** part of the capital of the business and are treated in the same way as any other loan.

Partnership Accounts

When a loan is obtained from a partner

Debit bank account   Credit loan from partner X account

When a loan is repaid to a partner

Debit loan from partner X account   Credit bank account

The loan account appears as a non-current liability in the balance sheet

Interest on loan paid

Debit interest on loan account   Credit bank account

Interest on loan due but not paid

Debit interest on loan account   Credit partner X current account*

The interest on loan account is transferred to the debit of the income statement

Preparation of a Profit and Loss Appropriation Account of a Partnership Business

The profit and loss appropriation account for the financial year is prepared after the income statement and shows how the profit for the year is shared between the partners.

The profit for the year is transferred to this account from the income statement. Any interest on drawings charged to the partners increases the amount available to share and this must be added to the profit. The **appropriations** (profit shares) detailed in the partnership agreement for interest on capital and partners' salaries are deducted. The remaining figure is known as the **residual profit** and is shared between the partners in the agreed profit-sharing ratio.

Example 19.1

Sumit and Padma are in partnership. Their financial year ends on 31 May. They provide the following information.

---

*See later in this Chapter.

		$
Capital on 1 June 20-8 – Sumit		40 000
Padma		20 000
Drawings for the year ended 31 May 20-9 –	Sumit	11 000
	Padma	8 000
Profit for the year ended 31 May 20-9		24 680

The partnership agreement includes the following terms:

Interest on capital is allowed at 5% per annum
Interest on drawings is charged at 3% per annum
Padma is entitled to a partnership salary of $9500 per annum
Residual profits are shared in proportion to capital invested

Prepare the profit and loss appropriation account for the year ended 31 May 20-9.

Sumit and Padma
Profit and Loss Appropriation Account for the year ended 31 May 20-9

			$	$	$
Profit for the year					24 680
Add Interest on drawings –	Sumit			330	
	Padma			240	570
					25 250
Less Interest on capital –	Sumit		2 000		
	Padma		1 000	3 000	
Partner's salary –	Padma			9 500	12 500
					12 750
*Profit shares –	Sumit			8 500	
	Padma			4 250	12 750

*The profit shares are calculated.

Sumit $\dfrac{40\ 000}{60\ 000} \times \dfrac{12\ 750}{1}$ Padma $\dfrac{20\ 000}{60\ 000} \times \dfrac{12\ 750}{1}$

Partnership Accounts

> **Test your understanding**
> 1. Explain why partners may agree to charge interest on drawings.
> 2. Explain why partners may agree to allow interest on capital.
> 3. Explain the term residual profit.

Partners' Ledger Account

Capital accounts

Similar to a sole trader each member of the partnership business has their own capital account in the nominal ledger. These usually record permanent increases or decreases in the capital invested by the individual partner. Capital accounts prepared in this way are referred to as **fixed capital accounts**.

A capital account has a credit balance as the business owes this to the partner.

Current accounts

Each member of a partnership business also has a current account. Anything which the partner becomes entitled to such as interest on capital, interest on loan, partner's salary, and profit share is credited to this account. Anything which the partner is charged with, such as drawings and interest on drawings is debited to this account.

A credit balance on a current account represents the amount owed to the partner and a debit balance represents the amount owed by the partner to the business. If a partner's drawings are more than his/her total share of profit, the current account will have a debit balance as the partner owes this to the business. If a partner's drawings are less than his/her total share of profit, the current account will have a credit balance as the business owes this to the partner.

If current accounts are not maintained interest on capital, partners' salaries, profit share, drawings and interest on drawings are recorded in the capital account.

Drawings accounts

A drawings account is maintained for each partner. The total of this account is transferred to the partner's current account at the end of the financial year.

Example 19.2

Sumit and Padma are in partnership. Their financial year ends on 31 May. They provide the following information.

	Sumit $	Padma $
On 1 June 20-8:		
Capital account	40 000	20 000
Current account	130 cr	910 dr
For the year ended 31 May 20-9:		
Drawings	11 000	8 000
Interest on drawings	330	240
Interest on capital	2 000	1 000
Partner's salary		9 500
Profit share	8 500	4 250

Prepare the capital account and the current account of Sumit for the year ended 31 May 20-9.

Sumit and Padma
Sumit Capital account

Date	Details	Folio	$	Date	Details	Folio	$
				20-8			
				June 1	Balance	b/d	40 000

Partnership Accounts

Sumit Current account

Date	Details	Folio	$	Date	Details	Folio	$
20-9 May 31	Drawings		11 000	20-8 June 1	Balance	b/d	130
	Interest on drawings		330	20-9 May 31	Interest on capital		2 000
					Profit share		8 500
					Balance	c/d	700
			11 330				11 330
20-9 June 1	Balance	b/d	700				

In examinations, it saves time to show partners' capital accounts and current accounts side-by-side using a column for each partner.

Example 19.3

Using the information in **Example 19.2** prepare the capital and current accounts of Sumit and Padma for the year ended 31 May 20-9. Prepare the accounts in columnar format.

Sumit and Padma
Capital accounts

			Sumit	Padma				Sumit	Padma
Date	Details	Fo	$	$	Date	Details	Fo	$	$
					20-8 June 1	Balance	b/d	40 000	20 000

Current accounts

Date	Details	Fo	Sumit $	Padma $	Date	Details	Fo	Sumit $	Padma $
20-8					20-8				
June 1	Balance	b/d		910	June 1	Balance	b/d	130	
20-9					20-9				
May 31	Drawings		11 000	8 000	May 31	Interest on capital		2 000	1 000
	Interest on drawings		330	240		Salary			9 500
	Balance	c/d		5 600		Profit share		8 500	4 250
						Balance	c/d	700	
			11 330	14 750				11 330	14 750
20-9					20-9				
June 1	Balance	b/d	700		June 1	Balance	b/d		5600

Test your understanding

1. A partner has a debit balance on her current account.
   (a) Explain what may have caused this.
   (b) Explain whether it represents money owed by the business to the partner or by the partner to the business.

Preparation of a Balance Sheet of a Partnership Business

A balance sheet of a partnership is same as that of a sole trader with the exception of the capital section. This must show that the capital account and current account balances for each partner separately.

It is not necessary to show all the details of the transactions affecting the current accounts. It is adequate to show the closing balance on each account.

Example 19.4

Sumit and Padma are in partnership. Their financial year ends on 31 May. Their current accounts are shown in **Example 19.3**.

Prepare a relevant extract from the balance sheet of Sumit and Padma at 31 May 20-9.

Partnership Accounts

Sumit and Padma
Extract from Balance Sheet at 31 May 20-9

	$ Sumit	$ Padma	$ Total
Capital accounts	40 000	20 000	60 000
Current accounts	(700)*	5 600	4 900
	39 300	25 600	64 900

* The debit balance on Sumit's current account is shown as a minus, which reduces the amount owed by the business to Sumit.

Sometimes the partners may wish to show the full details of the current accounts in the balance sheet. An examination question may also ask for details to be shown (this may also be necessary if current accounts are not prepared as part of the answer).

Example 19.5

Sumit and Padma are in partnership. Their financial year ends on 31 May. Their current accounts are shown in **Example 19.3**.

Prepare a relevant extract from the balance sheet of Sumit and Padma on 31 May 20-9 showing full details of their current accounts.

Sumit and Padma
Extract from Balance Sheet at 31 May 20-9

	$ Sumit	$ Padma	$ Total
Capital accounts	40 000	20 000	60 000
Current accounts			
Opening Balance	130	(910)	
Interest on capital	2 000	1 000	
Partner's salary		9 500	
Profit share	8 500	4 250	
	10 630	13 840	
Less Drawings	11 000	8 000	
Interest on drawings	330	240	
	11 330	8 240	
	(700)	5 600	4 900
			64 900

Points to Remember

1. A partnership is a business in which two or more people work together as owners with a view to making profits.
2. There are both advantages and disadvantages of being a member of a partnership business.
3. It is advisable to draw up a partnership agreement when the partnership is formed.
4. A partner may make a loan to the business. This is treated in a similar way to all other loans.
5. A profit and loss appropriation account is prepared after the income statement to share out the profit between the partners.
6. Each partner usually has a capital account and a current account.
7. In the balance sheet of a partnership the balances on each partner's capital account and current account must be shown separately.

Review Questions

1. Frankie and Johnny are in partnership. Their financial year ends on 31 August. After the preparation of their income statement for the year ended 31 August 2003, the following balances remained on the books.

		$
Capital accounts:	Frankie	50 000
	Johnny	30 000
Current accounts:	Frankie	15 000
	Johnny	5 000 Dr
Non-current assets at cost		85 000
Provision for depreciation of non-current assets		10 000
Inventory		8 000
Trade receivables		14 000
Bank balance		5 000 Dr
Trade payables		12 000

Partnership Accounts

Prepare the balance sheet of the partnership at 31 August 2003. Show the working capital.

[IGCSE 2003]

2. Smith and Travers are in partnership sharing profits and losses in accordance with their partnership agreement which states the following:
   1. Interest on capital is allowed at 5% per annum
   2. Salary to be paid to Smith of $15 000 per annum
   3. Interest to be charged on each partner's drawings for the year at 4% per annum
   4. Travers and Smith share the balance of profits in the ratio 3:2.

   The balances on the partners' capital accounts at 1 October 2005 were:

Smith	$30 000
Travers	$40 000

   The partners' drawings for the year ended 30 September 2006 were:

Smith	$35 000
Travers	$15 000

   The profit of the partnership for the year ended 30 September 2006 was $89 000.

   Required

   (a) Prepare the profit and loss appropriation account for the partnership for the year ended 30 September 2006.

   Smith's current account in the partnership books showed a balance of $2300 credit at 1 October 2005.

   Required

   (b) Using the information above and your answer to Part (a), calculate the balance on Smith's current account at 30 September 2006.

   [IGCSE 2006]

*3 Raminder and Vijay Singh formed a partnership and drew up a partnership agreement.

   Required

   (a) State **two** advantages of being in partnership rather than being a sole trader.

(b) State why, in addition to agreeing the profit-sharing ratio, partners should draw up a partnership agreement.

On 1 April 2007 the balances of the partners' current accounts were as follows.

	$
Raminder Singh	4 660 debit
Vijay Singh	1 820 credit

During the year ended 31 March 2008 the partners made the following drawings.

	$
Raminder Singh	21 000
Vijay Singh	28 000

The following information was extracted from the profit and loss appropriation account for the year ended 31 March 2008.

		$	$
Profit for the year			58 040
Interest charged on drawings –	Raminder	840	
	Vijay	1 120	1 960
Interest allowed on capital –	Raminder	6 000	
	Vijay	3 000	9 000
Partner's salary –	Vijay		20 000

Profits and losses are shared equally.

Required

(c) (i) Calculate the profit available for distribution between the partners.
  (ii) Calculate **each** partner's share of the profit available for distribution.
  (iii) Prepare the partners' current accounts as they would appear in the ledger for the year ended 31 March 2008.

On 1 April 2008 the credit balances on the partners' capital accounts were as follows.

	$
Raminder Singh	200 000
Vijay Singh	100 000

Partnership Accounts

On 1 April 2008 Raminder transferred the balance on his current account to his capital account. He also withdrew $45 000 of his capital from the business bank account.

On 30 April 2008 Vijay paid an amount into the business bank account so that his capital was equal to Raminder's.

Required

(d) Prepare the partners' capital accounts as they would appear in the ledger for the month of April 2008.

[IGCSE Specimen Paper]

4. Ruth and Lucy Lebengo formed a partnership on 1 October 2003. They share profits and losses 2:1. They agreed that a current account and a capital account would be kept for each partner.

The income statement for the year ended 30 September 2004 showed a profit for the year of $12 000.

Lucy has very little knowledge of bookkeeping, but attempted to prepare a balance sheet at 30 September 2004. The balance sheet she prepared, containing errors, is shown below.

Balance Sheet at 30 September 2004

	$	$	$
Premises at cost			35 000
Motor vehicles at cost		15 000	
Less Depreciation		1 500	13 500
Office equipment			3 000
Inventory			9 300
Trade receivables			5 900
			66 700
Capital – Ruth		30 000	
Lucy		20 000	50 000
Profit for the year		12 000	
Less Drawings – Ruth	4 000		
Lucy	4 400	8 400	3 600
Trade payables			7 400
Bank overdraft			5 100
			66 100

The following matters were then discovered.
1 No adjustment had been made in the balance sheet for the following:

	$
Depreciation of office equipment	300
Provision for doubtful debts	200

These items had been correctly charged in the income statement.
2 Cash in hand, $100, had been omitted from the balance sheet.
3 The overdraft shown on the bank statement had been entered in the balance sheet instead of the overdraft of $5300 shown in the cash book.

Taking the above matters into account, prepare a corrected balance sheet for Ruth and Lucy at 30 September 2004.

The balance sheet should be shown using a suitable form of presentation, showing the different types of assets and liabilities, the net current assets, and the capital and current accounts of each partner.

[IGCSE 2004]

*5. Archer and Bowman are partners.

Their income statement for the year ended 31 August 2003 showed a profit for the year of $18 490.

It was then found that the following errors had been made.
1 No entry had been made for inventory of stationery, $30, on 31 August 2003.
2 The inventory of goods for re-sale on 31 August 2003 had been valued at selling price, $8400, instead of cost price, $7000.
3 No entry had been made for depreciation of equipment. The equipment cost $13 000 and was estimated to have a scrap value of $1000 after 6 years. All the non-current assets of the partnership are depreciated using the straight line (fixed instalment) method.
4 Discount received of $210 has been included in the expenses instead of the income in the income statement.
5 A provision for doubtful debts is maintained equal to 5% of the trade receivables at the end of each financial year. On

Partnership Accounts

1 September 2002 the provision was $400. On 31 August 2003 the trade receivables totalled $8400. No adjustment has been made to the provision for doubtful debts.

(a) Prepare a statement to show the effect of correcting each of the errors 1-5 on Archer and Bowman's original profit for the year. Calculate the corrected profit for the year. The first one has been completed as an example.

Archer and Bowman
Statement of corrected profit for the year ended 31 August 2003

	Effect on profit		$
Profit for the year before corrections			18 490
	+	–	
	$	$	
Error 1	30		
2			
3			
4			
Corrected profit for the year			

Archer and Bowman's partnership agreement states that
  Interest is to be allowed on capital at 5% per annum
  Interest is to be charged on drawings at 5% per annum
  Archer is to receive an annual salary of $6000
  Profits and losses are to be shared equally.
On 31 August 2003 the following balances appeared in the partnership books.

		$
Capital account (at 1 September 2002) – Archer		40 000
Bowman		80 000
Drawings during the year ended 31 August 2003 – Archer		7 000
Bowman		3 000

(b) Using the corrected profit for the year calculated in (a), prepare the profit and loss appropriation account of Archer and Bowman for the year ended 31 August 2003.

[IGCSE 2003]

*6. Ebor and Olicana are in partnership trading in sports goods. Their financial year ends on 31 July. After the preparation of their income statement for the year ended 31 July 2005 the following errors were discovered.
1. Olicana had taken goods costing $500 for her own use. This had not been recorded.
2. $15 paid for carriage inwards had been debited to the carriage outwards account.
3. The purchase of computer paper, $30, had been debited to the purchases account.
4. Motor vehicle repairs of $200 had been debited to the motor vehicles account. Motor vehicles are depreciated by 25% on the cost of motors held at the end of each financial year.

Required
(a) Complete the following table to show the effect of **correcting the errors** on the gross profit and the net profit. If the correction of the error does not affect the profit write 'no effect'.
The first one has been completed as an example.

Error	Effect of correcting the error	
	on the gross profit	on the net profit
1	+$500	+$500
2		
3		
4		

Ebor and Olicana maintain a full set of books of account.
The following transactions took place on 31 August 2005.
1. Olicana took further goods costing $400 for her own use.
2. Ebor brought his own computer, valued at $900, into the business
3. Ebor's current account showed a credit balance of $10 000. It was agreed that he should transfer half of this to his capital account.

Partnership Accounts

> **Required**
>
> (b) Prepare the necessary journal entries to record the above transactions. Narratives **are** required.
>
> [IGCSE 2005]
>
> 7. Salim and Rita Jaffer are in partnership. Their financial year ends on 31 July. They share profits and losses equally. It was agreed that a current account and a capital account would be kept for each partner.
>
> Their income statement for the year ended 31 July 2008 showed a profit for the year of $15 500. The accountant was unable to prepare the balance sheet immediately because of illness.
>
> Salim has very little knowledge of bookkeeping, but attempted to prepare a balance sheet at 31 July 2008. The balance sheet he prepared, containing errors, is shown below.
>
> Balance Sheet at 31 July 2008
>
> | | | $ | $ |
> |---|---|---:|---:|
> | Premises at cost | | | 95 000 |
> | Equipment at book value at 1 August 2007 | | | 13 000 |
> | Inventory 31 July 2008 | | | 8 200 |
> | Trade receivables | | | 6 600 |
> | Drawings – Salim Jaffer | | 7 700 | |
> | Rita Jaffer | | 6 220 | 13 920 |
> | | | | 136 720 |
> | Trade payables | | | 6 800 |
> | Provision for doubtful debts | | | 330 |
> | Profit for the year | | | 15 500 |
> | Capital accounts 1 August 2007 – | Salim Jaffer | 40 000 | |
> | | Rita Jaffer | 60 000 | 100 000 |
> | Current accounts 1 August 2007 – | Salim Jaffer | 3 400 Cr | |
> | | Rita Jaffer | 6 100 Cr | 9 500 |
> | | | | 132 130 |
> | Balancing figure | | | 4 590 |
> | | | | 136 720 |

The following matters were then discovered.
1 No adjustment had been made in the balance sheet for the following:

	$
Other payables	620
Other receivables	430
Depreciation of equipment	1500

These items had been correctly recorded in the income statement.

2 The bank balance had been omitted from the balance sheet. On 31 July 2008 the cash book showed a bank overdraft of $2900 and the bank statement showed an overdraft of $2200.

All the transactions appearing on the bank statement had been recorded in the cash book.

Required

(a) Prepare a corrected balance sheet for Salim and Rita Jaffer at 31 July 2008.

The balance sheet should be shown using a suitable form of presentation, showing the different types of assets and liabilities, the net current assets and the capital and current accounts of each partner.

The calculation of the current account balances may either be shown within the balance sheet or as separate calculations.

On 1 August 2008 the balances on the partners' capital accounts were the same as those on 1 August 2007.

On 1 August 2008 Rita transferred $4000 from the credit balance on her current account to her capital account.

On 31 August 2008 Salim paid an amount into the business bank account so that his capital was equal to Rita's.

Required

(b) Write up the partners' capital accounts as they would appear in the ledger for the month of August 2008.

Partnership Accounts

Salim Jaffer suggests that it would be easier to maintain only a capital account for each partner instead of both a capital account and a current account.

Required

(c) State and explain **one** advantage of maintaining both a capital and a current account for each partner.

[IGCSE 2008]

Chapter 20 Accounts of Manufacturing Businesses

In this chapter you will learn to:
- understand the purpose of a manufacturing account
- understand the elements of cost
- prepare a manufacturing account
- calculate prime cost and cost of production
- prepare an income statement of a manufacturing business
- prepare a balance sheet of a manufacturing business.

Introduction

The previous chapters (except Chapter 18) relate to about businesses which are involved in trading (such as wholesale or retail businesses which buy goods and sell them without changing the goods in any way) or service businesses. There are, of course, manufacturing businesses which buy raw materials and convert these into finished products which they then sell.

A manufacturing business will maintain double entry records similar to those of retail and wholesale businesses. At the end of the financial year, in addition to an income statement (and possibly an appropriation account) and balance sheet, a manufacturing business will also prepare a **manufacturing account**. The purpose of preparing this account is to calculate how much it has cost the business to manufacture the goods produced in the financial year.

Accounts of Manufacturing Businesses

The Elements of Cost

The cost of manufacture is made up of four main elements. These are:

Direct material

The first thing a manufacturer needs is raw material to make the finished goods. This raw material takes many forms depending on the type of business – a baker will need flour, a furniture maker will need wood, a car maker will need steel and so on.

Direct labour

The next essential cost for a manufacturer is the cost of the wages of the people who are employed in the factory making the goods. Depending on the type of business, these may be bakers, carpenters, machine operators and so on. This cost is sometimes referred to as **direct wages**.

The term direct labour includes only those people who are actually involved in the production of the finished goods. It does not include the wages of supervisors, maintenance staff, factory cleaners etc. These people have an important role to play within the factory, but are regarded as indirect labour.

Direct expenses

These are any expenses which a manufacturer can directly link with the product being manufactured. It may be that, for every item produced, a manufacturer has to pay a fee (known as a **royalty**) to the person who originally invented the product. A manufacturer may have to hire a special piece of equipment to complete the manufacturing process. Such expenses are regarded as direct expenses.

Factory overheads

These are sometimes referred to as **indirect factory expenses**. They include all the costs involved in operating the factory which cannot be directly linked with the product being manufactured. Expenses such as factory rent and rates, factory heat and light, factory machinery repairs, depreciation of factory machinery, indirect factory wages etc. are all regarded as factory overheads.

> **Test your understanding**
> 1. Explain the difference between direct factory wages and indirect factory wages.
> 2. Give two examples of direct expenses.
> 3. For **each** of the following state whether it is direct material, direct labour, or a factory overhead of a clothing factory:
>   (a) electricity used in the factory
>   (b) purchase of suiting fabric
>   (c) wages of factory supervisors
>   (d) wages of sewing machinists
>   (e) purchase of spare parts for machine
>   (f) purchase of buttons and threads

Preparation of a Manufacturing Account

The cost of manufacturing the goods produced is calculated in the manufacturing account.

The first item in a manufacturing account is **direct material**. The cost of the raw material used during the year is calculated in a similar way to that in which a retailer calculates the cost of goods sold. The cost of raw material actually used during the year is calculated:

>   Opening inventory of raw material
> + Purchases of raw material
> + Carriage inwards on raw material
> − Closing inventory of raw material

The cost of the **direct labour** is then added to the direct material. Any **direct expenses** are then added.

The total of these three elements of cost is known as the **prime cost**.

| Direct material | + | Direct labour | + | Direct expenses | = | Prime cost |

The total **cost of production** is found by adding the **factory overheads** to the prime cost.

| Prime cost | + | Factory overheads | = | Cost of production |

Accounts of Manufacturing Businesses

Example 20.1

The following information was provided by the Kapoor Manufacturing Company on 30 April 20-6.

	$
Raw materials – Inventory 1 May 20-5	14 900
Inventory 30 April 20-6	15 300
Purchases	181 200
Carriage on purchases	3 300
Factory wages – Direct	166 100
Indirect	93 800
Royalties	10 000
Factory insurance	2 070
Factory rent and rates	2 930
Factory general expenses	6 350
Depreciation of factory machinery	9 500

Prepare the manufacturing account of the Kapoor Manufacturing Company for the year ended 30 April 20-6.

Kapoor Manufacturing Company
Manufacturing Account for the year ended 30 April 20-6

	$	$
Cost of material consumed		
Opening inventory of raw material	14 900	
Purchases of raw material	181 200	
Carriage on purchases	3 300	
	199 400	
Less Closing inventory of raw material	15 300	184 100
Direct wages		166 100
Direct expenses		
Royalties		10 000
Prime Cost		360 200
Factory overheads		
Indirect wages	93 800	
Insurance	2 070	
Rent and rates	2 930	
General expenses	6 350	
Depreciation of machinery	9 500	114 650
Production cost of goods completed		474 850

> **Test your understanding**
> 1. Explain the term prime cost.
> 2. State an alternative term for factory overheads.

Work in Progress

Goods which are partly completed at the end of the financial year are known as **work in progress**. The work in progress is excluded from the cost of production as these goods cannot be sold until they are completed. They do have some value however, as it has cost something to get them to their present condition – some material has been used and some direct wages have been incurred and so on. It is therefore necessary to place a value on the work in progress.

The partly-made goods at the end of the financial year are known as **closing work in progress**. These goods will, of course, become the **opening work in progress** at the start of the following financial year.

In a manufacturing account, it is necessary to adjust the cost of production so that it represents only the cost of goods actually completed in the year. This adjustment is done in the same way as for any other type of inventory – the opening inventory is added and the closing inventory is deducted.

Example 20.2

The following information was provided by the Kapoor Manufacturing Company on 30 April 20-6.

		$
Prime cost		360 200
Factory overheads		114 650
Work in progress –	Inventory 1 May 20-5	8 790
	Inventory 30 April 20-6	8 640

Prepare the manufacturing account of the Kapoor Manufacturing Company for the year ended 30 April 20-6.

Accounts of Manufacturing Businesses

Kapoor Manufacturing Company
Manufacturing Account for the year ended 30 April 20-6

	$	$
* Prime Cost		360 200
* Factory overheads		114 650
		474 850
Add Opening work in progress		8 790
		483 640
Less Closing work in progress		8 640
Production cost of goods completed		475 000

* Full details would be shown as in **Example 20.1**.

> **Test your understanding**
> 1. Explain the term "work in progress".
> 2. State why it is necessary to adjust the cost of production for work in progress.

Calculation of Unit Cost

Where a manufacturer makes only one identical product, the cost of making one article can be found by dividing the cost of goods completed by the number of articles manufactured.

Example 20.3

The Kapoor Manufacturing Company makes one identical product. The production cost of goods completed during the year ended 30 April 20-6 was $475 000, and a total of 20 000 articles were completed.
Calculate the unit cost.

$$\text{Unit cost} = \frac{\text{Production cost of goods completed}}{\text{Number of units produced}} = \frac{\$475\,000}{20\,000} = \$23.75$$

Preparation of a Trading Account Section of an Income Statement of a Manufacturing Business

The gross profit of a manufacturing business is calculated in the trading account section of the income statement. This is very similar to that prepared by a wholesale or retail business. The main difference is that, because the business actually makes the goods it sells, the item for purchases is replaced by the production cost of goods completed. Sometimes, however, a manufacturing business may purchase some finished goods which it does not manufacture itself. This may occur:

- when production does not meet demand
- when it is cheaper to buy the goods rather than make them
- when those particular items cannot be made by the business.

Purchases of finished goods are added to the production cost of goods completed in the trading account.

In the trading account the proceeds from the sale of finished goods is compared with the cost of those finished goods. This means that the inventories included in a trading account are the inventories of finished goods held by the manufacturer at the start and end of the financial year.

Example 20.4

The following information was provided by the Kapoor Manufacturing Company on 30 April 20-6.

		$
*Production cost of goods completed		475 000
Revenue (sales)		661 500
Finished goods – Inventory 1 May 20-5		31 000
Inventory 30 April 20-6		23 250
Purchases		15 500

*Calculated in the manufacturing account.

Prepare the trading account section of the income statement of the Kapoor Manufacturing Company for the year ended 30 April 20-6.

Accounts of Manufacturing Businesses

Kapoor Manufacturing Company
Income Statement for the year ended 30 April 20-6

	$	$
Revenue (sales)		661 500
Less Cost of sales		
Opening inventory of finished goods	31 000	
Production cost of goods completed	475 000	
Purchases of finished goods	15 500	
	521 500	
Less Closing inventory of finished goods	23 250	498 250
Gross profit		163 250

> **Test your understanding**
> 1. Explain why the production cost of goods completed appears in a trading account section of the income statement of a manufacturing business.
> 2. Explain why a manufacturer may sometimes purchase finished goods from another manufacturer.

Preparation of a Profit and Loss Account Section of an Income Statement of a Manufacturing Business

The net profit of a manufacturing business is calculated in the profit and loss account section of the income statement. This is very similar to that prepared by a wholesale or retail business. Expenses relating to the manufacturing process have already been entered in the manufacturing account, so only administration expenses, selling and distribution expenses, and financial expenses will appear in the profit and loss account.

Where an expense relates to the whole of the business it may be necessary to share this out between the factory and the offices. Expenses such as insurance of buildings, rent and rates, and heat and light often have to be apportioned in this way. For example the insurance of the buildings may be apportioned 2/3 to the factory and 1/3 to the offices. This means that if the total cost of insurance was $900 an amount of $600 would be included in the manufacturing account and $300 in the profit and loss account.

Preparation of a Balance Sheet of a Manufacturing Business

The balance sheet of a manufacturing business is similar to that prepared by a wholesale or retail business. There is only one main difference which is that a manufacturer may have three different inventories – raw material, work in progress and finished goods. It is usual to show each of these inventories are shown separately in the current asset section of the balance sheet.

Example 20.5

On 30 April 20-6 the Kapoor Manufacturing Company had inventories valued as follows:

	$
Raw material	15 300
Work in progress	8 640
Finished goods	23 250

Prepare a relevant extract from the balance sheet of the Kapoor Manufacturing Company at 30 April 20-6.

Kapoor Manufacturing Company
Balance Sheet at 30 April 20-6

		$	$
Current assets			
Inventories –	raw materials	15 300	
	work in progress	8 640	
	finished goods	<u>23 250</u>	47 190

Year-end Adjustments

This Chapter has concentrated on the difference between the financial statements of a manufacturing business and those of a trading business. In order to emphasise these differences none of the examples included year-end adjustments. A manufacturer may well have to make year-end adjustments for such things as accruals, prepayments, provision for doubtful debts and so on. These should be treated as described in earlier chapters.

Accounts of Manufacturing Businesses

Points to Remember

1. A manufacturing account is used to calculate the cost of making goods produced in the financial year. It consists of direct materials + direct labour + direct expenses + factory overheads.
2. Direct materials + direct labour + direct expenses = prime cost
3. The cost of goods produced may have to be amended for the goods partly made at the end of the financial year (known as work in progress).
4. In the trading account section of the income statement of a manufacturer, the cost of goods produced is included together with any purchases of finished goods.
5. In the balance sheet of a manufacturer, it may be necessary to show three different inventories.

Review Questions

1. The financial year of Leeford Manufacturers Ltd ends on 30 September. They supplied the following information.

	$
At 1 October 20-7	
Inventory of raw materials	41 800
Inventory of finished goods	62 300
Work in progress	18 600
For the year ended 30 September 20-8	
Purchases of raw materials	495 800
Purchases of finished goods	4 300
Revenue (sales)	824 000

Wages – factory direct wages	52 750
factory indirect salaries	29 760
office and sales salaries	36 890
Factory expenses	41 840
At 30 September 20-8	
Inventory of raw materials	43 200
Inventory of finished goods	60 750
Work in progress	17 850

(a) Select the relevant figures and prepare the manufacturing account of Leeford Manufacturers Ltd for the year ended 30 September 20-8.

(b) Select **two** of the items in the above list which should **not** appear in a manufacturing account and explain why they are not included.

2. The Playground Company makes equipment for children's playgrounds. It was formed on 1 January 2003 by Ismail Nasser.

The following information was extracted from the books at the end of the first financial year.

	$
Revenue (sales)	151 400
Purchases of raw materials	48 500
Direct factory wages	26 900
Indirect factory wages	18 400
Factory general expenses	4 930
Factory fuel and power	4 700

On 31 December 2003 the following additional information was provided.

	$
1. Fuel and power accrued amounted to	150
2. Direct factory wages accrued amounted to	650
3. Inventories were valued at – raw material	2 700
work in progress	1 920
finished goods	4 910

Accounts of Manufacturing Businesses

4. Factory machinery was valued at $19 550. It had been purchased for $21 000 on 1 January 2003. There were no other purchases or sales of machinery during the year.

   (a) Prepare the manufacturing account of the Playground Company for the year ended 31 December 2003.

   (b) Prepare the trading account section of the income statement of the Playground Company for the year ended 31 December 2003.

   [IGCSE 2004]

*3. (a) Explain the difference between
   (i) direct costs and indirect costs
   (ii) prime cost and cost of production.

   (b) Explain the meaning of the term "work in progress".

   (c) Explain why a manufacturer may purchase finished goods as well as raw materials.

Iftikhar is a manufacturer. He provided the following information for the year ended 31 May 20-9.

		$
1 June 20-8	Inventory of raw materials	4 750
	Work in progress	5 600
31 May 20-9	Inventory of raw materials	4 850
	Work in progress	4 300
For the year ended 31 May 20-9		
	Purchases of raw materials	49 590
	Direct factory wages	61 940
	Indirect factory wages	29 660
	Carriage on raw materials	3 710
	Factory direct expenses	2 960
	Factory indirect expenses	48 930

   (d) (i) Calculate the prime cost.
       (ii) Calculate the cost of production.

*4. (a) Explain why it is necessary for a manufacturing business to prepare a manufacturing account in addition to an income statement.

(b) Explain **each** of the following terms in connection with a manufacturing business.
   (i) Cost of materials consumed
   (ii) Prime cost
   (iii) Production cost.

(c) The financial year of El Sayed Manufacturing Company ends on 31 August. The following information is provided.

Inventories	On 1 September 2002 $	On 31 August 2003 $
Raw material	7040	6220
Work in progress	810	950
Finished goods	5780	6100

For the year ended 31 August 2003:

	$
Revenue (sales)	180 500
Purchases of raw materials	43 820
Wages – factory operatives	40 190
factory supervisors	18 400
office and sales staff	37 000
General expenses – factory	5 340
office	3 600
Rates and insurance	7 500

Additional information:
1. The factory machinery cost $42 000 and the office machinery cost $23 000. In each case the annual depreciation charge is 20% on cost.
2. The rates and insurance are to be apportioned – factory 4/5 and office 1/5.
3. On 31 August 2003 wages due were – factory operatives $1170 office staff $600.

Extract the necessary information from the above figures and prepare the manufacturing account of El Sayed Manufacturing Company for the year ended 31 August 2003.

[IGCSE 2003]

Accounts of Manufacturing Businesses

5. Gideon Yeboah is a manufacturer. He provided the following information.

	At 1 April 2007 $	At 31 March 2008 $
Inventory – raw materials	21 230	19 410
work in progress	11 680	12 130
finished goods	46 900	53 170

For the year ended 31 March 2008

	$
Revenue (sales)	825 000
Purchases of raw materials	255 620
Purchases of finished goods	13 200
Direct factory wages	194 060
Factory general expenses	133 910

The following additional information is available on 31 March 2008.
1. Direct factory wages accrued amounted to $4800.
2. The factory general expenses include insurance on the factory which is prepaid by $210.
3. The factory machinery was valued at $92 000.
   On 1 April 2007 the factory machinery was valued at $103 000. Additional machinery costing $21 000 was purchased during the year. There were no sales of machinery during the year.

Required
(a) (i) State the basis on which Gideon Yeboah should value his inventories.
    (ii) Name one accounting principle Gideon Yeboah is applying by valuing his inventories on this basis.
(b) Prepare the manufacturing account of Gideon Yeboah for the year ended 31 March 2008.
(c) Prepare the trading account section of the income statement of Gideon Yeboah for the year ended 31 March 2008.

[IGCSE 2008]

Chapter 21

Limited Company Accounts

In this chapter you will learn to:
- understand the nature of a limited company
- understand the terms issued share capital, called up share capital and paid up share capital
- understand the difference between ordinary shares, preference shares and debentures
- prepare a profit and loss appropriation account of a limited company and understand its purpose
- understand the capital structure of a limited company.

Introduction

A limited company is a legal entity which has a separate identity from its shareholders, whose liability for the company's debts is limited.

Sometimes a new business is formed as a limited company: sometimes a limited company is formed when a sole trader or partnership wishes to expand their business.

The Nature of a Limited Company

One person acting alone can from a limited company and there is no maximum numbers of members. The **capital of a company is divided into units known as shares** which can be of any monetary amount. The **members (shareholders) of the company are only liable for the debts of the company up to the amount they agree to pay for their shares**. Since a company can have a large number of members whose liability is limited, a large amount of capital can be raised. The shares of a company have a face value (par value) such as $5, $1, $0.50 etc. **Profits are distributed**

Limited Company Accounts

among the members in the form of dividends which are often stated in terms of a percentage of the face value of the shares.

Example 21.1

Dass Limited has a total capital of 200 000 shares of $2 each and decides to pay the shareholders a dividend of 10%.
  (a) What is the total amount payable?
  (b) What is the amount payable per share?

(a) Total amount payable is $40 000 ($400 000 x 10%)
(b) Amount payable per share is $0.20

It is obviously not practical for all the members to take part in the running of the company, so it is usually managed by an elected board of directors. Unlike a sole trader or the partnership business, a limited company has a separate identity from its owners (shareholders), so any legal actions can be taken against the company rather than the members of the company.

There are two types of limited company – a **public limited company** which may offer its shares to the public and a **private limited company** which is usually a smaller company and is not allowed to offer its shares to the public.

There are many legal requirements in relation to the formation and running of a limited company. In addition to the usual accounting records several other records must be maintained. Companies are also required to publish accounts annually. These legal requirements, additional records and published accounts are outside the scope of this book.

Test your understanding
1. Define a limited liability company.
2. "A member of a company has limited liability". Explain.
3. Name **two** types of limited company.
4. State the name for profits distributed to members of a limited company.

Share Capital

Traditionally, when a limited company was formed the amount of its share capital had to be stated. This was known as the **authorised share capital** and was the maximum amount of share capital the company was allowed to issue. It is not now necessary for a limited company to have an authorised share capital. The amount of share capital actually required will be issued to the shareholders (members) and this is known as the **issued share capital**. If more capital is required at a later date, further shares can be issued.

A company may not immediately require all the money due on the shares it issues. In this case shareholders may be allowed to pay in "instalments" at times and amounts fixed by the company. The total amount a company has requested from the shareholders is known as the **called up capital**. This may be less than the issued capital as a company may only "call up" the amount it actually requires at that date. The term **paid up capital** refers to that part of the called up capital for which a company has actually received cash from its shareholders.

Example 21.2

Mishra Limited was formed on 1 January 20-8. A total of 300 000 shares was issued immediately and shareholders were asked to pay 50% of the sum due immediately and the other 50% in January 20-9.
By 1 May 20-8 holders of 290 000 shares had paid the amount due.

State – (a) The issued capital of Mishra Limited on 1 May 20-8.
(b) The called up capital of Mishra Limited on 1 May 20-8.
(c) The paid up capital of Mishra Limited on 1 May 20-8.

(a) The issued capital is $300 000 consisting of 300 000 shares of $1 each.

(b) The called up capital is $150 000 consisting of $0.50 called up on 300 000 shares.

(c) The paid up capital is $145 000 consisting of $0.50 paid up on 290 000 shares.

Limited Company Accounts

Types of Shares

The authorised share capital of a limited company is divided into different types of shares. The most common ones are **preference shares** and **ordinary shares**.

Preference Shares

As the name implies, these get preference over the ordinary shares. They receive a fixed rate of dividend (based on the face value of the shares) which is payable before any dividend is payable to the ordinary shareholders. The dividend is same every year (provided that the profit of the company is enough to cover this amount). Preference share dividend was previously regarded as an appropriation of profit, but now should be included in the profit and loss account section of the income statement. If a company is wound up (closed down) any money left after paying outside liabilities is used to pay back the preference shareholders before anything is returned to the ordinary shareholders. Preference shareholders are not usually entitled to vote at shareholders' meetings. There are several types of preference shares, but these are outside the scope of this book.

Ordinary Shares

These are also known as **equity shares**. The dividend on ordinary shares is only payable after that on the preference shares has been accounted for. The dividend is not a fixed amount, but can vary according to the profits of the company. If the trading results are poor the ordinary shareholders may receive no dividend at all, but if trading results are good they may be awarded high dividends. If a company is wound up the outside liabilities and the preference shareholders are repaid before any monies are returned to the ordinary shareholders. This may result in very little being returned to the ordinary shareholders if the company was short of funds. However, the ordinary shareholders may receive a return higher than their original capital investment if the company had adequate funds. Ordinary shareholders are usually entitled to vote at shareholders' meetings on the basis of one vote per share.

Debentures (Loan Notes)

In addition to the funds provided by the owners (shareholders), a company may also obtain funds from debentures, which are long-term loans. Like most loans, debentures carry a fixed rate of interest, which is payable whether or not the company makes a profit. This loan interest appears in the profit and loss account section of the income statement as an expense. If the company is wound up the debenture holders will be repaid before any capital is repaid to shareholders. Debenture holders are not members of the company and so are not entitled to vote at shareholders' meetings.

> **Test your understanding**
> 1. State **three** differences between preference shares and ordinary shares.
> 2. State **three** differences between ordinary shares and debentures.

Profit and Loss Appropriation Account of a Limited Company

Chapter 19 explained how it was necessary to prepare a profit and loss appropriation account for a partnership business to show how the profit was divided between the partners. In a similar way, a limited company must prepare an account or statement showing how the profit for the year is used. Public limited companies are required to prepare a **statement of changes in equity**. However non-public limited companies can continue to prepare a profit and loss appropriation account. The published accounts of public limited companies are outside the scope of this book. CIE guidelines state that, for IGCSE, the traditional approach will be followed.

It has already been explained that profits are distributed to the shareholders of a limited company in the form of dividends. Preference share dividend is included in the income statement but ordinary share dividend is recorded in the profit and loss appropriation account. At the end of the financial year the directors of a company propose that ordinary share dividends are paid and these will be paid early in the following year. These proposed ordinary share dividends will appear as a note to the financial statements of public limited companies and will not be

Limited Company Accounts

included within the statements. Non-public limited companies following the traditional approach will show the proposed ordinary share dividends in the profit and loss appropriation account and also in the balance sheet as current liabilities (or Creditors: amounts falling due within one year). Sometimes the directors will recommend an **interim ordinary dividend** (half way dividend) to be paid during the year. This is still an appropriation of profit, but, as it has already been paid, is not included in the liabilities at the end of the year.

Very often limited companies do not distribute the whole of the net profit as dividends. Even if a limited company wished to distribute the whole profit it would not be possible if there was not enough cash available. Any profit that is not appropriated for dividends remains as a balance on the profit and loss appropriation account and is carried forward to the following year. This may be referred to as **retained profits** or **profit and loss account balance**. This will appear in the balance sheet as part of the **reserves** which are added to the share capital.

In addition to leaving a balance of undistributed profit in the profit and loss appropriation account, many companies will transfer an amount from the profit and loss appropriation account to a general reserve. This is another means of **ploughing back profits** into the company to help it grow. The general reserve also appears in the reserves section of the balance sheet which is added to the share capital.

Example 21.3

Anand Ltd was formed on 1 July 20-3. By 30 June 20-6 200 000 5% preference shares of $1 each and 600 000 ordinary shares of $0.50 each had been issued and were fully paid.

The profit for the year ended 30 June 20-6 *before* the preference share dividend was $58 000. On that date the retained profit brought forward amounted to $21 000.

Half of the preference share dividend was paid on 31 December 20-5. On 30 June 20-6 the remaining preference share dividend is to be accrued.

It was agreed to transfer $8000 to general reserve and to pay an ordinary share dividend of 8%.

(a) Prepare a relevant extract from the income statement for the year ended 30 June 20-6.

(b) Prepare the profit and loss appropriation account for the year ended 30 June 20-6.

(a)
Anand Ltd.
Extract from Income Statement for the year ended 30 June 20-6

	$
Expenses – Preference share dividend (5000 + 5000)	10 000

(b)
Anand Ltd.
Profit and Loss Appropriation Account for the year ended 30 June 20-6

	$	$
Profit for the year		48 000
Less Transfer to general reserve	8 000	
Ordinary share dividend – proposed	24 000	32 000
Retained profit for the year		16 000
Retained profit brought forward		21 000
Retained profit carried forward		37 000

> **Test your understanding**
> 1. State an alternative name for retained profits brought forward.
> 2. Explain the term interim dividend.
> 3. Explain the difference between dividends paid and dividends proposed.

Balance Sheet of a Limited Company

A balance sheet needs to be modified so that it is suitable for a limited company. Current liabilities are usually referred to as Creditors: amounts falling due within one year. Long-term liabilities are usually referred to as Creditors: amounts falling due after more than one year.

Where a limited company has raised funds from the issue of debentures, these are shown with the other long-term liabilities under the heading of Creditors: amounts falling due after more than one year.

In the capital section of the balance sheet, the share capital is shown, with details of the different types of shares. Any reserves such as general reserve and retained profits balance are added to the share capital. These

Limited Company Accounts

represent profits which have been ploughed back into the company and, as such, belong to the ordinary shareholders. The total of the share capital and the reserves is known as **shareholders' funds**.

Example 21.4

Anand Ltd. was formed on 1 July 20-3. By 30 June 20-6 200 000 5% preference shares of $1 each and 600 000 ordinary shares of $0.50 each had been issued and were fully paid.

At 30 June 20-6 the general reserve amounted to $34 000 (including $8000 transferred on 30 June 20-6).

The balance of retained profit after the preparation of the profit and loss appropriation account for the year ended 30 June 20-6 was $37 000.

Prepare an appropriate extract from the balance sheet of Anand Ltd. at 30 June showing the shareholders' funds.

Anand Ltd.
Balance Sheet at 30 June 20-6

	$
Capital and Reserves	
5% Preference shares of $1 each	200 000
Ordinary shares of $0.50 each	300 000
General reserve	34 000
Retained profits	37 000
Shareholders' funds	571 000

- The general reserve represents $26 000 brought forward from the previous year plus $8000 transferred from the profit and loss appropriation account for the year ended 30 June 20-6.
- The item for retained profits represents the balance of retained profits on the profit and loss appropriation account on 30 June 20-6 (see Example 21.3).
- Any share dividends agreed but not yet paid would be included in the balance sheet with the other current liabilities in the section headed Creditors: amounts falling due within one year.

Test your understanding
1. Explain how debentures are recorded in the balance sheet of a limited company.
2. Explain why reserves such as general reserve and retained profits are added to the share capital in the balance sheet of a limited company.
3. State what shareholders' funds consist of.

POINTS TO REMEMBER

1. A limited company is a legal entity which has a separate identity from its shareholders, whose liability is limited.
2. The share capital actually issued to shareholders is known as the issued capital.
3. There are two main types of shares – preference shares and ordinary shares.
4. Debentures are a form of long-term loan.
5. A profit and loss appropriation account shows how the profit for the year has been used.
6. The total of the issued share capital and the reserves is known as the shareholders' funds.

REVIEW QUESTIONS

1. (a) Explain the difference between the following
    (i) Called-up share capital and paid-up share capital
    (ii) Preference shares and ordinary shares
    (iii) Ordinary share dividend paid and ordinary share dividend proposed.

Limited Company Accounts

(b) Silsford Ltd provided the following information.

	Issued Capital $
6% Preference shares of $1 each	50 000
Ordinary shares of $1 each	80 000

During the financial year ended 31 December 20-9 an interim dividend of $2400 was paid on the ordinary shares.
The profit for the year ended 31 December 20-9 was $33 000.
On 31 December 20-9 it was decided to
   pay the dividend due on the preference shares
   pay a final dividend of 5% on the ordinary shares.

Calculate
  (i) The total preference share dividend (in $) for the year ended 31 December 20-9
  (ii) The total ordinary share dividend (in $) for the year ended 31 December 20-9
  (iii) The profit retained in the year ended 31 December 20-9.

2. The balance sheet of a limited company often includes the following items as sources of funds:
   (a) Ordinary share capital
   (b) Preference share capital
   (c) Debentures
   (d) Bank overdraft
   (e) Retained profits
   (f) General reserve
   Explain the main features of **each** of these sources of funds.

3. Bose Ltd. provides the following information.

Issued share capital	100 000 6% $1 preference shares
	300 000 $1 ordinary shares
General reserve 1 January 20-6	$130 000
Retained profits 1 January 20-6	$22 000 (credit)
Profit for the year ended 31 December 20-6 before preference dividend	$125 000

During the year ended 31 December 20-6 an interim dividend of 3% was paid on the preference shares, but no interim dividend was paid on the ordinary shares.

On 31 December 20-6:

1. The final dividend on the preference shares is to be accrued.
2. The directors decided to transfer $25 000 to the general reserve.
3. It was decided that an ordinary share dividend of 8% would be paid.

(a) Calculate the profit for the year after the preference share dividend. Show your workings.
(b) Prepare the profit and loss appropriation account of Bose Ltd for the year ended 31 December 20-6.

*4. Kinto Limited are in business as printers. The following trial balance (after calculating the profit for the year) has been prepared from the company's accounting records for the year ended 30 June 2010.

Kinto Limited
Trial Balance at 30 June 2010

	$	$
Machinery at cost	17 000	
Office equipment at cost	2 500	
Provision for depreciation		
Machinery		1 900
Office equipment		500
Other payables		300
Bank	25 000	
Cash	200	
Trade payables		1 800
Trade receivables	33 500	
Bank loan repayable 2016		5 000
Other receivables	600	
Inventory 30 June 2010	3 900	
Share capital (10 000 ordinary $1 shares)		10 000
Retained profit at 1 July 2009		47 200
Profit for the year		16 000
	82 700	82 700

Limited Company Accounts

On 30 June 2010 it was decided to pay a dividend of $0.25 per share and to transfer $5000 to a general reserve.

Required
(a) Prepare the profit and loss appropriation account of Kinoto Limited for the year ended 30 June 2010.
(b) Prepare Kinoto Limited's balance sheet at 30 June 2010.

[IGCSE Specimen Paper]

*5. Tiwari & Company Ltd. have issued 100 000 5% preference shares of $1 each and 600 000 ordinary shares of 50c each. All the shares are fully paid.

Tiwari and Company Ltd. provide the following information relating to the year ended 30 June 20-8.

20-7				$
July	1	Retained profits		9 500
		General reserve		12 000
Dec	31	Dividends paid:		
		Half year dividend on preference shares		
		Interim dividend of 5% on ordinary shares		
20-8				
June	30	Profit for the year before preference share dividend		59 000
		Dividend paid:		
		Half year dividend on preference shares		

On 30 June 20-8 it was decided to transfer $10 000 to general reserve and to pay a final dividend of 10% on the ordinary shares.

The directors decided not to apply the IAS rules regarding proposed ordinary share dividend.

Required
(a) Calculate the profit for the year ended 30 June 20-8 after the preference share dividend. Show your workings.
(b) Prepare the profit and loss appropriation account of Tiwari & Company Ltd. for the year ended 30 June 20-8.
(c) Prepare a relevant extract from the balance sheet of Tiwari & Company Ltd. at 30 June 2008 showing the share capital and reserves of the company.

(d) Explain which dividends (if any) would appear in the balance sheet of Tiwari and Company Ltd. at 30 June 10-8. Give reasons for your answer.

6. The financial year of Srivastava Ltd. ends on 31 May. The following information is provided.

	$
Issued share capital	
150 000 6% $1 preference shares	150 000
450 000 $1 ordinary shares	450 000
On 1 June 20-5	
General reserve	50 000
Retained profits	70 000
During the year ended 31 May 20-6	
Interim dividend paid – preference	4 500
ordinary	13 500
Final dividend paid – preference	4 500
Profit for the year before the preference share dividend	105 500
On 31 May 20-6 it was agreed to	
Transfer to general reserve	20 000
Pay a final dividend on ordinary shares	31 500

Required

(a) Prepare a relevant extract from the income statement of Srivastava Ltd for the year ended 31 May 20-6.
(b) Prepare the profit and loss appropriation account of Srivastava Ltd for the year ended 31 May 20-6.
(c) Prepare a relevant extract from the balance sheet of Srivastava Ltd at 31 May 20-6 showing the total shareholders' funds.

Chapter 22 Analysis and Interpretation

In this chapter you will learn to:
- understand and calculate the accounting ratios which measure profitability
- understand and calculate the accounting ratios which measure liquidity
- prepare simple statements showing inter-firm comparison and recognise their limitations
- understand how owners and other interested parties use accounting statements
- recognise the limitations of accounting statements.

Introduction

It is necessary to analyse and interpret the financial statements of a business in order to assess its performance and progress. **Analysis** consists of a detailed examination of the information in a set of financial statements of a business. The results of this analysis are then interpreted in order to assess the performance of the business. **Interpretation** can include comparing the results of other similar businesses and also comparing within the business (with the results for previous years and with targets and budgets).

To enable this comparison to be carried out in a meaningful way the results are usually expressed as accounting ratios. This is a general term which includes calculations in the form of ratios, percentages and time periods. Ratios are usually divided into two main groups - profitability ratios and liquidity ratios.

The main types of assets and liabilities have been explained earlier.

Working capital is the difference between the current assets and the current liabilities and is the amount available for the day-to-day running of the business (it is also known as **net current assets**). **Capital owned** is the amount owed by a business to the owner of the business on a certain date. **Capital employed** is the total funds which are being used by a business. This may be calculated as the owner's capital plus any non-current liabilities (alternatively, it may be calculated as non-current assets plus net current assets). Capital employed can be defined in several ways - the figure at the start of the year, the figure at the end of the year, or an average of the two.

> **Test your understanding**
> 1. Name the two main groups of ratios.
> 2. Define working capital.
> 3. State what is meant by capital owned.
> 4. State **two** ways in which capital employed can be calculated.

Example 22.1

Arun is a trader who has been in business for several years. His financial year ends on 31 December.

The following financial statements will be used in **Example 22.2** to **Example 22.10**

Arun
Income Statement for the year ended 31 December 20-7

	$	$
Revenue (sales) - Cash sales	10 000	
Credit seales	110 000	120 000
Less Cost of sales		
Opening inventory	7 500	
Purchases (all on credit)	97 000	
	104 500	
Less Closing inventory	8 500	96 000
Gross profit		24 000
Less Expenses		9 000
Profit for the year		15 000

Analysis and Interpretation

Balance Sheet at 31 December 20-7

	$	$
Non-current assets (at book value)		124 250
Current assets		
Inventory	8 500	
Trade receivables	10 500	
Bank	12 250	
	31 250	
Current liabilities		
Trade payables	12 500	
Net current assets		18 750
		143 000
Non-current liabilities		
Loan - AB Finance Ltd.		20 000
		123 000
Financed by		
Capital		
Opening balance		130 000
Plus Profit for the year		15 000
		145 000
Less Drawings		22 000
		123 000

Profitability Ratios

These are used to relate the profit figures to other figures within the same set of financial statements.

Return On Capital Employed (ROCE)

This is calculated using the following formula:

$$\frac{\text{net profit (profit for the year)}}{\text{capital employed}} \times \frac{100}{1}$$

Example 22.2

Using the financial statements shown in **Example 22.1** calculate Arun's return on capital employed.

Assume that capital employed equals the total of capital owned and non-current liabilities on 31 December 20-7.

$$\frac{\$15\,000}{\$143\,000} \times \frac{100}{1} = 10.49\%$$

This is a very important ratio as it shows the profit earned for every $100 invested in the business in order to earn that profit. The higher the return, the more efficiently the capital is being employed within the business.

Gross profit as a percentage of sales (gross profit/sales)

This is calculated using the following formula:

$$\frac{\text{gross profit}}{\text{sales (revenue)}} \times \frac{100}{1}$$

Example 22.3

Using the financial statements shown in **Example 22.1** calculate Arun's gross profit as a percentage of sales.

$$\frac{\$24\,000}{\$120\,000} \times \frac{100}{1} = 20\%$$

This is also called **gross profit as a percentage of turnover** (turnover equals net sales less sales returns). This ratio shows the gross profit earned for every $100 of sales. Different types of industries and trades tend to have different gross profit percentages. The same business may have a similar gross profit percentage from year to year. The higher the return, the more profitable is the business. However, by reducing selling prices slightly (and so reducing the gross profit percentage), a business may achieve a higher monetary gross profit.

The gross profit percentage can be improved by measures such as:

- increasing selling prices
- obtaining cheaper supplies
- increasing advertising and sales promotions
- changing the proportions of different types of goods sold

Analysis and Interpretation

However, these measures may have some adverse effects. For example, increasing the selling price may result in customers going elsewhere; obtaining cheaper goods may result in a lower quality of goods, and so on.

If the gross profit percentage changes significantly from one year to another the cause should be investigated. A fall in the gross profit percentage may be caused by:

- increasing the rate of trade discount
- selling goods at cheaper prices
- not passing on increased costs to customers

Net profit as a percentage of sales (net profit/sales)

This is calculated using the following formula:

$$\frac{\text{net profit (profit for the year)}}{\text{sales (revenue)}} \times \frac{100}{1}$$

Example 22.4

Using the financial statements shown in **Example 22.1** calculate Arun's net profit as a percentage of sales.

$$\frac{\$15\,000}{\$120\,000} \times \frac{100}{1} = 12.50\%$$

This ratio shows the net profit earned for every $100 of sales. The higher the return, the more profitable is the business. This ratio acts as an indicator of how well a business is able to control its expenses. If the net profit percentage of a business increases it indicates that the operating expenses are being controlled. This ratio will be influenced by the different types of expense: some expenses increase in proportion to the sales e.g. commission paid on sales made, but other expenses remain the same whatever the sales be e.g. insurance of buildings. Any change in the gross profit percentage will also affect the net profit percentage.

Test your understanding
1. Explain what is shown by the rate of return on capital employed.
2. State **two** factors which may increase the gross profit percentage.
3. State the expenses as a percentage of the sales if the gross profit/sales is 25% and the net profit/sales is 14%.

Liquidity Ratios

In business, the term "liquidity" relates to money and liquidity ratios measure the ease and speed with which assets can be turned into cash.

Current ratio

This is calculated using the following formula:
$$\text{current assets} : \text{current liabilities}$$

Example 22.5

Using the financial statements shown in **Example 22.1** calculate Arun's current ratio.
$$\$31\,250 : \$12\,500 = 2.50 : 1$$

This is also referred to as the **working capital ratio**. It compares the assets which are in the form of cash, or which can be turned into cash relatively easily within the next 12 months, with the liabilities which are due for repayment within the that period of time. This measures the ability of a business to meet its current liabilities when they fall due.

Ratios between 1.5 : 1 and 2 : 1 are generally regarded as satisfactory, but it is important to consider the size and type of business. Some businesses necessarily need a large amount of non-current assets whereas other businesses have a higher proportion of current assets; some businesses always purchase goods on credit whereas others always pay cash; some businesses obtain long-term loans whereas others make use of short-term loans or a bank overdraft. If the current ratio is over 2 : 1 it may indicate poor management of the current assets.

The working capital of a business must be adequate to finance the day-to-day trading activities. A business which is short of working capital may encounter the following problems:

- cannot meet liabilities when they are due
- experiences difficulties in obtaining further supplies on credit
- cannot take advantage of cash discounts
- cannot take advantage of business opportunities when they arise

Analysis and Interpretation

Ways to improve the working capital position include:
- introduction of further capital by the owner(s)
- obtaining non-current loans
- selling surplus non-current assets
- reducing drawings by the owner(s) (or reduction in dividends).

The actual cash position can also be improved by measures such as delaying the payment of creditors, increasing the proportion of cash sales, and reducing the period of credit allowed to debtors. These measures may also have some adverse effects such as the refusal of further supplies on credit, customers moving to other suppliers where longer credit is allowed etc.

Quick ratio

This is calculated using the following formula:

current assets – less inventory : current liabilities

Example 22.6

Using the financial statements shown in **Example 22.1** calculate Arun's quick ratio.

($31 250 – $8500) : $12 500 = 1.82 : 1

This is also known as the **acid test ratio**. It compares the assets which are in the form of money, or which will convert into money quickly, with the liabilities which are due for repayment in the near future. This is a similar calculation to the current ratio, but the quick ratio excludes inventory as this is not regarded as a liquid asset. Inventory is two stages away from being money: the goods have to be sold and then the money has to be collected from the debtors.

A ratio of 1 : 1 is usually regarded as satisfactory, but, as with the current ratio, the size and type of business should also be considered. A ratio of 1 : 1 indicates that the immediate liabilities can be met out of the liquid assets without having to sell inventory. (Where inventory has to be sold immediately it can sometimes only be done at a reduced price.) If the quick ratio is over 1 : 1 it may indicate poor management of liquid assets such as having too high a balance on a bank current account.

> **Test your understanding**
> 1. State **two** disadvantages of a shortage of working capital.
> 2. State **two** ways of improving the working capital.
> 3. Explain the difference between the current ratio and the quick ratio.

Rate of inventory turnover

This is calculated using the following formula:

$$\frac{\text{cost of sales}}{\text{average inventory}}$$ to give the number of times inventory is sold and replaced in the period

An alternative calculation uses the following formula:

$$\frac{\text{average inventory}}{\text{cost of sales}} \times \frac{365}{1}$$ to give the number of days on average the inventory is held before being sold

Example 22.7

Using the financial statements shown in **Example 22.1** calculate Arun's rate of inventory turnover to show the following:
(a) the number of times in the year inventory is replaced
(b) the number of days inventory is held before being sold

(a) $\dfrac{\$96\,000}{(\$7\,500 + \$8\,500) \div 2} = 12$ times

(b) $\dfrac{\$8\,000}{\$96\,000} \times \dfrac{365}{1} = 30.42$ days $= 31$ days

The rate of inventory turnover is sometimes referred to as **inventory turn**. This ratio calculates the number of times a business sells and replaces its inventory in a given period of time. The rate of inventory turnover will obviously vary according to the type of business. Businesses selling luxury goods such as expensive jewellery and private jet planes will have a low rate of inventory turnover whereas businesses selling low value "everyday" requirements such as fresh bread and newspapers will have a high rate of inventory turnover. The same business may have a similar rate of inventory turnover from year to year. If the rate increases it may indicate improved efficiency: if the rate decreases if may indicate that the

Analysis and Interpretation

business has too much inventory or that the sales are slowing down. The quicker the rate of inventory turnover, the less time funds are tied up in inventory which is regarded as the least liquid of the current assets.

A lower rate of inventory turnover can be caused by factors such as:
- lower sales (resulting in higher inventory levels)
- inventory over-purchased
- too high selling prices
- falling demand
- business activity slowing down
- business inefficiency

Collection period for trade receivables

This is calculated using the following formula:

$$\frac{\text{trade receivables}}{\text{credit sales}} \times \frac{365}{1} \quad \text{to give an answer in days}$$

$$\frac{\text{trade receivables}}{\text{credit sales}} \times \frac{52}{1} \quad \text{to give an answer in weeks}$$

$$\frac{\text{trade receivables}}{\text{credit sales}} \times \frac{12}{1} \quad \text{to give an answer in months}$$

Example 22.8

Using the financial statements shown in **Example 22.1** calculate (to the nearest whole day) Arun's collection period for trade receivables.

$$\frac{\$10\,500}{\$110\,000} \times \frac{365}{1} = 34.84 \text{ days} = 35 \text{ days}$$

This is also referred to as the **trade receivables/sales ratio**. It measures the average time the debtors take to pay their accounts. The answer to this calculation - the length of time debtors actually take to pay their accounts - should be compared with the term of credit allowed to debtors. The quicker the debtors pay their accounts, the better it is: the money can then be used for other purposes within the business. The longer a business has to wait for a debt to be paid the greater the risk of it becoming a bad debt.

The same business may have a similar collection period from year to year. If the period decreases it may indicate that the credit control policy is being applied more effectively: if the period increases it may indicate that the credit control policy is inefficient, or that longer credit terms are being allowed in order to maintain the quantity of credit sales.

The collection period for trade receivables can be improved by measures such:
- improving credit control policy (sending regular statements of account, "chasing" overdue accounts and so on)
- offering cash discount for early settlement
- charging interest on overdue accounts
- refusing further supplies until any outstanding debt is paid
- invoice discounting and debt factoring*

*For a fee, a debt factor will maintain the sales ledger, collect the debts and advance money against those debts. For a fee, a discounter will advance money against certain debts, but does not maintain the sales ledger.

Payment period for trade payables

This is calculated using the following formula:

$$\frac{\text{trade payables}}{\text{credit purchases}} \times \frac{365}{1} \quad \text{to give an answer in days}$$

$$\frac{\text{trade payables}}{\text{credit purchases}} \times \frac{52}{1} \quad \text{to give an answer in weeks}$$

$$\frac{\text{trade payables}}{\text{credit purchases}} \times \frac{12}{1} \quad \text{to give an answer in months}$$

Example 22.9

Using the financial statements shown in **Example 22.1** calculate (to the nearest whole day) Arun's payment period for trade payables.

$$\frac{\$12\,500}{\$97\,000} \times \frac{365}{1} = 47.04 \text{ days} = 48 \text{ days}$$

This is also known as the **trade payables/purchases ratio**. It measures the average time taken to pay the creditors' accounts. The answer to this

Analysis and Interpretation

calculation should be compared with the term of credit allowed by creditors.

The same business may have a similar payment period from year to year. If the period decreases, the business is paying the creditors more quickly: if the period increases it may indicate that the business is short of immediate funds and is finding it difficult to meet debts when they fall due. This ratio can also be influenced by the collection period for trade receivables: if the debtors do not settle their accounts promptly the business may not be able to pay the creditors promptly. Taking longer to pay the creditors means that the business can use the funds for other purposes, but there can be adverse effects such as:

- the supplier refusing credit in the future
- the supplier refusing further supplies
- the loss of any cash discount for early settlement
- damage to the relationship with the supplier

Test your understanding
1. State the formula for calculating rate of inventory turnover.
2. State **two** reasons why the rate of inventory turnover may fall.
3. State the formula for calculating the collection period for trade receivables.
4. A trader allows his debtors 30 days credit. The collection period is 40 days. State whether the trader will be satisfied. Give a reason for your answer.
5. A trader's creditors allow him 45 days credit. State **one** advantage and **one** disadvantage to the trader if he pays after 60 days.

Inter-firm Comparison

Comparing the ratios calculated for the current financial year with those of previous years can measure the progress and performance of a business and indicate the trends in profitability, liquidity and so on.

Another useful comparison is to compare the ratios with those of a similar business.

Example 22.10

Arun is a trader who has been in business for several years. Renu started a similar business in another town two years ago. The financial year for both businesses ends on 31 December.

Renu allows Arun access to her financial records. The following information is available.

	Arun $	Renu $
On 1 January 20-7:		
Inventory	7 500	5 100
For the year ended 31 December 20-7:		
Revenue - cash sales	10 000	–
credit sales	110 000	100 000
Purchases - cash	–	26 600
credit	97 000	50 000
Cost of sales	96 000	76 000
Expenses	9 000	13 500
On 31 December 20-7:		
Inventory	8 500	5 700
Trade receivables	10 500	10 900
Bank	12 250	–
Bank overdraft	–	6 600
Trade payables	12 500	5 000
Capital employed	143 000	115 000

(a) For **each** business calculate the following ratios:
   (i) Return on capital employed
   (ii) Gross profit as a percentage of sales
   (iii) Net profit as a percentage of sales
   (iv) Current ratio
   (v) Quick ratio
   (vi) Rate of inventory turnover
   (vii) Collection period for trade receivables
   (viii) Payment period for trade payables

(b) Using the ratios calculated in (a), compare the performance of the two businesses.

Analysis and Interpretation

(a)

	Arun $	Renu $
(i) Return on capital employed	10.49%	$\dfrac{\$10\,500}{\$115\,000} \times \dfrac{100}{1} = 9.13\%$
(ii) Gross profit as a percentage of sales	20%	$\dfrac{\$24\,000}{\$100\,000} \times \dfrac{100}{1} = 24\%$
(iii) Net profit as a percentage of sales	12.50%	$\dfrac{\$10\,500}{\$100\,000} \times \dfrac{100}{1} = 10.50\%$
(iv) Current ratio	2.50 : 1	$16\,600 : \$11\,600 = 1.43 : 1$
(v) Quick ratio	1.82 : 1	$10\,900 : \$11\,600 = 0.94 : 1$
(vi) Rate of inventory turnover	12 times	$\dfrac{\$76\,000}{\$5\,400} = 14.07$ times
(vii) Collection period for trade receivables	35 days	$\dfrac{\$10\,900}{\$100\,000} \times \dfrac{365}{1} = 40$ days
(viii) Payment period for trade payables	48 days	$\dfrac{\$5\,500}{\$50\,000} \times \dfrac{365}{1} = 37$ days

- The detailed calculations for Arun's business have been shown earlier in this chapter.

(b) Comparison of the ratios

Profitability

Arun is employing more capital and has a higher return on capital employed than Renu. For every $100 of capital employed Arun had a return of $10.49 whereas Renu only achieved $9.13. This may indicate that Renu is not employing the capital in the most effective way.

Both businesses earned the same amount of gross profit, but Renu achieved a higher gross profit as a percentage of sales. It may be that Arun failed to pass on increased costs, or sold goods at cheaper prices in order to achieve greater sales. Renu may have been selling the goods at higher prices or buying goods at a cheaper price than Arun.

Despite both businesses earning the same amount of gross profit, Arun achieved a higher amount of net profit by controlling his expenses. Arun's expenses as a percentage of sales were 8.50% compared with 13.50% for Renu. This resulted in Arun having a higher net profit as a percentage of sales.

Liquidity

Arun's current ratio of 2.50 : 1 is quite satisfactory as his current assets are two and a half times the current liabilities. Renu's current ratio of 1.43: 1 may be regarded as too low as her current assets are only 1.43 times greater than her current liabilities. Renu may find it difficult to meet her current liabilities when they fall due and may not be able to take advantage of cash discounts or business opportunities when they arise. The introduction of additional capital or a long-term loan to replace part (or all) of the bank overdraft would improve her working capital position.

Arun's quick ratio is also satisfactory (some may even regard it as a little too high). Renu's quick ratio is quite reasonable as her liquid assets and her current liabilities are almost equal. However, her only liquid asset is trade receivables, so she is dependent on debtors paying their accounts before she is able to pay her current liabilities.

Renu has achieved a slightly quicker rate of inventory turnover than Arun. This may indicate that Renu is more efficient. Arun could consider reducing his inventory levels and try to increase his rate of sales.

Arun's credit sales are only slightly higher than Renu's. The amount of trade receivables of each business is very similar. Arun's debtors are paying their accounts in an average of 35 days: Renu's debtors are taking an average of 40 days to pay their accounts. It may be that Renu's credit control policy is inefficient or that she is not offering cash discounts. To be more meaningful, these figures should be compared to the credit allowed by each business.

The amount of Arun's credit purchases was much higher than that of Renu. The total of Arun's trade payables is much greater than that owed by Renu. Arun's creditors are being paid in an average of 48 days: Renu takes an average of 37 days to pay her creditors. This may be linked to the fact that Renu is relying on a bank overdraft for short-term finance, and her trade payables much less than Arun's.

Analysis and Interpretation

Problems of inter-firm comparison

A business can often obtain valuable information by comparing their accounting ratios with those of another business, but the business must be aware of the limitations of such a comparison. Every business is different and has different requirements and accounting policies. A comparison is only meaningful if it is between two or more businesses of the same type, of the same size and in the same trade. The problems of comparison include the following:
- The businesses may apply different accounting policies, for example they may use different methods of depreciation.
- The businesses may apply different operating policies such as renting premises or purchasing premises, obtaining long-term finance from capital only or using capital and long-term loans. Such policies will affect both the profit for the year and the balance sheet.
- Non-monetary items such as the skill of the work-force, the goodwill of the business and so on do not appear in the accounting records, but are very important in the success of the business.
- It is not always possible to obtain all the information about another business which is needed to make a true comparison. For example, the inventory shown in the financial stateemnts may not represent the average amount held during the year; the financial statements do not show the age of the non-current assets and when they need replacing.
- The information relating to other businesses may be for one financial year only, so it is not possible to calculate business trends. That particular year may also not be a "typical" year.
- The financial years may end on different dates which can make comparison difficult. For example, the year end for one business may be at a time when inventories are particularly low; the year end for another business may be when inventories are particularly high.
- The accounts are based on historic cost and do not show the effects of inflation.

> **Test your understanding**
> 1. State and explain **four** problems of inter-firm comparison

Users of Accounting Statements

It is not only the owner who is interested in analysing and interpreting the financial statements of a business. Various other people are also interested in different aspects of the accounts. The users of accounting statements can be divided into two main groups - internal users and external users.

Internal users

1. Owner(s)
   The owners of a business such as a sole trader or partners will be interested in all aspects of the business, both profitability and liquidity in order to assess the business's performance and progress. Any potential partners are interested in the profitability of the business. The owners of a limited company, the shareholders, and potential shareholders, are interested in the profitability of the company and also in various investment ratios (which are outside the scope of this book).
2. Manager(s)
   In many small businesses, the owners manage the business. In some cases, management may be carried out by an employee. Like the owners, managers are interested in all aspects of the business. They may use ratios to assess past performance, plan for the future and take remedial action where necessary.

External users

1. Bank manager
   If a business requests a bank loan or an overdraft facility the bank manager will require the financial statements of the business. The bank manager will need to know whether there is adequate security to cover the amount of the loan or overdraft, whether it can be repaid when due, and whether interest can be paid when due.
2. Other lenders
   Anyone who has made a loan to a business (and any potential lenders) will be interested in the security available, the repayment of the loan when due, and the payment of interest when due.

Analysis and Interpretation

3. **Creditors**
   Anyone who has supplied a business with goods on credit terms (and any potential creditor) is interested in the liquidity position and the payment period for trade payables. These factors may be considered when determining the credit limit and the length of credit allowed. In practice, it may not be possible to obtain the accounts of sole traders and partnership businesses, so other means of checking credit-worthiness are employed.
4. **Potential buyers of the business**
   Anyone with an interest in purchasing the business or making a take over bid will be interested in the profitability of the business and the market value of the assets of the business.
5. **Customers**
   Customers of the business are interested in ensuring the continuity of supplies.
6. **Employees and trade unions**
   Employees and trade unions want to know that the company is able to continue operating, and so maintain jobs and continue to pay adequate wages (and, in some cases, contribute to pension schemes).
7. **Government departments**
   This may be for purposes such as compiling business statistics and checking that the correct amount of tax is being paid.

Limitations of Accounting Statements

Accounting statements and the ratios calculated from them provide valuable information about a business. They do, however, have limitations and are not able to provide a complete picture of the performance and position of a business. Their limitations include:

Time factor

The accounting statements are a record of what has happened in the past, not a guide to the future. Additionally, there is a gap between the end of the financial year and the preparation of the accounting statements. In that time significant events such as changes in inventory levels, purchasing of non-current assets may have taken place.

Historic cost

The only way to record financial transactions is to use the actual cost price. However, comparing transactions taking place at different times can be difficult because of the effect of inflation. For example, in times of inflation, it would cost more to buy a machine in 20-8 identical to one purchased in 20-1.

Accounting policies

All businesses should apply the accounting principles of **prudence** and **consistency** which should help in making comparisons. However, there are several acceptable accounting policies which may be applied, for example there are several different methods of calculating depreciation. Where businesses have used different accounting policies it is difficult to make a meaningful comparison of their results. Similarly, where a business changes its policy, a comparison with the results of previous years is difficult.

Different definitions

The figure of profit for the year may be adjusted for loan interest, and sometimes preference share dividends in a limited company (these adjustments are outside the scope of this book). A comparison of results is only meaningful if "like is compared with like" and the same definitions are applied.

Money measurement

Accounts only record information which can be expressed in monetary terms. This means that there are many important factors which influence the performance of a business which will not appear in the accounting statements.

The factors which are within the control of the business include the quality of management, the skill and reliability of the workforce, the goodwill of the business, the age and condition of the non-current assets, and the ability to adapt in response to changing market conditions.

Other factors are outside the control of the business. These include government policies, competition, impact of new technology, and future long-term prospects for the particular trade or industry.

Analysis and Interpretation

Test your understanding

1. Name **three** business people who would be interested in the accounts of a sole trader. Explain the reason for their interest in each case.
2. Explain **three** limitations of the accounting statements of a business.

Points to Remember

1. There are three ratios which measure profitability - return on capital employed, gross profit as a percentage of sales and net profit as a percentage of sales.
2. There are five ratios which measure liquidity - current ratio, quick ratio, rate of inventory turnover, collection period for trade receivables and payment period for trade payables.
3. Ratios can be used to compare the current year with previous years and with other similar businesses. Problems can arise when making inter-firm comparisons.
4. Certain aspects of the accounting statements of a business are of interest to users such as owner(s), managers, lenders, creditors, potential buyers, customers, employees and trade unions, and government departments.
5. Accounting statements and the ratios calculated from them provide valuable information, but they have limitations and are not able to provide a complete picture of the performance and position of a business.

Review Questions

*1. On 31 December 2008 Morag MacDonald had money in the bank but her working capital as lower than it was at the start of the year.

   Required
   (a) Explain why it is important for Morag MacDonald to have an adequate amount of working capital.
   (b) State **two** ways in which Morag MacDonald could increase her working capital.
   (c) State and explain the effect of **each** of the following transactions on Morag MacDonald's working capital.
       The first one has been completed as an example.
       (i) Office equipment, $10 000, was purchased by cheque
           Effect   Working capital decreases by $10 000
           Explanation   The current assets decrease by $10 000 as the bank balance decreases.
                         There is no change in the current liabilities
       (ii) An increase in the provision for doubtful debts of $50.
       (iii) Payment of $200 by a debtor in cash.
       (iv) Payment of $96 by cheque to a creditor in full settlement of $100 owing. [IGCSE 2009]

*2. Miriam Rajah is a trader. She is concerned that she often has a bank overdraft. She believes that this may be connected to the rate at which she pays her trade payables and the rate at which she collects her trade receivables.

   All Miriam Rajah's sales and purchases are made on credit terms. She allows her debtors 30 days credit and is allowed 21 days credit by her creditors.

   The following information is available at 31 January 2008:

	$
For the year ended 31 January 2008	
credit sales	268 500
credit purchases	242 500

Analysis and Interpretation

At 31 January 2008	
trade receivables	30 000
trade payables	20 200

Required

(a) Suggest **one** way in which the collection period for trade receivables may affect the payment period for trade payables.
(b) Calculate Miriam Rajah's collection period for trade receivables. Show your workings. Round up your answer to the nearest whole day.
(c) Calculate Miriam Rajah's payment period for trade payables. Show your workings. Round up your answer to the nearest whole day.
(d) State **two** possible advantages to Miriam Rajah of paying her trade payables before the due date.

[IGCSE 2008]

3. Mona El Tawil is a sole trader. Her financial year ends on 31 December. She provided the following information:

For the year ended 31 December 2006

		$	$
Sales –	cash	115 000	
	credit	275 000	390 000
Purchases –	cash	5 000	
	credit	465 000	470 000

At 31 December 2006

	$
Trade receivables	29 000
Trade payables	40 000
Inventory	34 000
Bank	7 000 debit
Non-current assets	180 000

Mona El Tawil decides to compare her position with that at the end of the previous financial year.

Required

(a) Complete the following table to show the ratios for Mona El Tawil's business for the year ended 31 December 2006.

Calculations should be correct to **two** decimal places for (i) and (ii) and should be rounded up to the next whole day for (iii) and (iv).

Ratio	Year ended 31 December 2005	Year ended 31 December 2006
(i) Current ratio	2.25:1	....
(ii) Quick ratio	0.75:1	....
(iii) Collection period for trade receivables	30 days	.... days
(iv) Payment period for trade payables	24 days	.... days

(b) Explain why the quick ratio is more reliable than the current ratio as an indicator of liquidity.
(c) State whether Mona El Tawil will be satisfied with the change in the quick ratio.
(d) Suggest **one** possible reason which could account for the change in the current ratio.
(e) State and explain whether you think Mona El Tawil will be satisfied with the change in the trade receivables collection period.
   (i) Will she be satisfied?
  (ii) Explanation
(f) Explain how the change in the trade receivables collection period may have affected the payment period for trade payables.
(g) Name one other ratio which would help Mona El Tawil assess the liquidity position.

Mona El Tawil would like to compare her results with those of other businesses.
She is aware that even comparing with a business of a similar size dealing in similar goods can produce misleading results.

Required

(h) List **four** things Mona El Tawil should consider when comparing her results with those of a similar business.

Analysis and Interpretation

The first one has been completed as an example.
(i) *There may be differences that affect profitability e.g. one business may rent premises and the other business may own premises.*
[IGCSE 2007]

4. State how **each** of the following may be regarded as a limitation of accounting statements.
The first one has been completed as an example.
   (a) Historic cost
   All transactions are recorded at the actual cost price. It is difficult to compare transactions taking place at different times.
   (b) Money measurement
   (c) Time factor   [IGCSE 2009]

5. Jones Shilango is a trader. He provided the following information for the year ended 31 July 2007.

	$
Revenue (sales)	72 000
Purchases	54 400
Inventory 1 August 2006	5 200
Inventory 31 July 2007	4 900

Expenses were 15% of sales.

Required

(a) (i) Calculate to two decimal places, the percentage of gross profit to sales. Show your workings.
   (ii) State **two** ways in which the percentage of gross profit to sales could be improved.
(b) (i) Calculate to two decimal places the percentage of net profit to sales. Show your workings.
   (ii) State **two** ways in which the percentage of net profit to sales could be improved.

Jones Shilango's accountant advises his that it is necessary to make decisions in relation to accounting policies.

Required

(c) (i) State which accounting policy is described in the following statement.

"It must be recognised that a financial report can only be compared with reports for other periods if similarities and differences can be identified."

(ii) Explain the meaning of the accounting term "reliability".

In addition to Jones Shilango, the owner, other people are also interested in the financial statements of Jones Shilango's business.

Required

(d) List **three** business people (excluding the owner) who would be interested in Jones Shilango's financial statements.
In each case state one reason why that person would be interested in the statements.

[IGCSE 2007]

6. On 1 October 2008 Maria Maziya had the following current assets and current liabilities.

	$
Inventory	5020
Trade receivables	4710
Trade payables	3280
Bank overdraft	3620
Cash	200

Required

(a) Calculate Maria Maziya's working capital. Show your workings.
(b) State **two** ways in which Maria Maziya could increase her working capital.
(c) State **two** disadvantages to Maria Maziya of having insufficient working capital.

Maria Maziya's financial year ends on 30 September.

Her return on capital employed (ROCE) for the financial year ended 30 September 2007 was 19.50%.

Maria Maziya's profit for the year ended 30 September 2008 was $6465.

On 30 September 2008 her capital employed was $41 100.

Analysis and Interpretation

Required

(d) Calculate, to two decimal places, the return on capital employed (ROCE) for the year ended 30 September 2008. Show your workings.

(e) State and explain whether you think Maria Maziya will be satisfied with the change in the return on capital employed (ROCE).

[IGCSE 2008]

7. In addition to the owner of a business, various other business people are interested in the financial statements.

   Explain why **each** of the following business people would be interested in the financial statements.

   (a) Bank manger
   (b) Creditor

[IGCSE 2009]

8. Kalpna Khan started a business on 1 April 2007. On that date she rented premises larger than she required so that she had space for future expansion. She employs ten staff to make exclusive hand-made sweets and chocolates, which are sold to department stores and personal customers.

   She provided the following information:

Ratio	Year ended 31 March 2008	Year ended 31 March 2009
Percentage of gross profit to sales	25%	21%
Percentage of net profit to sales	10%	9%

Required

(a) Suggest **two** reasons for the fall in the percentage of **gross** profit to sales.

(b) Explain one way in which the percentage of **net** profit to sales could be increased.

Kalpna Khan is interested in the effect of expenses on her profitability.

Required

(c) Using the information in the table above, calculate the percentage of expenses to sales for **each** year. Show your calculations.

(d) Explain how the change in the percentage of expenses to sales has affected the efficiency of the business.

Kalpna Khan is allowed a period of 60 days in which to pay her creditors. She allows her debtors a period of 30 days in which to pay their accounts.

On 31 March 2009 Kalpna Khan's trade payables amounted to $44 500 and her trade receivables amounted to $38 500.

Kalpna Khan's purchases and sales for the year ended 31 March 2009 were:

		$
Purchases –	cash	4 000
	credit	320 000
Sales –	cash	50 000
	credit	400 000

Required

(e) Complete the table below to show the ratios for the year ended 31 March 2009. Calculations should be rounded up to the next whole day.

Ratio	Year ended 31 March 2008	Year ended 31 March 2009
Payment period for trade payables	61 days	.... days
collection period for trade receivables	29 days	.... days

(f) Using the figures in the table above, explain the effect of the change in the ratios on the liquidity of Kalpna Khan's business.

(g) Explain **two** ways in which Kalpna Khan could improve the collection period for trade receivables.

Kalpna Khan wishes to compare her results with those of a similar business. She is aware that there are problems in making such a comparison.

Analysis and Interpretation

> **Required**
>
> (h) Explain how **each** of the following affects inter-firm comparison. Use examples to illustrate your answers.
> The first has been completed as an example.
>   (i) Different type of expense
>   *One business may own premises, another may rent premises. This affects the expenses and the profit and the profitability ratios – making comparison difficult.*
>   (ii) Non-monetary factory
>   (iii) Accounting policies [IGCSE 2009]
>
> *9. Ebor and Olicana are partners and have invited Lindum to join the partnership and have given him their financial statements for the year ended 31 July 2005.
>
> Lindum is aware that these financial statements will not provide all the relevant information he needs.
>
> State and explain **two** limitations Lindum should be aware of when he is studying the financial statements Ebor and Olicana have provided.
> [IGCSE 2005]

Answers to Review Questions

Chapter 1

Question 3

Transaction	Effect on assets		Effect on liabilities	
		$		$
(b)	Inventory	Increase	Trade payables	Increase
(c)	Trade receivables Bank	Decrease Increase		
(d)	Trade receivables Inventory	Increase Decrease		
(e)	Cash	Decrease	Loan	Decrease

Chapter 2

Question 3

Mumtaz
Bank account

Date	Details	Folio	$	Date	Details	Folio	$
20-6				20-6			
July 1	Capital		50 000	July 2	Premises		25 000
9	Sales		200	4	Equipment		4 000
				7	Advertising		60
				14	Mayur Vihar Traders		1 000
					Balance	c/d	20 140
			50 200				50 200
20-6							
July 15	Balance	b/d	20 140				

Answers to Review Questions

Capital account

Date	Details	Folio	$	Date	Details	Folio	$
				20-6 July 1	Bank		50 000

Premises account

Date	Details	Folio	$	Date	Details	Folio	$
20-6 July 2	Bank		25 000				

Equipment account

Date	Details	Folio	$	Date	Details	Folio	$
20-6 July 4	Bank		4 000				

Purchases account

Date	Details	Folio	$	Date	Details	Folio	$
20-6 July 6	Mayur Vihar Traders		1 500				

Mayur Vihar Traders account

Date	Details	Folio	$	Date	Details	Folio	$
20-6 July 14	Bank Balance	c/d	1 000 500 1 500	20-6 July 6	Purchases		1 500 1 500
				20-6 July 15	Balance	b/d	500

Advertising account

Date	Details	Folio	$	Date	Details	Folio	$
20-6 July 7	Bank		60				

Sales account

Date	Details	Folio	$	Date	Details	Folio	$
				20-6 July 9	Bank		200
				12	Ridhima		310

Ridhima account

Date	Details	Folio	$	Date	Details	Folio	$
20-6 July 12	Sales		310	20-6 July 13	Sales returns		20
			___	14	Balance	c/d	290
			310				310
20-6 July 15	Balance	b/d	290				

Sales returns account

Date	Details	Folio	$	Date	Details	Folio	$
20-6 July 13	Ridhima		20				

Question 4

Rahman
Manish account

Date	Details	Folio	Debit $	Credit $	Balance $
20-1					
May 1	Balance		920		920 dr
14	Sales		440		1 360 dr
16	Sales returns			175	1 185 dr
19	Cash			100	1 085 dr
21	Sales		93		1 178 dr
26	Bank			900	278 dr

Answers to Review Questions

Chapter 3

Question 3

(a)

Hilota
Trial Balance at 31 March 2006

	$	$
Non-current assets	12 700	
Inventory	3 200	
Bank	4 550	
Sales		56 000
Purchases	34 200	
Carriage outwards	950	
Rent	4 000	
Wages	7 200	
General expenses	2 600	
Trade receivables	2 100	
Trade payables		3 000
Capital		20 000
Drawings	7 500	
	79 000	79 000

(b) A trial balance only proves that the total of the debit balances is equal to the total of the credit balances, it does not prove that the double entry is error-free.

(c) A trial balance can assist in locating arithmetical errors.
A trial balance is a useful list from which to prepare financial statements.

Chapter 4

Question 3

(a)

Jonah
Cash Book

Date	Details	Folio	Discount Allowed $	Cash $	Bank $	Date	Details	Folio	Discount Received $	Cash $	Bank $
2004						2004					
July 1	Balance	b/d		600	2 500	July 7	Cash	c			200
3	H Syde		10		490	10	J Teime		15		385
7	Bank	c		200		12	Wages			400	
14	B Sharp		20		780	17	P Mulder		25		975
20	Sales				350	24	Wages			250	
21	M Yaveli				630	29	Electricity				600
							M Yaveli (dishonoured cheque)				630
					31	Balance	c/d		150	1 960
			30	800	4 750				40	800	4 750
2004											
Aug 1	Balance	b/d		150	1 960						

Answers to Review Questions

(b) **Jonah**
Discount allowed account

Date	Details	Folio	$	Date	Details	Folio	$
2004 July 31	Total for month		30				

Discount received account

Date	Details	Folio	$	Date	Details	Folio	$
				2004 July 31	Total for month		40

Question 5

(a) June 1 Balance b/d (debit side)
The business had a total of $240 in cash on this date left over from May
Double entry – credit side of cash column in cash book for May

June 1 Balance b/d (credit side)
The business had a bank overdraft of $3130 as this is owing to the bank at the end of May
Double entry – debit side of bank column in cash book for May

June 2 Cash (debit side)
This is a contra entry when $200 cash was paid into the bank from surplus office cash
Double entry – credit side of cash column in cash book

June 2 Bank (credit side)
The other entry for the contra item taking $200 surplus office cash to pay into the bank
Double entry – debit side of bank column in cash book

June 3 Rohit
A cheque received from Rohit was paid into the bank

Double entry – credit side of Rohit's account in the sales ledger

June 7 ADT Ltd.
$390 paid to ADT Ltd. by cheque after a cash discount received of $10
Double entry – debit side of ADT Ltd.'s account in the purchases ledger

June 10 Rohit (dishonoured cheque)
The cheque received from Rohit on 3 June has been returned unpaid by the bank
Double entry – debit side of Rohit's account in the sales ledger

(b) Discount columns provide a convenient place in which to note the cash discount allowed and received at the time the payment is recorded in the cash book. Only the totals for the period are posted to the ledger so that there are only a limited number of entries in the discount accounts in the ledger.

Answers to Review Questions

Chapter 5

Question 1

(a)

Mel Rose
Petty Cash Book

Total Received	Fo.	Date	Details	Vo. No.	Total Paid	Stationery	Postage	Travel	Cleaning
$		2002			$	$	$	$	$
100	b/d	Mar 1	Balance						
		3	Travelling expenses		10			10	
		6	Office expenses		12	12			
		10	Postage		5		5		
		14	Cleaner's wages		20				20
		17	Envelopes		3	3			
		22	Bus fares		6			6	
		25	Postages		4		4		
		28	Cleaner's wages		20				20
					80	15	9	16	40
		31	Balance	c/d	20				
100					100				
20	b/d	2002 Apl 1	Balance						
80			Cash/Bank						

Question 5

(a)

Shilpa
Petty Cash Book

Total Received	Date	Details	Fo	Date	Details	Vo	Total Paid	Refresh-ments	Cleaning expenses	Motor expenses	Ledger accounts
$	20-9			20-9			$	$	$	$	$
50	Feb 21	Balance	b/d	Feb 26	Window cleaner		7		7		
					Petrol		11			11	
					Refreshments		5	5			
				27	Ghandi Stores		12				12
							35	5	7	11	12
50					Balance	c/d	15				
							50				
15	20-9	Balance	b/d								
35	Feb 28	Bank									

Answers to Review Questions

(b)

Shilpa
Cash Book

Date	Details	Folio	Discount Allowed	Bank	Date	Details	Folio	Discount Received	Bank
20-9			$	$	20-9			$	$
Feb 21	Balance	b/d		3 120	Feb 21	South West Traders		29	721
24	Janpath Stores		15	410	26	Speedy Motors			85
	AB Trading			220	28	Petty cash			35
						Balance	c/d		2 909
			15	3 750				29	3 750
20-9									
Mar 1	Balance	b/d		2 909					

Chapter 6

Question 2

(a) Invoice   Credit note   Statement of account   Receipt

(b) A debit note may be issued for request a reduction of an invoice in case of an overcharge, damaged or faulty goods etc.

(c) Any four from - Customer's name and address, date, total sales, invoice numbers, total sales returns, credit note numbers, cash/cheques received, any discounts allowed, net amount due, date amount due, terms of business etc.

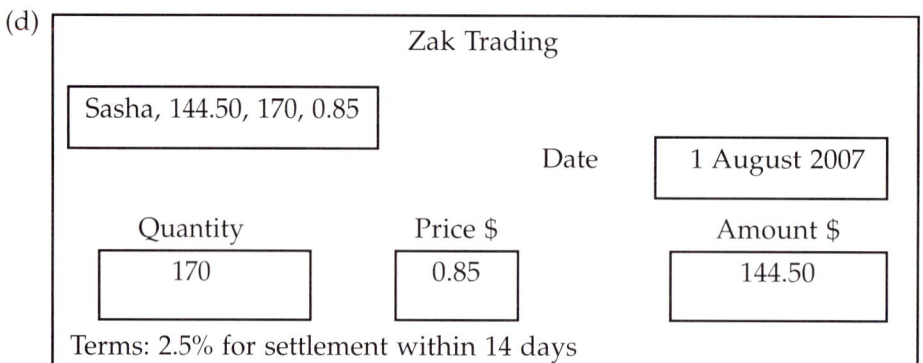

(d)

Zak Trading

Sasha, 144.50, 170, 0.85		
	Date	1 August 2007

Quantity	Price $	Amount $
170	0.85	144.50

Terms: 2.5% for settlement within 14 days

(e)
Cash book (debit)

Date 2007	Details	Discount allowed $	Bank $
Aug 12	Sasha	3.61	140.89

(f) (i) (250 × $0.85) × 5% = $10.62
    (ii) $212.50 − $10.62 = $201.88
    (iii) $201.88 × 2.5% = $5.05

Question 5

(a) (i) 3000   (ii) $100
    (iii) $1300   (iv) cash discount
(b) (i) $75   (ii) $2425
    (iii) $0   (iv) $1300

Answers to Review Questions

(c)

Pieter Burg
Purchases Ledger
General Supply Company account

Date	Details	Folio	$	Date	Details	Folio	$
2005				2005			
Sept 5	Bank		2 425	Sept 1	Balance	b/d	2 500
30	Discount		75	25	Purchases		1 300
	Balance	c/d	1 300				
			3 800				3 800
2005				2005			
Oct 3	Bank		1 300	Oct 1	Balance	b/d	1 300
			1 300				1 300

Chapter 7

Question 2

Redd
Purchases Ledger
Block account

Date	Details	Folio	$	Date	Details	Folio	$
2005				2005			
Mar 8	Purchases returns		100	Mar 5	Purchases		320
30	Bank		220	29	Purchases		270
31	Balance	c/d	270				
			590				590
				2005			
				Apl 1	Balance	b/d	270

Quayle account

Date	Details	Folio	$	Date	Details	Folio	$
2005				2005			
Mar 30	Bank		485	Mar 17	Purchases		500
	Discount		15				
			500				500

Question 4

(a)

		(i)	(ii)
Date	Transaction	Business document used by Billy	Billy's prime entry book
20-1 September 1 September 10	Goods bought Goods returned	Invoice Credit note	Purchases journal Purchases returns journal

(b) Discount received = 2½% × ($1000 – $200) = $20
Amount paid = $800 – $20 = $780

(c) 1. The total of the sales journal is posted to the credit side of the sales account.
2. The total of the sales returns journal is posted to the debit side of the sales returns account.

(d)

Joseph
Sales Ledger
Billy Jones account

Date	Details	Folio	$	Date	Details	Folio	$
2001				2001			
Sept 1	Sales		1000	Sept 10	Sales returns		200
				25	Bank		780
					Discount		20
			1000				1000

Answers to Review Questions

Chapter 8

Question 2

Piyush
Income Statement for the year ended 31 October 20-6

	$	$
Commissions earned		72 100
Add Interest received		2 900
		75 000
Less Staff salaries	28 500	
Rent	9 400	
Postages and telephone expenses	5 700	
Light and heat	1 100	
Insurance	800	
General expenses	3 500	49 000
Profit for the year		26 000

Question 3

(a)

Rani
Income Statement for the year ended 31 December 20-9

	$	$
Gross profit		35 000
Add Discount received		870
Rent received		6 000
		41 870
Less Wages and salaries	23 000	
General expenses	13 500	
Loan interest	1 000	
Discount allowed	500	
Advertising	680	
Property tax	1 240	
Motor expenses	2 550	42 470
Loss for the year		600

(b)

General Ledger
Sales Ledger
Capital account

Date	Details	Folio	$	Date	Details	Folio	$
20-9				20-9			
Dec 31	Drawings		17 000	Jan 1	Balance	b/d	46 000
	Loss		600				
	Balance		28 400				
			46 000				46 000
				20-0			
				Jan 1	Balance	b/d	28 000

Chapter 9

Question 4

Y Singh
Income Statement for the year ended 30 November 20-7

	$	$	$
Revenue (sales)		9 300	
Less Sales returns		103	9 197
Less Cost of sales			
Opening inventory		1 184	
Purchases	5 937		
Less Purchases returns	161		
	5 776		
Carriage inwards	100	5 876	
		7 060	
Less Closing inventory		980	6 080
Gross profit			3 117
Less Carriage outwards		160	
Wages		1 933	
Rent and insurance		235	
Motor vehicle expenses		440	
General expenses		240	3 008
Profit for the year			109

Answers to Review Questions

Balance Sheet at 30 November 20-7

	$	$	$
Non-current assets			
Equipment			3 500
Motor vehicle			2 975
			6 475
Current assets			
Inventory		980	
Bank		240	
		1 220	
Current liabilities			
Trade payables		866	
Net current assets			354
			6 829
Financed by			
Capital			
Opening balance			7 320
Plus Profit for the year			109
			7 429
Less Drawings			600
			6 829

Question 5

(a)

Pathan Stores
Income Statement for the year ended 31 December 20-1

	$	$
Gross profit		58 500
Add Commission received		3 000
		61 500
Less Wages	19 150	
Office expenses	1 300	
Rent and property tax	5 170	
Insurance	910	
Carriage outwards	4 270	
Motor expenses	7 770	
Sundry expenses	410	38 980
Profit for the year		22 520

(b)
Balance Sheet at 31 December 20-1

	$	$
Non-current assets		
Machinery		20 000
Motor vehicles		11 000
		31 000
Current assets		
Inventory	25 000	
Trade receivables	13 350	
Bank	9 400	
Cash	1 000	
	48 750	
Current liabilities		
Trade payables	8 430	
Net current assets		40 320
		71 320
Non-current liabilities		
Loan – AB Finance		20 000
		51 320
Financed by		
Capital		
Opening balance		38 800
Plus Profit for the year		22 520
		61 320
Less Drawings		10 000
		51 320

Chapter 10

Question 6

(a) Compare with results of other businesses of a similar size/type.
(b) One from – Improve profitability, analyse results and make decisions, identify and solve problems, increase sales, review inventory levels etc.
(c) Two from – capable of being independently verified, free from bias, free from significant errors, prepared with suitable caution being applied to any judgements and estimates.

Answers to Review Questions

Question 9

(a) (i) Capital expenditure is money spend on acquiring, improving and installing non-current assets.
Revenue expenditure is money spent on running a business on a day-to-day basis.
(ii) Capital receipts are amounts received from the sale of non-current assets.
Revenue receipts are sales and other items of income which are recorded in the income statement.

(b)
Michael Ong
Statement of corrected profit for the year ended 30 June 2009

	$	$
Profit for the year		15 000
Add Purchase of motor vehicle (CD357)	8 000	
Commission received	500	8 500
		23 500
Less Sale of motor vehicle (AB 246)	2 000	
Purchases of stationery	200	2 200
Corrected profit for the year		21 300

Question 10

			$
Inventory Code BD20 300 units × ($1.50 + $0.05)	=		465.00
Inventory Code BD23 119 units × $0.80	=		95.20
Inventory Code BD29 410 units × 1.78	=		729.80
			1290.00

Chapter 11

Question 4

(a)

Ramon
Sales account

Date	Details	Folio	$	Date	Details	Folio	$
2007				2007			
Apl 30	Income statement		500	Apl 3	Cash		500
			500				500

(b)

Ahmed account

Date	Details	Folio	$	Date	Details	Folio	$
2007				2007			
Apl 1	Balance	b/d	2850	Apl 12	Bank		1200
				29	Bank		650
				30	Balance	c/d	1000
			2850				2850
2007							
May 1	Balance	b/d	1000				

(c)

Rent account

Date	Details	Folio	$	Date	Details	Folio	$
2007				2007			
Apl 1	Bank		900	Apl 30	Income statement		300
					Balance	c/d	600
			900				900
2007							
May 1	Balance	b/d	600				

Answers to Review Questions

(d) Electricity account

Date	Details	Folio	$	Date	Details	Folio	$
2007				2007			
Apl 6	Bank		120	Apl 30	Income		
30	Balance	c/d	60		statement		180
			180				180
				2007			
				May 1	Balance	b/d	60

(e) Drawings account

Date	Details	Folio	$	Date	Details	Folio	$
2007				2007			
Apl 21	Cash		800	Apl 30	Capital		800
			800				800

(f) Wages account

Date	Details	Folio	$	Date	Details	Folio	$
2007				2007			
Apl 29	Cash		700	Apl 30	Income		
					statement		700
			700				700

Question 7

Mirian
Income Statement for the year ended 30 September 20-4

	$	$
Fees from clients		40 900
Commission receivable (5600 + 250)		5 850
		46 750
Less Office expenses (7250 – 250 + 45)	7 045	
Wages	27 500	
Insurance (1800 – 360)	1 440	
Property tax (800 + 160)	960	
Motor vehicle expenses (1840 – 920)	920	
Bank charges	115	37 980
Profit for the year		8 770

Chapter 12

Question 3

(a)
Joe
Equipment account

Date	Details	Folio	$	Date	Details	Folio	$
2001				2002			
Sept 1	Balance (A)	b/d	40 000	July 31	Balance	c/d	90 000
	Bank (B)		30 000				
2002							
Mar 1	Bank (C)		20 000				
			90 000				90 000
2002							
Sept 1	Balance	b/d	90 000				

Provision for depreciation of equipment account

Date	Details	Folio	$	Date	Details	Folio	$
2002				2001			
Aug 31	Balance	c/d	23 000	Sept 1	Balance	b/d	15 000
				June 30	Income statement		
					(A) 4 000		
					(B) 3 000		
					(C) 1 000		8 000
			23 000				23 000
				2002			
				July 1	Balance	b/d	23 000

Answers to Review Questions

(b)
Joe
Extract from Balance Sheet at 31 August 2002

Non-current assets	$ Cost	$ Depreciation to date	$ Book value
Equipment	90 000	23 000	67 000

(c) Prudence is observed:

In the income statement
The profit is not overstated as depreciation is shown as an expense. This means that the profit/loss is shown at a more realistic amount.

In the balance sheet
The non-current assets are not overstated as depreciation is deducted from the cost of the assets. This means that the non-current assets are shown at more realistic values.

Question 5

(a)
(i)
Mustafa and Syed
Equipment account

Date	Details	Folio	$	Date	Details	Folio	$
2000 Apl 1	AB Ltd.		10 000	2001 Oct 1	Disposal		5 000
				2002 Mar 31	Balance	c/d	5 000
			10 000				10 000
2002 Apl 1	Balance	b/d	5 000				

(ii) **Provision for depreciation of equipment account**

Date	Details	Folio	$	Date	Details	Folio	$
2001				2001			
Mar 31	Balance	c/d	2 000	Mar 31	Income statement		2 000
			2 000				2 000
2001				2001			
Oct 1	Disposal		1 000	Apl 1	Balance	b/d	2 000
2002				2002			
Mar 31	Balance	c/d	2 000	Mar 31	Income statement		1 000
			3 000				3 000
				2002			
				Apl 1	Balance	b/d	2 000

(iii) **Disposal of equipment account**

Date	Details	Folio	$	Date	Details	Folio	$
2001				2001			
Oct 1	Equipment		5 000	Oct 1	Provision for depreciation		1 000
					Zeta Ltd.		3 500
				2002			
				Mar 31	Income statement		500
			5 000				5 000

(b) The method of calculating depreciation should not be changed because:
1. This would be contrary to the principle of consistency.
2. Should spread the cost of the asset as fairly as possible to each period benefiting from the use of the asset.
3. Should not change method in order to manipulate profits.
(Any two points)

Answers to Review Questions

Chapter 13

Question 1

(a)

K Dhoni
Income Statement for the year ended 30 September 20-1

	$	$	$
Income from clients			75 300
Add Rent received (5400 – 1800)			3 600
			78 900
Less Bad debts		100	
Provision for doubtful debts (200 – 150)		50	
Insurance (2400 – 600)		1 800	
Printing and stationery (3150 + 150)		3 300	
Wages		47 000	
Office expenses		2 950	
Loan interest		500	
Depreciation of office equipment		1 900	57 600
Profit for the year			21 300

(b)

Balance Sheet at 30 September 20-1

	$	$	$
Non-current assets	Cost	Depreciation to date	Book value
Premises	82 000		82 000
Office equipment	19 000	3 800	15 200
	101 000	3 800	97 200
Current assets			
Trade payables	5 000		
Less Provision for doubtful debts	200	4 800	
Other receivables		600	
Bank		12 700	
Cash		200	
		18 300	
Current liabilities			
Other payables (150 + 500)	650		
Income prepaid	1 800	2 450	
Net current assets			15 850
			113 050

	$	$	$
Non-current liabilities			
Loan (repayable 20-9)			10 000
			103 050
Capital			
Opening balance			94 000
Plus Profit for the year			21 300
			115 300
Less Drawings			12 250
			103 050

Question 2

(a) Prudence
    Accruals

(b)

Maria Van Zly
Nominal Ledger
Provision for doubtful debts

Date	Details	Folio	$	Date	Details	Folio	$
2005				2004			
July 31	Income statement		90	Aug 1	Balance	b/d	990
	Balance	c/d	900				
			990				990
				2005			
				Aug 1	Balance	b/d	900

(c) Any two:

    Looking at each individual debtor's account and estimating which ones will not be paid.

    Estimating, on the basis of past experience, the percentage of the total amount owing by debtors that will not be paid.

    Considering the length of time debts have been outstanding by means of an ageing schedule.

Answers to Review Questions

(d) 2. Net profit for the year ended 31 August 2005
Overstated
Omission of a loss in the income statement means the profit is overstated
3. Current assets at 31 August 2005
Overstated
Trade receivables are shown at a higher value than will actually be received

Chapter 14

Question 2

Mary
Bank Reconciliation Statement at 31 January 2003

	$
Balance shown on bank statement	(2310)
Add Amounts not yet credited	800
	(1510)
Less Cheques not yet presented – David	270
Balance shown in cash book	(1780)

Question 3

(a) (i) Any two – Opening bank balance, closing bank balance, amounts paid into bank, amounts withdrawn from bank, bank charges, standing orders, credit transfers, direct debits, dishonoured cheques.

(ii) Any two – find accurate bank balance, identify any errors and omissions in cash book or bank records, identify amounts not credited and cheques not presented, assists in detecting fraud, identifies any "stale" cheques.

(b)

Sara Perez
Cash Book (Bank columns only)

Date	Details	Folio	$	Date	Details	Folio	$
2000				2000			
Nov 1	Balance	b/d	5264	Nov 1	Motor insurance		26
	Error correction		100		Bank charges		88
					Fine Fabrics (dishonoured cheque)		242
					Balance	c/d	5008
			5364				5364
2000							
Nov 1	Balance	b/d	5008				

(c)   **Bank Reconciliation Statement at 31 October 2000**

	$
Balance shown on bank statement	4145
Add Amounts not yet credited – Sales	1078
	5223
Less Cheques not yet presented – Thai Exports	240
	4983
Add Bank error – Rent	25
Balance shown in cash book	5008

(d) Current asset - $5008

Chapter 15

Question 2

(a) (i) A narrative consists of a brief explanation of what is being recorded and why the entry is being made.

    (ii) It is impossible to remember the reason for every entry and the entries in the journal sometimes involve "out of the ordinary" transactions.

Answers to Review Questions

(b)

Ruth
Journal

Date	Details	Folio	Debit $	Credit $
	Drawings		60	
	Purchases			60
	Goods taken for own use			
	Motor vehicle		15 000	
	Motor vehicle expenses		600	
	PJ Motors			15 600
	Purchase of new motor vehicle on credit and repairs to old motor vehicle			
	Stationery		20	
	Purchases			20
	Error in posting stationery to purchases now corrected			

Question 4

(a)

Maria Matsa
Journal

Date	Details	Folio	Debit $	Credit $
	Stationery		50	
	Suspense			50
	Suspense		1 000	
	Sales			1 000
	Abdulla Ahmed		240	
	Abdul Ahmed			240
	Suspense		28	
	Discount allowed			14
	Discount received			14
	Joe Jones		190	
	Suspense			190

(b)

Suspense account

Date	Details	Folio	$	Date	Details	Folio	$
2002				2002			
Sept 30	Sales		1000	Sept 30	Difference on trial balance		788
	Discount allowed		14		Stationery		50
	Discount received		14		Joe Jones		190
			1028				1028

(c) Error 2 Increase by $1000
Error 3 No effect
Error 4 Increase by $28
Error 5 No effect

Chapter 16

Question 2

Ruth Tembe
Purchases ledger control account

Date	Details	Folio	$	Date	Details	Folio	$
2009				2009			
July 1	Balance	b/d	15	July 1	Balance	b/d	3680
31	Bank		4650	31	Purchases		4800
	Discount received		90				
	Purchases returns		30				
	Inter ledger transfer		105				
	Balance	c/d	3590				
			8480				8480
				2009			
				Aug 1	Balance	b/d	3590

Answers to Review Questions

Question 6

(a) See Chapter 16

(b) (i) Credit sales — sales journal
 (ii) Discount allowed — cash book
 (iii) Bad debts — journal

(c) Any one – debtor returned goods after settling account, debtor overpaid account, cash discount not deducted before account paid, payment made in advance.

(d)

David Odoyo
Purchases ledger control account

Date	Details	Folio	$	Date	Details	Folio	$
2002				2002			
Oct 31	Purchases returns		135	Oct 1	Balance	b/d	2950
	Bank		4120	31	Purchases		5050
	Discount received		85		Cash		100
	Balance	c/d	3760				
			8100				8100
				2002			
				Nov 1	Balance	b/d	3760

Chapter 17

Question 1

(a)

Rebecca Tan
Statement of Affairs at 30 June 2005

	$ Cost	$ Depreciation for year	$ Book value
Non-current assets			
Equipment	13 900	1 200	12 700
Motor vehicles	7 500	1 500	6 000
	21 400	3 700	18 700
Current assets			
Inventory		7 250	
Trade receivables	5 200		
Less Provision for doubtful debts	104	5 096	
Other receivables		122	
		12 468	
Current liabilities			
Trade payables	4 800		
Other payables	146		
Bank overdraft	250	5 196	
Net current assets			7 272
			25 972
Financed by			
Capital			
Balance			25 972

(b) Calculation of profit for the year ended 30 June 2005

	$	$
Capital at 30 June 2005		25 972
Less Capital at 1 July 2004		27 000
		(1 028)
Add Drawings – cash	3 150	
goods	1 250	4 400
		3 372
Less Capital introduced		5 000
Profit for the year		(1 628)

Alternatively the calculation could be presented in the form of a capital account.

Answers to Review Questions

Question 3

(a) Calculation of credit sales

	$
Total bank deposits	15 270
Less Cash sales	2 680
	12 590
Less Trade receivables 1 April 2004	3 140
	9 450
Plus Trade receivables 31 March 2005	4 080
Credit sales for the year	13 530

(b) William
Income Statement for the year ended 31 March 2005

	$	$	$
Revenue – cash sales		2 680	
credit sales		13 530	16 210
Less Cost of sales			
Opening inventory		1 780	
Purchases	9 560		
Carriage inwards	280	9 840	
		11 620	
Less Closing inventory		1 920	9 700
Gross profit			6 510
Less Rent		600	
Electricity		360	
Motor expenses		800	
Insurance		580	
Wages		1 370	3 710
Profit for the year			2 800

(c) Gross profit margin = $\dfrac{\text{Gross profit}}{\text{Sales}} \times \dfrac{100}{1} = \dfrac{5\,510}{16\,510} \times \dfrac{100}{1} = 40.16\%$

(d) (i) Gross profit will increase by $90.

(ii) $\dfrac{(6\,510 + 90)}{16\,210} \times \dfrac{100}{1} = 40.49\%$

Question 6

(a)
Jane Joda
Income Statement for the year ended 31 March 2005

	$	$
Revenue – cash sales	6 600	
credit sales	10 900 *	17 500 100%
Less Cost of sales		
Opening inventory	9 500	
Purchases	22 000	
	31 500	
Less Closing inventory	17 500	14 000 80%
Gross profit		3 500 20%

Chapter 18

Question 2

(a)
Safat Judu Club
Income and Expenditure Account for the year ended 31 January 2006

	$	$
Income		
Subscriptions (10 650 – 250 – 400)		10 000
Competition – entrance fees	800	
cost of prizes	210	590
		10 590
Expenditure		
General expenses	2 645	
Travelling expenses	830	
Rent (2600 – 50 – 100)	2 450	
Loss on sale of motor vehicle (2000 – 1750)	250	
Depreciation – Motor vehicle (10 000 – 8500)	1 500	7 675
Surplus for the year		2 915

Answers to Review Questions

(b) **Balance Sheet at 31 January 2006**

	$	$
Non-current assets		
Motor vehicle at valuation		8 500
Current assets		
Other receivables	100	
Bank (3150 + 13 200 – 16 285)	65	
	165	
Current liabilities		
Subscriptions prepaid by members	(400)	
		(235)
		8 265
Financed by		
Accumulated fund		
Opening balance (3150 + 2000 + 250 – 50)		5 350
Add Surplus for year		2 915
		8 265

(c) Any two from –
The receipts and payments account shows the total money paid and received
The income and expenditure account adjusts figures for accruals and prepayments
The income and expenditure account includes non-monetary items such as depreciation
The income and expenditure account includes only revenue items

Question 3

(a) (i) The income and expenditure account is equivalent to a profit and loss account of a trading organisation. It is used to calculate the annual surplus or deficit.

(ii) The accumulated fund is equivalent to the capital of a trading organisation, the difference between the assets and liabilities. The annual surpluses (less any deficits) accumulate within a non-trading organisation to form the accumulated fund.

(b) Siltones Music Society
Receipts and Payments Account for the year ended 31 March 2005

	Receipts		$		Payments		$
2004				2005			
Apl 1	Balance	b/d	2 210	Mar 31	Expenses of concert		1 250
2005					Rent of premises		1 820
Mar 31	Subscriptions		5 800		General expenses		215
	Receipts from concert		1 900		Insurance		325
	Proceeds of sale of				Musical instruments		3 350
	instruments		700		Balance	c/d	3 650
			10 610				10 610
2005							
Apl 1	Balance	b/d	3 650				

(c) Subscriptions account

Date	Details	Folio	$	Date	Details	Folio	$
2004				2005			
Apl 1	Balance	b/d	1 000	Mar 31	Bank		5 800
2005							
Mar 31	Balance	c/d	800				
	Income & expenditure		4 000				
			5 800				5 800
				2005			
				Apl 1	Balance	b/d	800

Answers to Review Questions

Chapter 19

Question 3

(a) Any two from –
   Share losses
   Share responsibilities
   Share risks
   Additional finance is available
   Discussion can take place before decisions are made

(b) To avoid any misunderstandings/disagreements later

(c) (i)

		$	$
Profit for the year			58 040
Add Interest on drawings			1 960
			60 000
Less Interest on capital		9 000	
Partner's salary		20 000	29 000
Profit available for distribution			31 000

(ii) Share of profit – Raminder Singh 1/2 × $31 000 = $15 500
    Vijay Singh 1/2 × $31 000 = $15 500

(iii) Current accounts

		R Singh	V Singh			R Singh	V Singh
2007		$	$	2007		$	$
Apl 1	Balance b/d	4 660		Apl 1	Balance b/d		1 820
2008				2008			
Mar 31	Drawings	21 000	28 000	Mar 31	Interest on capital	6 000	3 000
	Interest on drawings	840	1 120		Salary		20 000
	Balance c/d	11 200			Profit share	15 500	15 500
					Balance c/d	5 000	
		26 500	40 320			26 500	40 320
2008				2008			
Apl 1	Balance b/d	5 000		Apl 1	Balance b/d		11 200

(d)   Capital accounts

	R Singh $	V Singh $		R Singh $	V Singh $
2008			2008		
Apl 1 Current a/c	5 000		Apl 1 Balances b/d	200 000	100 000
Bank	45 000		30 Bank		50 000
30 Balance c/d	150 000	150 000			
	200 000	150 000		200 000	150 000
			2008		
			May 1 Balance b/d	150 000	150 000

Question 5

(a)   **Archer and Bowman**
       Statement of corrected profit for the year ended 31 August 2003

			$
Profit for the year before correction			18 490

Effect on profit

	+ $	– $	
Error 1	30		
Error 2		1 400	
Error 3		2 000	
Error 4	420		
Error 5		20	
	450	3 420	2 970
Corrected profit for the year			15 520

(b)   **Archer and Bowman**
       Profit and Loss Appropriation Account for the year ended 31 August 2003

	$	$	$
Profit for the year			15 520
Add Interest on drawings – Archer		350	
Bowman		150	500
			16 020
Less Interest on capital – Archer	2 000		
Bowman	4 000	6 000	
Partner's salary – Archer		6 000	12 000
			4 020
Profit shares – Archer		2 010	
Bowman		2 010	4 020

Answers to Review Questions

Question 6

(a)

Error	Effect of correcting the error	
	on the gross profit	*on the net profit*
2	–$15	No effect
3	+$30	No effect
4	No effect	–$200
		+$50

(b)

Ebor and Olicana
Journal

Date	Details	Folio	Debit $	Credit
2005 Aug 31	Drawings - Olicana Purchases Goods taken by partner for own use		400	400
	Office equipment Capital – Ebor Computer introduced into the business by partner		900	900
	Current - Ebor Capital – Ebor Transfer from current account to capital account		5 000	5 000

Chapter 20

Question 3

(a) (i) Direct costs are those costs in a manufacturing business which can be traced directly to the item being manufactured. They include direct material, direct labour and direct expenses.
Indirect costs are those costs in a manufacturing business which cannot be traced directly to the item being manufactured. They include factory overheads.

(ii) Prime cost is the total of the direct materials, the direct labour and the direct expenses.
Cost of production is the prime cost plus the factory overheads.

(b) A manufacturer may purchase finished goods if production does not meet demand, if it is cheaper to buy than to make and if he cannot manufacture those particular items.

(c) (i) Calculation of prime cost

	$
Opening inventory of raw material	4 750
Purchases of raw material	49 590
Carriage on purchases	3 710
	58 050
Less Closing inventory of raw material	4 850
	53 200
Direct factory wages	61 940
Direct factory expenses	2 960
	118 100

Answers to Review Questions

(ii) Calculation of cost of production

	$
Prime cost	118 100
Factory overheads –	
Indirect factory wages	29 660
Factory indirect expenses	48 930
	196 690
Add Opening work in progress	5 600
	202 290
Less Closing work in progress	4 300
	197 990

Question 4

(a) A manufacturing account is used to calculate how much it cost to make the goods produced in the financial year. This figure is then used in the trading account section of the income statement in order to calculate the gross profit.

(b) (i) The cost of materials consumed is the total cost of the raw materials actually used in the production during the financial year. It consists of the net purchases of raw material, adjusted for opening and closing inventories of raw materials, and plus carriage on raw material.

(ii) The prime cost is the total of the three main elements of cost i.e. direct materials, direct labour and direct expenses. It is the basic cost of manufacturing the goods.

(iii) The production cost is the total cost of manufacturing the goods produced in the financial year. It consists of prime cost plus factory overheads. An adjustment is made for the opening and closing work in progress.

(c)	El Sayed Manufacturing Company
Manufacturing Account for the year ended 31 August 2003

	$	$
Cost of material consumed		
Opening inventory of raw material	7 040	
Purchases of raw material	43 820	
	50 860	
Less Closing inventory of raw material	6 220	44 640
Direct wages (40190 + 1170)		41 360
Prime Cost		86 000
Factory overheads		
Indirect wages	18 400	
General expenses	5 340	
Rates and insurance (7500 x 4/5)	6 000	
Depreciation of machinery (42000 x 20%)	8 400	38 140
		124 140
Add Opening work in progress		810
		124 950
Less Closing work in progress		950
Production cost of goods completed		124 000

Chapter 21

Question 4

(a)	Kinto Limited
Profit and Loss Appropriation Account for the year ended 30 June 2000

	$	$
Profit for the year		16 000
Less Transfer to general reserve	5 000	
Dividends – Ordinary proposed	2 500	7 500
Retained profit for the year		8 500
Retained profit brought forward		47 200
Retained profit carried forward		55 700

Answers to Review Questions

(b)   Balance Sheet at 30 June 2010

	$ Cost	$ Depreciation to date	$ Book value
Non-current assets			
Machinery	17 000	1 900	15 100
Office equipment	2 500	500	2 000
	19 500	2 400	17 100
Current assets			
Inventory		3 900	
Trade receivables		33 500	
Other receivables		600	
Bank		25 000	
Cash		200	
		63 200	
Creditors: amounts falling due within one year			
Trade payables	1 800		
Other payables	300		
Proposed dividends	2 500	4 600	
Net current assets			58 600
			75 700
Creditors: amounts falling due after more than one year			
Bank loan (repayable 2016)			5 000
			70 700
Financed by			
Capital and reserves			
Ordinary shares of $1 each			10 000
General reserve			5 000
Retained profits			55 700
Shareholders' funds			70 700

Question 5

(a)

	$
Profit for the year before preference share dividend	59 000
Preference share dividend paid	5 000
Profit for the year after preference share dividend	54 000

(b)
Tiwari & Company Ltd.
Profit and Loss Appropriation Account for the year ended 30 June 20-8

	$	$	$
Profit for the year			54 000
Less Transfer to general reserve		10 000	
Ordinary share dividend – paid	15 000		
proposed	30 000	45 000	55 000
Retained profit for the year			(1 000)
Retained profit brought forward			9 500
Retained profit carried forward			8 500

(c)
Tiwari & Company Ltd.
Extract from Balance Sheet at 30 June 20-6

	$
Capital and reserves	
5% Preference shares of $1 each	100 000
Ordinary shares of $0.50 each	300 000
General reserve (12 000 + 10 000)	22 000
Retained profits	8 500
Shareholders' funds	430 500

(d) As the directors decided not to apply the IAS rules regarding proposed dividends, the proposed ordinary share dividend of $30 000 which has been decided upon would appear in the balance sheet at 30 June 20-8. This would appear under Creditors: amounts falling due within one year (or current liabilities). The dividends already paid do not appear in the balance sheet as they are not liabilities.

Answers to Review Questions

Chapter 22

Question 1

(a) To be able to meet debts when they fall due
To be able to take advantage of cash discounts
To be able to take advantage of business opportunities as they arise
To ensure that there is no difficulty in obtaining further supplies

(b) Any two from –
Introduce further capital
Reduce drawings
Sell surplus non-current assets
Obtain long-term loans

(c) (i) Effect — Working capital decreases by $50.
Explanation — Current assets decrease by $50 as trade receivables decrease.
There is no change in the current liabilities.
(ii) Effect — Working capital does not change.
Explanation — The current assets do not change as the cash increases and the trade receivables decrease by $200. There is no change in the current liabilities.
(iii) Effect — Working capital increases by $4.
Explanation — Current assets decrease by $96 and the current liabilities decrease by $100.

Question 2

(a) One from –
If debtors delay payment the business may be forced to delay paying the creditors unless liquid funds are available.
If debtors pay with the set time the business may be able to pay its creditors within the set time without any significant impact on the bank balance.

(b) $\dfrac{30\,000}{268\,500} \times \dfrac{365}{1} = 40.78 = 48$ days

(c) $\dfrac{20\,200}{242\,500} \times \dfrac{365}{1} = 30.40 = 31$ days

(d) May be able to take advantage of cash discounts
Will improve the relationship with suppliers

Question 9

Reflect what has happened in the past – significant events may have taken place since the end of the financial year.
Transactions are recorded at their actual cost – inflation may affect these figures.
Accounts only include information that can be expresses in monetary terms – and so many factors will not appear in the financial statements.
The financial statements provided are for one year only – statements for previous years would allow meaningful ratios to be prepared.

Index

Accounting 1–2
Accounting entity 128
   equation 3–4
   period 132
   policies 133–134
   principles 128–132
   ratios 355–368
Accruals principle 130, 143, 146, 152, 155
Accrued expenses 143–146, 149–151
   Income 152–155, 157–159
Accumulated fund 292, 294, 297–298
Acid test ratio 361
Analysis columns 62–64
Appropriation account 308, 311–312, 346–348
Assets 2–5, 13–14, 43, 116–117, 360, 368
   current 117, 356, 361
   non-current 117, 166–167, 360

Bad debts recovered 190–192
   reducing possibility of 192
   written off 189–190
Balance sheet 2–3, 5–7, 99, 116–122, 143, 146, 153, 155, 177–179, 193–198, 234–235, 286, 291–293, 311, 316–317, 336, 347–349
Balance sheet equation 3
Bank overdraft 48–Bank reconciliation 207–216
Bank statement 207–209
Book-keeping 1, 7, 10–27, 31–32, 42–54
Business entity 128

Capital 3, 5, 7, 118, 128, 261–262, 292, 294, 297, 310–311, 342, 344, 348–349, 360
Capital account 12, 17, 109, 261, 265, 313
   employed 356, 357–358
   expenditure 134–135, 167, 179, 286, 289
   owned 356
   receipt 135, 179, 286, 289
Carriage inwards 25, 101, 136, 330
   outwards 25
Cash book petty 61–67
   three column 48–54
   two column 43–48
Cheque 51, 79–80, 208, 210
Clubs and societies 285–298
Comparability 134
Consistency 129–130, 168, 372
Contra entries 44, 251–252
Control account 243–252
   advantages 243–244
   purchases ledger 246–248, 252
   sales ledger 244–247, 249–250, 251
Cost elements of manufacture 329
   of production 330–333
Credit note 76–77
Creditor 5, 42–43, 50, 247, 347–348, 361, 365, 371
Current accounts 313–317
Current ratio 360–361

Debentures 346, 348
Debit note 74–75
Debtor 5, 22, 50–51, 63, 180, 189–190, 192, 244–245, 249, 361

Depreciation causes 167–168
   methods 168–172
   recording 172–179
Diminishing balance depreciation 170–171
Direct expenses 329–330
   labour 329–330
   material 329–330
Discount allowed 50, 80, 273
   cash 48, 50, 73
   received 50, 273
   trade 72–73, 90
Dishonoured cheque 51, 209, 245
Disposal of non-current assets 135, 179–181
Dividend 343, 345–347
Documents, business 12, 72–80
Double entry 1, 7, 10–27, 31–32, 42–54–4, 61, 64, 87–88, 106–108, 128, 143, 153, 155, 211, 260, 266, 308, 328
Doubtful debts provision 193–198
Drawings 17, 109, 120, 128, 261, 292, 310, 313–314
Duality 128

Errors
   bank 209–210, 216
   commission 37, 228
   compensating 37, 228
   complete reversal 37, 228
   omission 37, 228
   original entry 37, 228
   principle 37, 228
Errors correction 228–232
   effect on balance sheet 234–235
   effect on profit 232–234
   in trial balance 36–37, 229–230
Equity, owner's 3
   shares 345

Financial statements 1–2, 7, 99–111, 116–122, 134, 176–179, 234, 370–371
Fixed instalment depreciation 168–169
Folio numbers 11, 33

Going concern principle 131–132
Goods for own use 17, 101
Goodwill of the business 369, 372
Gross profit 99,101–102, 105, 108, 232, 273–288, 358–359
   to sales ratio 358–359

Historical cost 132, 167, 372

Imprest 62, 64
Income and expenditure account 286, 289–291, 294
Income statement 2, 99–111, 116, 130, 132, 135, 142–144, 146, 155, 167, 176–180, 189–190, 226–227, 232–234, 275, 287–289, 311, 334–335, 345–346
Inter-firm comparison 365–369
Interest on capital 310–312
Interest on drawings 310–312
Inventory 19, 101, 108–109, 117
   finished goods 334–336
   raw materials 330–331
   turnover rate of 275–276, 362–363, 368
   valuation 136–137
   work in progress 332
Invoice 72–75

Journal general 86, 222–232
   purchases 90–91, 225
   purchases returns 91–93
   sales 87, 225
   sales returns 87–90

Ledger 10
   accounts 11
   balancing accounts 18–19
   closing accounts 106–109
   general 43
   purchases 42
   nominal 43
   sales 42
   three column accounts 25–27

Index

Liabilities 2–5, 13–14, 43, 116, 118
   current 118
   non-current 118
Limitations of financial statements 371–372
Limited company 342–349
Limited liability 342
Liquidity ratios 360–365
Loan notes 346

Manufacturing businesses 328–336
Margin 273–276
Mark-up 273–276
Matching 130, 167
Materiality 131–132
Money measurement 128–129, 132, 372

Net current assets 121, 356
Net profit 99, 103–105, 109, 136, 232–234, 261–265, 289, 335, 357–359
Net profit to sales ratio 359
Non-trading organisations 285

Other receivables 142–159
Other payables 142–159
Overheads, factory 329
Original entry books 86

Partnership accounts 308–317
   advantages 309
   agreement 309–310
   disadvantages 309
Petty cash book 61–67
Prepaid income 155–157, 159
   expense 146–149, 151–152
Prepayments 143
Prime entry books 44, 86–93, 222, 225, 245, 247
Profit and loss account 2, 99, 103–105, 108, 142, 232, 273, 288–289, 294, 335, 345–347
Profit for the year 99, 103–105, 108–109, 120, 135–136, 167, 190, 232–234, 261–265, 294, 311, 346, 357–359

Profitability ratios 355, 357–359
Prudence, principle of 130–131, 136, 167, 190, 193, 372
Purchases 19–21, 42–43, 74, 86, 90–93, 99, 107, 225, 247, 269, 271–272, 330, 334, 364
Purchases returns 23–24, 77, 86, 90–93, 101, 222, 232, 234, 247

Quick ratio 361

Rate of inventory turnover 275–276, 362–363
Ratio analysis 355–368
Realisation 129
Receipt 80
Receipts and payments account 286–287, 294
Reducing balance depreciation 168, 170–171
Relevance 133
Reliability 133
Reserves 347–349
Retained profits 347–349
Return on capital employed 357–358
Returns inwards 23
Returns outwards 23
Revaluation method of depreciation 168, 171
Revenue 103
Revenue expenditure 127, 130, 135, 286, 289
Revenue receipt 135–136, 286, 289

Sales 19, 21–23, 43, 74, 86, 87–90, 99, 131, 245, 268, 271–272, 358, 363
Sales returns 23–24, 77, 86, 87–90, 99, 245
Service businesses 110–111
Share capital 344, 348–349
   authorised 344
   called-up 344
   issued 344
   paid-up 344

Shares
　preference 345
　ordinary 345
Shareholders' funds 348–349
Statement of account 77–78
Statement of affairs 260–273
Statement of changes in equity 346
Straight line depreciation 168–170
Subscriptions 285, 294–295
Subsidiary books 86
Suspense account 229–232

Total trade payables account 246, 269
Total trade receivables account 244, 268,
Trade payables 5, 118
Trade payables payment period 364–365
Trade payables to purchases ratio
　364–365

Trade receivables 5, 117
Trade receivables collection period
　363–364
Trade receivables to sales ratio
　363–364
Trading account 2, 99, 101–104, 232, 273,
　275, 286–289, 334–335
Trial balance 31–37, 100, 228–232,
　236, 243
Turnover 358
　inventory 273–276, 362–363, 368

Understandability 133–134
Users of accounting statements 370–371

Work in progress 332–336
Working capital 121, 356, 360–361
Working capital ratio 360